HOBBES'S
SCIENCE OF POLITICS

HOBBES'S
SCIENCE
OF POLITICS

M.M. Goldsmith

COLUMBIA UNIVERSITY PRESS

New York

M. M. Goldsmith is Assistant Professor of Government at Columbia University.

This study, prepared under the Graduate Faculties of Columbia University, was selected by a committee of those Faculties to receive one of the Clarke F. Ansley awards given annually by Columbia University Press.

Columbia University Press
New York   Guildford, Surrey
Copyright © 1966 Columbia University Press
All Rights Reserved

ISBN 0-231-02803-2 *(cloth)*
ISBN 0-231-02804-0 *(paperback)*

Library of Congress Catalog Card Number: 66-18860
Printed in the United States of America
Third cloth and first paperback printing.

TO MY MOTHER

AND TO THE

MEMORY OF MY FATHER

PREFACE

"Of making many books there is no end." To those who find yet another study of Hobbes a weariness of the flesh, I offer my apologies. It seemed to me when I began this study that Hobbes's attempt to create a philosophic system encompassing both natural and political science had been neither understood nor taken seriously by most commentators. I hope that this is no longer true.

Treating Hobbes's philosophy systematically forced me to study his method and his natural philosophy; understanding Hobbes's political philosophy as a part, albeit the most interesting part, of his philosophic system required a review of his political writings. In the concluding chapter, I attempt to test my thesis by showing how Hobbes's political science explains political phenomena.

It is a pleasure to acknowledge my debts; the largest of them I owe to Herbert A. Deane, who patiently guided my studies, matching scrupulous criticism with generous encouragement. I am also the appreciative recipient of Julian H. Franklin's trenchant and sympathetic criticism. I wish to thank Professors Robert Cumming, Thomas P. Peardon, and Robert K. Webb for their helpful suggestions. Rosalie L. Colie read the manuscript in its penultimate form; I have benefited greatly from her acute sense of style and from her extensive knowledge of seventeenth-century thought.

To the Social Science Research Council, which appointed me a Fellow in Political Theory and Legal Philosophy for 1959–60, I owe a valuable year of research and writing in England. The liberality of Columbia College in awarding me a Chamberlain Fellowship for the spring of 1965 has enabled me to revise the manuscript at leisure. The British Museum has, as always, been generous with its facilities.

I am grateful to His Grace the Duke of Devonshire for permitting me to examine the Hobbes MSS at Chatsworth; and also to Mr. T. S. Wragg, Keeper of the Devonshire Collections, both for his generous assistance (which included allowing me to use his catalogue of the Hobbes papers) and for his indulgence of my interest in Hobbes.

I am indebted to many acquaintances and friends who, tolerating my obsession with Hobbes, have contributed their help and their encouragement.

M. M. GOLDSMITH

New York
September, 1965

CONTENTS

CITATION OF
HOBBES'S WORKS

All page references to Hobbes's works are to the editions listed below, cited more fully in the Bibliography.

EW   *The English Works of Thomas Hobbes of Malmesbury*, edited by Sir William Molesworth.

LW   *Thomae Hobbes Malmesburiensis—Opera Philosophica quae Latine scripsit Omnia*, edited by Sir William Molesworth.

Behemoth   *Behemoth; or, The Long Parliament*, edited by Ferdinand Tönnies.

Elements of Law   *The Elements of Law, Natural and Politic*, edited by Ferdinand Tönnies, 1889.

Leviathan   *Hobbes's Leviathan*, with an essay by W. G. Pogson Smith.

Where possible, I have identified the relevant divisions: part, chapter, and section. Thus, a reference to *De Cive*, Chapter iii, Section 21, in Volume II of the Latin works at page 192 would read: *De Cive* (iii. 21), *LW* II, 192. I have cited *Philosophical Rudiments of Government and Society* by its original title in Latin, i.e., *De Cive*. Consequently the same passage cited in the English translation would read: *De Cive* (iii. 21), *EW* II, 42. A reference to the *Elements of Law*, Part I, Chapter ix, Section 12 on page 41 of Tönnies' edition (1889) would read: *Elements of Law* (I. ix. 12), p. 41. In referring to *Leviathan* or other works not divided into small sections, the number of the chapter or part is indicated in parentheses, e.g., *Leviathan* (17), p. 129.

INTRODUCTION

Hobbes's philosophy was designed to form a system. Hobbes explains in his Preface to *De Cive* that, having gathered the elements of philosophy, he had digested them into three sections: (1) of body and its properties, (2) of man and his special faculties and affections, (3) of civil government and the duties of subjects. These would have been presented in their proper order had the third section not been "ripened and plucked" by the controversies which preceded the Civil War. But because the country "was boiling hot with questions concerning the rights of dominion, and the obedience due from subjects, the true forerunners of an approaching war," the third section of Hobbes's philosophy, *De Cive,* was published in 1642 before the first two sections.[1]

Hobbes's literary career had begun in 1629 with the publication, for the instruction of his countrymen, of his translation of Thucydides' *History of the Peloponnesian War.*[2] However, his intention to make Englishmen more prudent had not led him to rush his translation into print, for although finished "it lay long by" him.[3] By 1630 Hobbes had become interested in natural philosophy and the problem of sensation.[4] After re-

[1] *De Cive* (Preface to the Reader), *EW* II, xx. This preface was written for the second edition published in 1647.
[2] *History of the Grecian War by Thucydides* (To the Readers), *EW* VIII, vii.
[3] *Ibid.,* p. ix.
[4] See "A Short Tract on First Principles," in *Elements of Law,* p. 193; and Brandt, pp. 9–85.

turning to England in 1637 from his third continental tour, he formulated his system:

> *Nam philosophandi*
> *Corpus, Homo, Civis continet omne genus.*
> *Tres super his rebus statuo conscribere libros;*
> *Materiemque mihi congero quoque die.*[5]

Nevertheless, *De Corpore* did not appear until 1655 and *De Homine* not until 1658, although both works were begun much earlier.[6]

During the period between 1636 and 1658, Hobbes produced two works on politics in English, as well as his philosophical system. *The Elements of Law* (1640) and *Leviathan* (1651) are related to each other and to his philosophical system. *The Elements of Law* was probably an early draft of *Leviathan*. At least, both begin with a discussion of man's faculties: sense, imagination, speech, reason, passion. This is followed by a description of man's natural condition, and the derivation of the nature and powers of commonwealth. The contents of the first parts of these works correspond to the prospectus of the second section of Hobbes's system in the Preface to *De Cive:* "*imagination, memory, intellect, ratiocination, appetite, will, good* and *evil, honest* and *dishonest,* and the like."* [7] In fact, when a pirated edition of the first thirteen chapters of the *Elements of Law* appeared in 1650 under the title *Humane Nature, or the Fundamental Elements of Policy,* it masqueraded as the second part of Hobbes's system.[8] Furthermore, the remainder of the *Elements of Law* and *Leviathan,* and *De Cive,* all deal with the same subjects, i.e., man's natural condition, commonwealth, and religion.

In spite of the circumstances that led Hobbes to finish *De Cive,* the *Elements of Law,* and *Leviathan* before he completed

---

[5] *Vita Carmine Expressa, LW* I, xc.

[6] Parts of both works survive in Hobbes's remaining papers at Chatsworth. They are in the same hand as the presentation copy of *De Cive* (also at Chatsworth) dated Paris, 1641. See also Aaron, pp. 342–56.

[7] *De Cive* (Preface), *EW* II, xx.

[8] *Humane Nature* (Publisher's note "To the Reader"), *EW* IV, xi.

his projected system of philosophy, and although civil philosophy may be severed from natural philosophy because its principles may be sufficiently known by experience,[9] Hobbes intended to create a unified philosophy. Does attending to this intention lead to a clearer understanding of Hobbes's political philosophy? [10]

It is true that *De Cive,* and *a fortiori* the *Elements of Law* and *Leviathan,* can be read and appreciated apart from the rest of the system. From such a reading, Hobbes's political position —Erastian, *politique,* royalist—should be apparent. He wrote to defend the king's peace and his right to govern both state and church. Consequently, he attacked opinions which were subversive of peace, opinions contrary to the necessary conditions of peace.[11]

What are the necessary conditions of peace? How can peace be established? How is it maintained? The necessary conditions of peace are the laws of nature. These laws can only be established by a sovereign power. Such a power is necessary if peace is to be maintained. This much is clear. But, if we are to understand how the laws of nature can be rules of reason, and commands of God, and grounded on principles known by experience, and if we are to understand why in Hobbes's opinion a sovereign state is necessary, then we must unravel the connections between reason, experience, and faith in his philosophy. We must discover, if possible, why Hobbes thought that he was writing something more than political pamphlets. We must determine how far he was correct in this supposition.

[9] *De Corpore* (vi. 7), *EW* I, 73; *De Cive* (Preface), *EW* II, xx.
[10] J. W. N. Watkins, in *Hobbes's System of Ideas,* agrees that it does. I regret that this book appeared too late for me to take account of its argument in preparing this study.
[11] See Stewart, pp. 547–65.

I

PHILOSOPHY

'Tis onely *God* can know
Whether the fair *Idea* thou dost show
Agree intirely with his *own* or no.
    This I dare boldly tell,
'Tis so like *Truth* 'twill serve our turn as well.
                ABRAHAM COWLEY, "TO MR. HOBS"

Hobbes defined philosophy, or science, as the knowledge of causal relations: either knowledge of the effects following from known causes, or of the possible causes of known effects.[1] Philosophy, then, is reasoning from previously known causes to their effects, or from previously known effects to their possible causes. Such a definition of philosophy is a definition in terms of method—the methods by which new knowledge can be generated out of old; philosophy itself is defined in terms of its causes.

Philosophy, to Hobbes, is knowledge generated by method, and the method by which knowledge is correctly generated is analytic-synthetic. The method of analysis, or resolution, begins from effects and discovers their possible causes; the method of synthesis, or composition, begins from causes and deduces their necessary effects. Hobbes accepted the method of science

---

[1] *De Corpore* (i. 2), *EW* I, 3.

—that of Galileo, Harvey, and the Paduan school [2]—and upon that method he built a general system of philosophy.

To explain Hobbes's use of analytic-synthetic method and his system of philosophy, some account must be given of how knowledge is possible, of how men can come to know the world, and of how they can come to explain it; this account of the operations of the human mind, of sensation, imagination, reasoning, etc., will rely on the results of the application of the analytic-synthetic method, i.e., on the findings of science.

The materials of all thinking and knowing originate in the process of sensation, the reaction of a sensing creature to external motion impinging on it. Natural philosophy can explain the mechanism of sensation: it is caused by external pressure on the sensing creature. This pressure, continued inward to the brain and heart, is resisted by a counterpressure outward. The result of this process is a sensation or phantasm that appears to be something outside of the sensing creature.

And this *seeming,* or *fancy,* is that which men call *Sense;* and consisteth, as to the Eye, in a *Light,* or *Colour figured;* To the Eare, in a *Sound;* To the Nostrill, in an *Odour;* To the Tongue and Palat, in a *Savour;* And to the rest of the body, in *Heat, Cold, Hardnesse, Softnesse,* and such other qualities, as we discern by *Feeling.*[3]

That is, the path taken by the pressure and reaction determines the kind of sensation that occurs. The originating pressure is motion (or endeavor) inward, and it is resisted by motion (or endeavor) outward. Motion produces motion; motion is resisted by motion. The resulting sensation may also be called a fancy, a seeming, an appearance, an image, a phantasm, or an idea (from *eidolon*). By this process are conceptions of

[2] On this method in general, see Randall, pp. 177–206; but for a more skeptical view of the development of these methods, see Gilbert. For an account in relation to Hobbes, see Watkins, *Hobbes's System of Ideas,* pp. 47–81.

[3] *Leviathan* (1), p. 11. *Cf. Elements of Law* (I. ii. 3), p. 3; *De Corpore* (xxv. 2), *EW* I, 390.

external objects produced; objects may not be as they appear, but appearances are our conceptions of objects.[4]

Imagination and memory are also fancy. Motion will continue indefinitely until it is stayed. Imagination and memory are results of the inertia of motions produced in sensation. These motions are obscured by subsequent motions and gradually worn away.

> This *decaying sense,* when wee would express the thing it self, (I mean *fancy* it selfe,) wee call *Imagination,* as I said before: But when we would express the *decay,* and signifie that the Sense is fading, old, and past, it is called *Memory.* So that *Imagination* and *Memory,* are but one thing, which for divers considerations hath divers names.[5]

Up to this point, the phantasms of sense and imagination have been treated as single moments, but both sense and imagination involve change; both require comparison and distinction between one phantasm and another. A man who always sees the same unchanging phantasm can no more be said to see than a human being can be said to feel his own bones.[6]

There are several sorts of sequences in which phantasms may occur. Phantasms of sense occur in the order in which they are caused in us. This order is not always the same. Trains of imaginations may occur in any order in which they previously occurred in sense or in imagination, or in an order guided by some desire or design, i.e., in an order dominated by some strong thought to which the other thoughts are related, and to which they keep returning. So we can think backward along a course of events, seek the means of effecting some result, or consider the consequences of an action.[7]

Memory of the succession of one event to another is an ex-

---

[4] *Elements of Law* (I. ii. 4–10), pp. 3–7.
[5] *Leviathan* (2), p. 14; *De Corpore* (xxv. 7), *EW* I, 397; *Elements of Law* (I. iii. 1, 7), pp. 8, 11.
[6] *De Corpore* (xxv. 5), *EW* I, 394.
[7] *Leviathan* (3), pp. 18–20; *Elements of Law* (I. iv. 1–5), pp. 13–14.

periment. The sequence of events may be natural, or contrived by the experimenter. To have many such memories is experience. Expectation of future events, or prediction of future events, is based on experience. The presumption is that actions will have consequences in the future like the consequences they have had in the past.

Which kind of thoughts is called *Foresight,* and *Prudence,* or *Providence;* and sometimes *Wisdome;* though such conjecture, through the difficulty of observing all circumstances, be very fallacious. But this is certain; by how much one man has more experience of things past, than another; by so much also he is more Prudent, and his expectations the seldomer faile him.[8]

In our conjectures about what will happen, or what has happened, observed antecedent and consequent events are taken to be signs of each other, signs the more certain the more often they are observed. To be more experienced than others in any kind of activity is to have more signs to guess by.

The natural operations of the minds of men (and of other animals as well)—sense, imagination, memory, and prudential expectation—provide a kind of knowledge about the world—experiential knowledge. Sensation is the basis of all knowledge, but neither sensation, nor memory, nor prudence is scientific knowledge, for science requires calculation in language.

Language consists of words connected with other words, *"Names* or *Appellations,* and their Connexion; whereby men register their Thoughts."[9] Names are marks, vocal or visual, by which men can register and recall thoughts; words are an arbitrary or conventional relation between a mark and a mental image. A system of such marks which would serve as a private notational device could be invented by a man. But words have a second more important function as signs by which men can communicate their conceptions to each other. A language, developed over time according to men's needs, and learned ex-

---

[8] *Leviathan* (3), p. 21; *Elements of Law* (I. iv. 7–10), pp. 15–16.
[9] *Leviathan* (4), p. 24.

perientially by individuals, provides a means by which one man, uttering certain sounds or making certain marks, can cause another to have a set of conceptions.[10]

Names may be distributed among four categories: (1) names of body or matter; (2) names of accidents; (3) names of phantasms; (4) names of names and speeches.[11] These categories are not necessarily categories of different kinds of things, but only of different ways of considering things or our conceptions of things. For example, we can talk of a hot thing, of heat in the abstract, of our perception of heat, and of the names "hot" and "heat" and our statements using these terms. In each case we may discuss a single situation in a different way, conceiving of, or focusing on, one or another aspect of it. In the first case we are concerned with a particular body and with the causes which make it what it is. In the second we abstract one type of accident, one set of causes, the set that produces the effect of heat. The third case involves an examination of the perception of heat by a sensing organism. Finally, we may discuss "heat" words and "heat" statements.

To reason is to join names; a proposition joins two names, a syllogism (in which two propositions are joined to imply a third) joins three names. By asserting a proposition (e.g., A man is a living creature), the speaker indicates that he thinks that the proposition is true, i.e., that the predicate (living creature) is the name of everything of which the subject (man) is the name. He states that the former name is comprehended by the latter. Since a proposition is true if the former name is so comprehended, truth consists in the proper use of names and not in things, "for, truth, and a true proposition, is all one." [12]

The method of analysis is reasoning back from the phenomena present to sense in order to discover "such causes as may

---

[10] *Ibid.*, pp. 24–25; *De Corpore* (ii. 2–4), *EW* I, 14–16; *Elements of Law* (I. v. 1–2, I. vi. 1), pp. 17–18, 24.

[11] *De Corpore* (v. 2), *EW* I, 57–58; *Leviathan* (4), pp. 29–30.

[12] *Elements of Law* (I. v. 10), p. 21; *De Corpore* (iii. 2, 7), *EW* I, 30, 35; *Leviathan* (4), pp. 27–28.

be." Analysis or resolution is the method used to arrive at universal principles, causal definitions in terms of motion. To discover the causes of some effect, we imagine all the accidents which accompany or precede the effect. (An *accident* is the faculty of a body by which it works in us a conception of itself.) [13] Then we examine our conception of this effect in conjunction with each of the accidents. If the effect can be conceived to occur without an accident, then that accident is not part of the cause.[14] A *cause* is the sum or aggregate of all the accidents, in the agent and in the patient which are necessary to produce the effect; if all these accidents exist, it cannot be understood that the effect will not exist, nor that the effect will occur if any one of them is absent. So, the first step in arriving at universal principles is to divide a conception into parts. If we begin with the conception of a *square,* we resolve it into a *plane, terminated with a certain number of equal and straight lines and right angles.* This can in turn be resolved into *line, plane, terminated, angle, straightness, rectitude, equality.* Compounding the causes of these elements will produce a square. Had we started with *gold,* we should have analyzed it into *solid, visible, heavy,* and so on. "And in this manner, by resolving continually, we may come to know what those things are, whose causes being first known severally, and afterwards compounded, may bring us to the knowledge of singular things." [15]

The method of resolution is to be pursued until universal principles are found. These have one universal cause, manifest of itself; that cause is motion, and motion itself cannot be understood to have any cause other than motion.[16]

The synthetic or compositive method, the method of demonstration, begins with the causes discovered by analysis. From these first principles, by a process of continued logical deduction, a science may be produced. To produce science—true

---

[13] *De Corpore* (viii. 2), *EW* I, 103.   [14] *Ibid.* (vi. 10), *EW* I, 77.
[15] *Ibid.* (vi. 4), *EW* I, 69.   [16] *Ibid.* (vi. 5), *EW* I, 69–70.

and correct philosophical knowledge—two things are necessary: proper definitions and correct reasoning. Of these two
necessities, correct reasoning is the easier to obtain. In reckoning, certain errors must be avoided. We must avoid equivocation, keeping the signification of the words constant. But this
is hindered because men's conceptions are affected by their
likes and dislikes, by their desires and detestations.

For seeing all names are imposed to signifie our conceptions; and
all our affections are but conceptions; when we conceive the same
things differently, we can hardly avoyd different naming of them.
For though the nature of that we conceive, be the same; yet the
diversity of our reception of it, in respect of different constitutions
of body, and prejudices of opinion, gives every thing a tincture
of our different passions. And therefore in reasoning, a man must
take heed of words; which besides the signification of what we
imagine of their nature, have a signification also of the nature, disposition, and interest of the speaker; such as are the names of
Vertues, and Vices; For one man calleth *Wisdome*, what another
calleth *feare*; and one *cruelty*, what another *justice*; one *prodigal-
ity*, what another *magnanimity*; one *gravity*, what another *stu-
pidicy*, &c. And therefore such names can never be true grounds
of any ratiocination.[17]

In reasoning, care must be taken that names joined together
produce a conceivable result. If a name (x) is added to its contradictory (not-x), we cannot imagine anything which has both
names.[18] Nor can we have any conception corresponding to an
untrue general proposition. So, if a proposition is asserted in
which the second name does not comprehend the first, the
result will be inconceivable. "And words whereby we conceive
nothing but the sound, are those we call *Absurd, Insignificant,*
and *Non-sense.*" [19] It is somewhat unusual for absurdity to be
completely undisguised. Contradictory conjunctions of words
usually employ roots from different languages, preferably from
Latin or Greek; an "incorporeal body" seems much more viable

[17] *Leviathan* (4), pp. 31–32; *cf. Elements of Law* (Ep. Ded.), p. xv.
[18] *Leviathan* (4), pp. 30–31; *De Corpore* (ii. 7–8), *EW* I, 18–19.
[19] *Leviathan* (5), p. 34.

than "immaterial matter" or "insubstantial substance." But
the most serious sort of absurdity is the category error involved
in joining words of two different types in a proposition, e.g.,
asserting that the name of a body is the name of a word or the
name of an accident. Notable examples of this mistake occur
in popular speech and in learned discourse: "body is extension," "a ghost is a thing," *"esse est ens," "genus est ens,"* "a
thing is as it appears," "a definition is the essence of a thing,"
"an idea is universal," "some things are necessary, other things
are contingent." Most of these absurdities are obvious if it is
remembered that only names are universals or "kinds," that
things are not appearances whereas phantasms are, that only
propositions are necessary or contingent.[20]

Correct reckoning—the adding and subtracting of words,
figures, or numbers—must be formally correct; it must also
produce a conceivable, an imaginable, result. Otherwise it
could not be understood.

When a man upon the hearing of any Speech, hath those thoughts
which the words of that Speech, and their connexion, were ordained and constituted to signifie; Then he is said to understand it:
Understanding being nothing else, but conception caused by
Speech.[21]

The second necessity for science is proper definitions. All
scientific conclusions are the results of reasoning, and reasoning
can never arrive at absolute certainty but only at conditional
truth: the conclusions are true if the premises from which
they have been correctly derived are true. To start from equivo-
cal terms, or from premises taken from other men's books, is
to tote up an account without any assurance of the accuracy

[20] *Ibid.* (4, 5), pp. 30–31, 35–36; *De Corpore* (v. 2–9), *EW* I, 57–61. See Engel,
"Hobbes's Table of Absurdity," pp. 533–43.

[21] *Leviathan* (4), p. 31. *Cf. Elements of Law* (I. vi. 3), p. 25: Evidence "is the
concomitance of a man's conception with the words that signify such conception in the act of ratiocination." Interpretations of Hobbes's theories of language and truth as purely nominalist seem to me to overlook the importance
of this point. See Krook, "Thomas Hobbes's Doctrine of Meaning and Truth,"
pp. 3–22, and Watkins, *Hobbes's System of Ideas*, pp. 138–50.

of the items, thus laying the account open to false or absurd results without being able to correct it.

For words are wise mens counters, they do but reckon by them: but they are the mony of fooles, that value them by the authority of an *Aristotle,* a *Cicero,* or a *Thomas,* or any other Doctor whatsoever, if but a man.[22]

The prime necessity, then, is for definitions.

Seeing then that *truth* consisteth in the right ordering of names in our affirmations, a man that seeketh precise *truth,* had need to remember what every name he uses stands for; and to place it accordingly; or else he will find himselfe entangled in words, as a bird in lime-twiggs; the more he struggles, the more belimed. And therefore in Geometry, (which is the onely Science that it hath pleased God hitherto to bestow on mankind,) men begin at settling the significations of their words; which settling of significations, they call *Definitions;* and place them in the beginning of their reckoning.[23]

The method of composition begins with definitions. But these definitions will not be merely verbal circumlocutions, lest the results fail to be a science useful to men. Philosophy must be knowledge of causation. Only if the first premises and definitions, the universal principles discovered by resolution, are stated in terms of the motions by which they are or could be produced, will the conclusions deduced be a causal science. In other words, by beginning with causal statements (the productive motions), we insure that the chain of reasoning that follows is reducible to causal statements—statements about a conceivable mechanical world. Definitions must be given in terms of conceivable generations. We must begin by imagining causal motions that produce the thing defined, for if generations are not contained in the definitions

they cannot be found in the conclusion of the first syllogism, that is made from those definitions; and if they be not in the first conclusion, they will not be found in any further conclusion deduced from that; and, therefore, by proceeding in this manner, we shall

[22] *Leviathan* (4), p. 29.   [23] *Ibid.,* p. 28.

never come to science; which is against the scope and intention of demonstration.[24]

From first principles defined in terms of conceivable motions, a causal science can be produced by continued deduction—the application of the method of synthesis. This is the method used for the demonstration (rather than the discovery) of science or philosophy. For Hobbes, the model of a demonstrative science was Euclidean geometry. It was the discovery of geometry which set him off in quest of science.[25] But Hobbes did not regard geometry as purely abstract deductions from a set of postulates. Geometry is an intermediate science; its first principles may be derived from principles still more basic, and in addition, they should be restated as Hobbes restates them —in terms of generative motions.[26] Hobbes had what may be called a geometric imagination as opposed to an algebraic one; he thought abstract symbolic reasoning neither valid nor useful because the symbols have no reference to any conceptions. Algebraic reasoning then is inconceivable; in his long battle against its exponents, Hobbes admitted only that algebra might be useful as a device for registering the inventions of geometricians.[27] Hobbes thought geometry the science of the figure and motion of bodies abstracted from all other considerations.[28]

In presenting his system of philosophy, Hobbes used the method of synthesis. From the definitions and explications of the fundamental principles of science (place, motion, cause, etc.), the effects of various motions are deduced (mechanics). This is followed by the investigation of the effects of the invisible motions of parts of bodies (physics), and the investigation of sense and its causes. Next come the science of human passion and action—psychology in its widest sense—and finally civil philosophy, the science of natural justice which was first

[24] *De Corpore* (vi. 13), *EW* I, 82–83.   [25] Aubrey, I, 332.
[26] *De Corpore* (xiv), *EW* I, 176–202; see also, *Six Lessons to the Professors of Mathematics* (Ep. Ded.), *EW* VII, 183–84, and Watkins, *Hobbes's System of Ideas*, pp. 68–71.
[27] *De Corpore* (xx. 6), *EW* I, 316–17.   [28] *Leviathan* (9, Table), p. 65.

presented by Hobbes himself in *De Cive*.[29] And civil philosophy
is like geometry because we make both lines and figures and
commonwealths ourselves; correct political construction is entirely in man's power.[30] Civil philosophy, however, has even
more important affinities with natural philosophy, for just
as the theorems of natural philosophy can be used to explain
the causes of natural phenomena, the theorems of political
philosophy can be used to explain social phenomena.[31]

There are two different types of knowledge: empirical—
knowledge of the facts of sense and memory; and scientific
—knowledge of a chain of reasoning.

No Discourse whatsoever, can End in absolute knowledge of Fact,
past, or to come. For, as for the knowledge of Fact, it is originally,
Sense; and ever after, Memory. And for the knowledge of Consequence, which I have said before is called Science, it is not Absolute, but Conditionall. No man can know by Discourse, that this,
or that, is, has been, or will be; which is to know absolutely: but
onely, that if This be, That is; if This has been, That has been;
if This shall be, That shall be: which is to know conditionally;
and that not the consequence of one thing to another; but of one
name of a thing, to another name of the same thing.[32]

Knowledge of the first kind is registered in books called histories; both natural histories and histories of human acts. "The
Registers of Science, are such *Books* as contain the *Demonstrations* of Consequences of one Affirmation, to another; and are
commonly called *Books of Philosophy*." [33]

Hobbes's conditional philosophic knowledge depends, as he
recognized, on its first principles. These were to be derived by

[29] *De Cive* (Preface), *EW* II, xx; *De Corpore* (Ep. Ded.), *EW* I, viii–ix; *A
Minute or first Draught of the Optiques*, *EW* VII, 470–71. *N.B.*, in the first two
references and in *Leviathan* (9 Table), p. 65, Hobbes's classification of the
branches of philosophy differ. It is divided into two parts (natural and civil) in
Leviathan and into three parts (nature, man, and society) in his systematic
works. In all these descriptions geometry holds a minor place, but *cf. De Cive*
(Ep. Ded.), *EW* II, iii–iv, where its importance is greater.
[30] *Six Lessons to the Professors of Mathematics* (Ep. Ded.), *EW* VII, 183–84.
[31] See below, pp. 35–47, 228–42.   [32] *Leviathan* (7), pp. 49–50.
[33] *Ibid.* (9), p. 64; *cf. ibid.* (5), pp. 36–37; *Elements of Law* (I. vi. 1), pp. 24–25;
De Corpore (i. 8), *EW* I, 10–11.

analysis; they were to be possible and conceivable causes. The premises themselves cannot be demonstrated, but they may be explicated.[34] A clear conception of what is meant is created in the hearer's mind when "motion" is described as the leaving of one place and the acquiring of another, or when "place" is defined as space possessed or filled by some body. Thus, the principles of the system are definitions given in terms of causes, with explications of these principles and terms which produce clear conceptions of what is meant.

Although Hobbes admits that these definitions, because they are principles, cannot be demonstrated, he argues that they need not be demonstrated because they are "known by nature." We have seen that knowledge acquired by sense is immediately known. In this sort of knowledge, we know the whole sense-conception first, and we know more about it than we know about the causes of the parts of this conception. But the first principles of a philosophic system are not immediately known by sense. When we have scientific knowledge of the causes of the conceptions compounded into the idea of man (figure, animal, rational, etc.), then we know more (scientifically) about the causes of these "universals" than we know about the causes of a particular human individual.[35]

Hobbes claimed that the causes of universal principles are manifest of themselves. This claim depends upon the assumptions of his system of thought, the assumptions implied by the adoption of analytic-synthetic method and reinforced by the use of that method. The method is centered on the problem of sensation. Sense-conception itself involves the necessity of, and the conception of, change or mutation. The absence of sensible change, absolutely constant sensation, would be indistinguishable from the absence of sensation. Sensation implies change, and every change must be caused. All events are effects having causes—or at least events can be understood only as

[34] *De Corpore* (vi. 12), *EW* I, 80–81.   [35] *Ibid.*, (vi. 2), *EW* I, 66–68.

effects. But if there is no movement, then everything must remain the same, without change. All change is motion; all causation is motion; rest cannot be the cause of anything.[36] The world is a world of uniformly necessary causation, and in this world every effect and every cause is motion. What else but motions could be the manifest causes of universal principles?

Philosophy, then, is systematic knowledge about a world of causal motions. One of the principles necessary to explain appearances is that there are bodies that exist independently of thought. Bodies can be observed, however, only indirectly through their effects on observers. The concept of substance is not given, but constructed for the purpose of scientific explanation.[37] Philosophy includes only that which can be compounded of causes and resolved into causes—"every body of which we can conceive any generation and which may be compared with other bodies, or which is capable of composition and resolution." [38] Philosophy cannot arrive at any knowledge about God, or about anything else that is unique, or eternal, or unchanging, or inconceivable. In spite of its limitations, philosophical knowledge can be used for the benefit of man. The knowledge of natural causes will enable us, when we have the causes in our power, to produce the results we desire. The knowledge of the science of civil government will enable us to avoid the catastrophes that occur when men are ignorant of this science.[39]

The problem of sensation is central to Hobbes's philosophy. Sense-conception is the starting point for resolution; the observable phenomena must ultimately be explained by the results of composition. The central problem in natural philosophy is the relation of the observer to the world. Hobbes made

[36] *Ibid.* (ix. 9), *EW* I, 126.
[37] *Objections III* (9) to Descartes's *Meditations, Philosophical Works of Descartes,* II, 70–71.
[38] *De Corpore* (i. 8), *EW* I, 10   [39] *Ibid.* (i. 6–7), *EW* I, 7–10

his first effort to deal with this problem systematically in his
first philosophic work, the "Short Tract on First Principles." [40]
His continued interest is exhibited in a series of optical treatises, and in his expositions of natural philosophy; even *The
Elements of Law* and *Leviathan* begin by establishing the
relations between the world and the observer, and between
sensation and knowledge.[41]

Natural philosophy must explain sensation. From the first
principles a causal science must be deduced which can explain
the phenomena observed in sensation and the mechanism of
sensation itself. The explanation of sensation provides the link
between man and the world; it is the link between the explanation of the physical world and the explanation of human
behavior. Hobbes thought that his civil philosophy was based
on his natural philosophy, for civil philosophy begins with a
model of human behavior provided by natural philosophy even
though the principles of human behavior may be independently
known by experience.[42] An examination of Hobbes's natural
philosophy should provide us with an example of a Hobbesian
science and with the principles that Hobbes believed were
the foundation of his political philosophy.

[40] *Elements of Law*, pp. 193–210. See Brandt, pp. 9–85, and Watkins, *Hobbes's
System of Ideas*, pp. 40–46.
[41] *De Corpore* (i. 2–4), *EW* I, 3–6; *Leviathan* (1, 2), pp. 11–18; *Elements of
Law* (I. i–ii), pp. 1–7.
[42] *De Cive* (Preface), *EW* II, xx.

2

NATURAL PHILOSOPHY

Omne quod est corpus est sui generis: nihil est incorporale nisi quod non est.

TERTULLIAN, *De Carne Christi*, 11

Hobbes divides his treatment of natural philosophy into three sections (Parts II, III, and IV of *De Corpore*). The first of these is called *Prima Philosophia,* or the First Grounds of Philosophy. The second concerns the Proportions of Motions and Magnitudes. In the third section Hobbes deals with Physics or the Phenomena of Nature.

These three sections have different functions. The first is Hobbes's analysis of the most general terms in which the world can be discussed. Here he establishes the definitions upon which the system rests. The second section takes the analysis a step farther. Motion and endeavor are considered in the abstract. The results are theories about the movement, balance, and collision of bodies. The third part, Physics, involves a shift of perspective. The first two sections have elaborated a theoretical framework; the purpose of the third section is to explain our experience of the world in terms of that framework. Explanations of the appearances of nature are constructed which use the theoretical framework.

Prima Philosophia

The first grounds of natural philosophy are space, time, body and accident, cause and effect, motion, and the explanation of some of the terms used in defining and comparing things.

SPACE AND TIME

In order to understand the world, we must conceive its possible generation; Part I of *De Corpore* attempts to describe the elements which constitute, or at least may constitute, the world. First we must imagine the world annihilated except for one man. This man, retaining his memory, would be able to consider the world as he had formerly perceived it, and as he could yet imagine it. (Unlike God, man cannot create a world *ex nihilo;* he can only reconstruct it out of sense perceptions.) The construction of a world out of remembered perceptions is what the scientist does when he calculates the motions of the heavens and the earth. He does it in his study, his closet, and not by taking observations in heaven. Science begins from sense perceptions (sense and memory); it considers sensations not only as internal motions of the mind, but as things that appear to exist outside the mind.[1]

If that solitary scientist imagined something existing outside himself, he would have a conception of space.[2] Fancy of succession, a before and after in motion, would be a conception of time.[3] Space and time are both phantasms. It is not surprising that Hobbes should describe time as a function of motion, always measured in comparison with motion. Aristotle, as Hobbes admits, had adopted a similar theory. But why is space imaginary?

The central problem of the Prima Philosophia is the problem

---

[1] *De Corpore* (vii. 1), *EW* I, 91–92. Hobbes used the annihilation argument for a similar purpose as early as 1640: *Elements of Law* (I. i. 8), p. 2.
[2] *De Corpore* (vii. 2), *EW* I, 93.   [3] *Ibid.* (vii. 3), *EW* I, 94–95.

of light. Hobbes sets up a set of abstract categories: space, time, motion, body, and cause. But the connections between these categories and the reasons for his taking the positions he does take on, e.g., space, can only be understood in relation to the construction of a satisfactory theory of light. Even if light is not the greatest puzzle for all theories of the world, it is the most difficult of the natural phenomena to explain in terms of bodies and motions.

The key to the solution of the problem of light for Hobbes was his radical suggestion that space is imaginary. The alternative was to accept space as real. Had he taken this position, Hobbes would have been forced to one of two conclusions: either objective space would have to be equivalent to extension, or space would have to be something that really exists but is nothing. Both conclusions were repugnant.

The first alternative was the position of Descartes: space is extension. This equates space and body; it makes a full universe (a plenum) logically necessary. Correlatively, vacuum is logically impossible. Although Hobbes argues against the existence of vacuum in his Physics,[4] his argument is not that vacuum is impossible, but that the phenomena explained by the vacuum hypothesis may be explained as well without it, and that there is at least one crucial experiment against it. The other alternative, that space is objective but empty, was equally unacceptable to Hobbes. He did not think that vacuum could be proved not to exist,[5] but he is very far from accepting it as a necessary and fundamental element of the world. Hobbes could not accept the real existence of empty space, of nothing. To assert that "Space is empty nothing having a real existence without the mind" would have implied that the concept of an incorporeal substance was not the objectionable nonsense that Hobbes held it to be.

Hobbes had additional philosophic reasons for rejecting objective empty space. Hobbes had once accepted a vacuum

[4] *Ibid.* (xxvi. 2–4), *EW* I, 414–26.   [5] *Ibid.* (viii. 9), *EW* I, 108–9.

hypothesis. As late as 1646, he had been willing to allow empty spaces between bodies.[6] Interstitial minute vacuums were acceptable, both theoretically and ontologically, but the production, in Torricelli's famous experiment, of an observable vacuum above the column of mercury led Hobbes to revise his opinion. Light apparently passes through such a space without the distortion which should be apparent if it were traveling around it, through the glass. Hobbes drew the consequence that such a space could not be empty in fact. Vacuum becomes an ontological impossibility, but Hobbes never adopted the view that vacuum was a theoretical absurdity.[7]

The experimental discovery of vacuum forced Hobbes to re-examine his position on the existence of vacuums (and paradoxically to deny the existence of vacuums) because of the connections between the vacuum theory and the possible theories of light transmission. Hobbes firmly denied the possibility of action at a distance; motion must always be transmitted through some material. Occult influences are excluded. There are two available theories of the transmission of light (light being some kind of motion): (1) the emanation theory and (2) the medium theory.

(1) The emanation theory. This theory is similar to the

[6] Hobbes defends the vacuum hypothesis in conjunction with his theory that the sun produces light by dilation and contraction. Against the objection that the dilation-contraction explanation requires that vacuum be admitted, in *A Minute or first Draught of the Optiques* (I. ii. 2), British Museum, *Harleian* MSS, 3360, fol. 9, Hobbes argues:

"To ye second [objection] I answer, That I suppose that there is vacuity made by such dilatation, but find no impossibility nor absurdity, nor so much as an improbability in admitting vacuity, for no probable argument hath ever beene produced to ye contrarie, unlesse we should take a space or extension for a body or thing extended and thence conclude because space is every where imaginable, Therefore bodie is in every space, ffor who knows not that Extension is one thing, and ye thing extended another, as hunger is one thing, & that w[hi]ch is hungry another."

[7] *De Corpore* (viii. 9), *EW* I, 108–9. See Brandt, pp. 201–7, for a discussion of the development of Hobbes's position on vacuum, including an analysis of Hobbes's letter to Mersenne of February 17, 1648 (see Tönnies, "Hobbes-Analekten II," pp. 172–73) in which the vacuum problem is raised. Brandt mistakenly holds however that "Hobbes, in his ultimate natural philosophy (1655), vigorously denies the possibility of vacuity." (p. 202.)

modern particle theory. Species or particles emanate from a moving body. They proceed to another body and affect it by causing motion, or change of motion, in it. The emanating species are bodily (and not incorporeal); consequently the body from which they emanate must diminish in size, or be replenished as a fire must be.

Hobbes presented the emanation theory in just this form in "the little treatise." He argued that the medium theory is contradicted in the case of light by the absence of observable effects on light in its motion through a possible medium of transmission, air. Replenishment is possible, for

we may with probability imagine, that as Fyery bodyes, which send out most Species, are manifestly and sensiblely supplyed with fuell: so other bodyes, sending out fewer, may have a supply of Nutriment, by converting other bodyes or Species adjacent, into themselves; though the way how this is done, as allmost all the wayes of Nature, be to us not so perceptible.[8]

Nevertheless, by 1640 Hobbes had abandoned the emanation theory for a medium theory.[9] Perhaps Hobbes was driven to the alternative hypothesis because replenishment was more difficult to imagine than he had originally supposed.[10]

(2) The medium theory. According to this theory, light is transmitted by successive motion through a medium. The motion of the light-producing body is transmitted to the contiguous part of the medium, from that part to the next part, and so on. If this theory is accepted, empty space, presumably non-transmitting, cannot exist between the earth and such visible light sources as the sun and the stars.

Having rejected the emanation theory, Hobbes had to accept the medium theory. He could then no longer accept the reality of vacuum, objective empty space, for if he had accepted

[8] "A Short Tract on First Principles," in *Elements of Law*, p. 201.
[9] *Elements of Law* (I. ii. 8), p. 5. Brandt dates the *Tractatus Opticus* (*Elements of Law*, Appendix II, pp. 211–26), which also adopts the medium theory, by 1641. (Brandt, pp. 92, 100 ff.)
[10] The emanation theory is rejected (because the sun would have been used up long ago) in *Seven Philosophical Problems* (iv), *EW* VII, 32.

it he would have been forced to explain why it did not exist. At the same time, Hobbes stubbornly refused to accept Descartes's solution, identifying body with extension, thereby making a full world logically inescapable. Faced with the dilemma of choosing between two objectionable alternatives, real empty space and real full space, Hobbes adopted a third theory, a theory which elegantly avoided some of the disadvantages of the other two—for in it neither vacuum nor plenum was necessary—and which was more consistent with his general approach: space is imaginary.[11]

Hobbes's theory of space commits him neither to the denial of the possibility of vacuum nor to the acceptance of vacuum as necessary. His adopting this position is connected with his positions on cause and effect, and on body and accident. If space were real, either it would have to be equivalent to body (the plenum theory), or it would exclude body; everything is either body or space. But if space is imaginary it neither excludes body nor is body. Since Hobbes could not accept action at a distance or action by intelligible (non-corporeal) species, his theory of space was the only one of the three theories compatible with both the emanistic and the mediumistic theories of light. The plenum theory is most compatible with the propagation of light by motion through a medium; the empty space theory is most compatible with an emanistic explanation. Hobbes's theory of space was the only one available to him that did not commit him to a theory of light.

BODY AND ACCIDENT

The second foundation of Hobbes's natural philosophy is his theory of body and accident. Let us, Hobbes says, now imagine something newly created or replaced in space. This is body. It is a self-subsisting subject; i.e., it exists without us, it is not dependent on our thought, and it is placed in and

---

[11] *De Corpore* (vii. 2), *EW* I, 93-94; see Brandt, pp. 253-54.

subjected to imaginary space.[12] Hobbes is making two points: (1) Body is real; it has real size: extension or magnitude. (2) Body is subject to imaginary space; it is always perceived or imagined as being in some place.

Body actually possesses real magnitude but it is imagined as occupying space, and so has an imaginary magnitude. For body does not displace space as it would if space were something real; it occupies space. The space that it occupies is "place." A body always keeps its magnitude, but it does not necessarily keep the same place. Place itself, imaginary position, does not move.[13] A body cannot be in two places at one time; nor can two bodies be in the same place at one time.[14]

The relation between real magnitude and imaginary magnitude raises the general problem of the relation between bodies and their accidents. If we imagine a thing existing independently of our minds, it must occupy some place; it must also be in motion or at rest. The "qualities" of extension, motion, and rest are accidents. Hobbes regards accidents as distinguishable from body, but not as parts of body capable of separate existence. That which is moved is always a body; that which is extended is always a body. The accidents of motion and extension, and other accidents as well, may be defined in two ways; an accident is *"the manner by which any body is conceived"* or *"that faculty of any body by which it works in us a conception of itself."* [15] Hobbes held that these two definitions were equivalent. The "manner by which a body is conceived" is a causal relation between the body and a percipient, the cause of a perception of motion, or hardness, or some other quality. The "faculty of any body by which it works in us a conception of itself" is also a description of a causal relation between a body and the perception of that body by a perceiver. Magnitude and figure are always accidents of any conceivable body.

[12] *De Corpore* (viii. 1), *EW* I, 101–2. [13] *Ibid.* (viii. 5), *EW* I, 105–7.
[14] *Ibid.* (viii. 8), *EW* I, 108. [15] *Ibid.* (viii. 2–3), *EW* I, 102–5.

After magnitude the most important accident of a body is motion. Motion is the continual relinquishing of one place and the acquiring of another. "I say a continual relinquishing, because no body how little soever, can totally and at once go out of its former place into another, so, but that some part of it will be in a part of a place which is common to both, namely, to the relinquished and the acquired places." [16] Nor is anything moved in no time at all. If this were possible, it would be moved without motion. Something is at rest if it remains in one place during any time; something is moved if it was formerly in another place. So, what is moved has been moved; what is moved will yet be moved; what is moved is not in one place in any time, no matter how small.[17]

Motion and rest are both inert. If a body is in motion, then it will continue to move unless something causes it to cease moving; if a body is at rest, it will always remain at rest *"unless there be some other body besides it, which, by endeavouring to get into its place by motion, suffers it no longer to remain at rest."* [18] Hobbes adopts a theory of inertia [19] and immediately connects it with his causal theory. Change from rest to motion, or from motion to rest, must be caused by something external, continuous, and moving.

Body itself is neither generated nor destroyed. Matter is conserved. When we say that some specific thing is generated or destroyed (a seed becomes a tree, a tree dies and rots), what we mean is that the accidents for which we named it are generated and destroyed.[20] Accidents are not bodies or parts of bodies; as we have seen, accidents are generated and they perish. In fact, every change of appearance involves the destruction of at least one accident or the creation of at least one new accident. When a bit of iron is melted, hardness is not still present in it invisibly; nor has the hardness been separated from the iron. Hardness (i.e., the cause of this appearance) has

[16] *Ibid.* (viii. 10), *EW* I, 109.   [17] *Ibid.* (viii. 11), *EW* I, 110–11.
[18] *Ibid.* (viii. 19), *EW* I, 115. *Cf. Leviathan* (2), p. 13.
[19] See Brandt, pp. 282 ff.   [20] *De Corpore* (viii. 20), *EW* I, 116–17.

perished; softness (i.e., the cause of this appearance) has been created.[21] This is equally true in the case of an optical illusion, though what perishes in this case may be an accident only of the observer, i.e., a phantasm. Accidents, not being bodies, cannot be moved about, or at least it is improper to say that they are moved about.[22] "Now that accident for which we give a certain name to any body, or the accident which denominates its subject, is commonly called the ESSENCE thereof. . . . And the same essence, in as much as it is generated, is called the FORM."[23] In respect to the "form," the body is called the "matter"; in respect to any accident, it is the "subject." Change is the production or the perishing of any accident. If the form is changed, the particular thing is said to be destroyed or generated. Hobbes has reduced "matter," "form," and "essence" to related names.

Hobbes carries the reduction of real relations even farther. He uses this reduction to suggest that the problem of identity is not insoluble and not as serious as it sometimes appears to be. Two bodies differ when something may be said of one which may not be said of the other at the same time.[24] Consequently, no two bodies can be identical, for they cannot both be in the same place at the same time.[25] How can we say that a thing is the same thing over a period of time? When is a thing still the same thing? When is it no longer the same thing? Is it the same if its form is the same although its matter has changed? Is it the same when its matter is the same although its form has changed? Or does it retain the same identity only if all its accidents are unchanged?

The answer to such a question is found by considering the name by which a thing is called when we make the inquiry. "Is Socrates the same man?" is one question. "Is Socrates the same body?" is another question. When the question is about the matter, then the thing is the same if the matter is the same.

---

[21] *Ibid.* (viii. 21), *EW* I, 117. [22] *Ibid.* (viii. 22), *EW* I, 117.
[23] *Ibid.* (viii. 23), *EW* I, 117–18. [24] *Ibid.* (xi. 1), *EW* I, 132.
[25] *Ibid.* (xi. 2), *EW* I, 133.

When the question is about form, then identity is preserved as long as the generated motion is continued after its initiation. Socrates is Socrates from his generation until his death. A river is the same river as long as it flows from the same source.[26] Heraclitus should have said that you can't step into the same water (not the same river) twice.

Identity, then, is not a separate accident of a body. It is a function of our consideration of a body and of our names for the body so considered. The problem of identity is a verbal problem; if our words are precise, it need not arise. Some sensible qualities are not accidents of the body to which they are generally attributed, e.g., colors (strictly speaking) are not accidents of objects but of percipients. Although color is a phantasm in the observer, it is causally related to the object, and to the medium transmitting the causing motion to the observer.[27] The relations of equality and inequality, similarity and difference, are not separate accidents of things. Two things are equal if their magnitudes are the same. Equality is a function of our comparison of the magnitudes; it is not a quality separable from the magnitude of the bodies. The similarity of the shape of one body to another, and its dissimilarity to a third, exists only because of the shapes of the bodies. The cause of the accident in these cases is the cause of the relation, i.e., without this accident the body would not be so related.[28] The relative terms are applied because the accidents are compared.

It is convenient to have a term for a conception of body without any accident other than magnitude and aptness to receive other accidents. This is what is meant by *materia prima* (body in general). This is a useful term although no particular thing can be said to be *materia prima*, or to be made of it rather than of iron or copper or wood.[29]

[26] *Ibid.* (xi. 7), *EW* I, 135–38.
[27] *Ibid.* (viii. 3; xxv. 3, 10), *EW* I, 104–5, 391–92, 404.
[28] *Ibid.* (xi. 6), *EW* I, 135.   [29] *Ibid.* (viii. 24), *EW* I, 118–19.

CAUSE AND EFFECT

The third base of Hobbes's natural philosophy is his theory of cause and effect. A body acts upon another body when it generates or destroys some accident in the other body. The acting body is the *agent;* the body acted upon is the *patient;* the accident generated or destroyed is the *effect.*[30] If one body acts upon a second which, in turn, acts upon a third, the mediating body is both patient and agent.[31]

[A] CAUSE simply, or *an entire cause, is the aggregate of all the accidents both of the agents, how many soever they be, and of the patient, put together; which when they are all supposed to be present, it cannot be understood but that the effect is produced at the same instant; and if any one of them be wanting, it cannot be understood but that the effect is not produced.*[32]

Hobbes discusses some of the other usages of the term "cause." Each accident without which the effect cannot be produced is a "cause *sine qua non.*" [33] The aggregate of necessary accidents in the agent is the "efficient cause"; the aggregate of necessary accidents in the patient is the "material cause." [34] Some thinkers have not been satisfied with these causes.

The writers of metaphysics reckon up two other causes besides the *efficient* and *material,* namely, the ESSENCE, which some call the *formal cause,* and the END, or *final cause;* both which are nevertheless efficient causes. For when it is said the essence of a thing is the cause thereof, *as to be rational is the cause of man,* it is not intelligible; for it is all one, as if it were said, *to be a man is the cause of man;* which is not well said. And yet the knowledge of the *essence* of anything, is the cause of the knowledge of the thing itself; for, if I first know that a thing is *rational,* I know from thence, that the same is man; but this is no other than an efficient cause. [I.e., it is the cause of the knowledge.] A *final cause* has no

---

[30] *Ibid.* (ix. 1), *EW* I, 120.   [31] *Ibid.* (ix. 2), *EW* I, 120–21.
[32] *Ibid.* (ix. 3), *EW* I, 121–22.   [33] *Ibid.*
[34] *Ibid.* (ix. 4), *EW* I, 122.

place but in such things as have sense and will; and this also I shall prove hereafter to be an efficient cause.[35]

So, a cause is the aggregate of all the accidents necessary to produce the effect. If the effect is not produced, the cause is not complete; no effect, no cause. Moreover this formula is reversible. Everything which is produced has a cause. There are no contingencies, no accidental happenings. An accident is contingent to another accident when it is not causally related to it.[36] All events happen with equal necessity; they are all necessarily caused. Necessary causation is as true of events in the future as it has been of events in the past. But that future events will be the effects of necessary causes does not mean that we necessarily know the causes of all events, or even that we are correct when we think that we know the cause of an effect. Although some accidents are not causally related to other accidents, although we confess that we do not perceive the causes of future events, nevertheless no events can occur without their necessary causes.[37]

If we consider causation in the future instead of in the past, the terms *power* and *act* are applied rather than *cause* and *effect*. The two sets of terms are otherwise equivalent. Every act produced will be produced by a power necessary and sufficient to produce it. *Plenary power* (the power of the agent plus that of the patient) necessarily produces the act.

Hobbes's analysis of cause and effect is not especially radical. He has done no more than to insist on a strict use of the terms "cause" and "effect." If a cause then its effect; if an effect, then it has been produced by a cause. Nevertheless, it is not the only conceivable position. He could have held that some events were not effects; e.g., he could have adopted Lucretius' view that atoms swerve from their courses in a random or accidental

[35] *Ibid.* (x. 7), *EW* I, 131–32. [36] *Ibid.* (ix. 10), *EW* I, 126–27.
[37] *Ibid.* (ix. 5), *EW* I, 122–23. *Cf. The Questions concerning Liberty, Necessity, and Chance* (xiv), *EW* V, 189: "But, because men for the most part think those things produced without cause, whereof they do not see the cause, they use to call both the agent and the action contingent, as attributing it to fortune."

way. Again (even if he had regarded all happenings to bodies as effects) he could have believed in the existence of non-bodily, uncaused things, i.e., souls or minds, which need not be subject to external causation. The immunity of the soul from external necessity—Descartes's position—is the basis of the theory of free will. All bodily events are caused; animals are regarded as mechanisms; but, soul events (or at least some of them) are determined by the soul itself. Minds are uncaused. Hobbes would not retreat from his mechanistic determinism. There are no incorporeal substances; all events are bodily events; all events are equally necessary effects of necessary causes.

A completely determined universe was not an especially new or unusual theory in the seventeenth century. Calvin's God provided, as the Divine Spirit of the Stoics had provided, for all the occurrences in the universe, past, present, and future. Hobbes, in fact, hinted in his controversy with Bishop Bramhall that it was blasphemous to deny that all things happened necessarily in accordance with God's foreknowledge and will.[38]

MOTION

To his materialism (all real things are bodies) and his determinism (all events have antecedent necessary causes), Hobbes added a third element that made this theory very radical indeed. An effect is the production or destruction of some accident in the patient, and this is what we mean by change. Hobbes insisted that all change is motion. Not only is all change motion, but all change is externally caused; thus all causes, all

[38] *Of Liberty and Necessity, EW* IV, 278: "To which [logical proof of necessity] I could add, if I thought it good logic, the *inconvenience* of denying *necessity*, as it destroyeth both the *decrees* and the *prescience* of God Almighty; for whatsoever God hath *purposed* to bring to pass by *man*, as an instrument, or foreseeth shall come to pass; a man, if he have *liberty*, such as his Lordship [Bishop Bramhall] affirmeth, from *necessitation*, might frustrate, and make not to come to pass, and God should either not *foreknow* it, and not *decree* it, or he should *foreknow* such things shall be, as shall never be, and *decree* that which shall never come to pass." See also *The Questions concerning Liberty, Necessity, and Chance, EW* V, 17–18

effects, all accidents (except perhaps magnitude) can be reduced
to motions and externally caused changes in motions.

Hobbes must set out to prove: (1) that all change is motion
or change in motion, and (2) that all change is externally
caused, i.e., that nothing can move itself. In fact he goes further than this by contending that motion can only be caused
by a contiguous and moving body, that is, there is no action
at a distance. Although it cannot be said that Hobbes rigorously
demonstrates these contentions, he does produce some very
interesting arguments in their favor. The first of these is based
on the continual interaction of causes and effects.

And from this, that whensoever the cause is entire, the effect is
produced in the same instant, it is manifest that causation and the
production of effects consist in a certain continual progress; so
that as there is a continual mutation in the agent or agents, by the
working of other agents upon them, so also the patient, upon
which they work, is continually altered and changed. For example:
as the heat of the fire increases more and more, so also the effects
thereof, namely, the heat of such bodies as are next to it, and again,
of such other bodies as are next to them, increase more and more
accordingly; which is already no little argument that all mutation
consists in motion only.[39]

The continuity of cause, effect, and further effect indicates
that causation involves some sort of constant transmission. Both
cause and effect, then, must be reducible to something in process. For Hobbes, this could only be motion. The argument is
based upon his fusion of motion and causation.

Hobbes's contention that all change is externally caused by
motion depends on his acceptance of the inertia of uniform
motion and of rest. It was mentioned above that Hobbes adopts
a principle of inertia and that this principle is connected with
his theory of causation. Suppose a body to be at rest, with
nothing else in space; "if now this body begin to be moved,
it will certainly be moved some way; seeing therefore there
was nothing in that body which did not dispose it to rest

[39] *De Corpore* (ix. 6), *EW* I, 123–24.

[otherwise it would not have been at rest], the reason why it is moved this way is in something out of it"; or if it had been moved another way, the reason for its motion that way would be something out of it. But we supposed nothing else in space, so "the reason of its motion one way would be the same with the reason of its motion every other way, wherefore it would be moved alike all ways at once; which is impossible." [40] Unless we suppose an external cause of motion, there is no sufficient reason why the body should begin to move at any particular time or in any particular direction.

Hobbes had already rejected the possibility of an internal cause of motion. He applied the same argument to internally caused motion in the "little treatise." If a body had power to move itself, then it would always be moving, since it is always applied to itself. Here there is no sufficient reason why it should move in one direction rather than another, or at one time rather than another. The same arguments apply to a body in motion; a moving body will continue to move in the same way and with the same velocity unless its motion is affected by another moving body.[41] Hobbes's arguments for effects being produced by external motion depend on the principle of sufficient reason. There must be some reason for every event; this reason must be a change in the situation. His argument that every cause of motion must be a body that is contiguous as well as moving lacks any substantial support.

For let there be any two bodies which are not contiguous, and betwixt which the intermediate space is empty, . . . and let one of the propounded bodies be supposed to be at rest; I say it shall always be at rest. For if it shall be moved, the cause of that motion . . . will be some external body; and, therefore, if between it and that external body there be nothing but empty space, then whatsoever the disposition be of that external body or of the patient itself, yet if it be supposed to be now at rest, we may conceive it will continue so till it be touched by some other body. But seeing cause, by the definition, is the aggregate of all such accidents, which being

---

[40] *Ibid.* (viii. 19), *EW* I, 115.   [41] *Ibid.* (ix. 7), *EW* I, 124–25.

supposed to be present, it cannot be conceived but that the effect will follow, those accidents, which are either in external bodies, or in the patient itself, cannot be the cause of future motion.[42]

Hobbes assumes that action at a distance cannot occur: contiguity is necessary to causation. Action at a distance was inconceivable to him, and even Newton did not wish to be thought foolish enough to suppose that it was possible.[43]

The concept of causation requires the assumption that nature is uniform over time. The same agent working on the same patient will produce the same effect at different times. If the conditions were unchanged, and the same effect were not produced, we should either have to discard regular causation or include time as a causal element. To do the latter would make time something more than the imagination of before and after in motion; it would have to become something real. Nature is uniform; the same cause will always produce the same effect. Hobbes uses the principle of uniformity to support his argument that all change is motion. If the principle is accepted, then all change is motion of the parts of the changed body. The argument deserves to be quoted:

[42] *Ibid.*

[43] See Isaac Newton to Richard Bentley, 25 February 1692/3, no. 406 in Newton, III, 253–54:

"Tis unconceivable that inanimate brute matter should (without ye mediation of something else wch is not material) operate upon & affect other matter without mutual contact; as it must if gravitation in the sense of Epicurus be essential & inherent in it. And this is one reason why I desired you would not ascribe innate gravity to me. That gravity should be innate inherent & essential to matter so yt one body may act upon another at a distance through a vacuum without the mediation of any thing else by & through wch their action or force may be conveyed from one to another is to me so great an absurdity that I believe no man who has in philosophical matters any competent faculty of thinking can ever fall into it."

Cf. Strauss, *The Political Philosophy of Hobbes*, p. 166: "His scientific explanation of sense-perception is characterized by the fact that it interprets perception of the higher senses by the sense of touch; and the preference for the sense of touch which this presupposes is already implied in Hobbes's original view of the fundamental significance of the antithesis between vanity and fear."

Strauss's contention that Hobbes's moral views are prior to his science is criticized by Watkins, *Hobbes's System of Ideas*, pp. 27–46.

For first, we do not say anything is changed, but that which appears to our senses otherwise than it appeared formerly. Secondly, both those appearances are effects produced in the sentient; and, therefore, if they be different, it is necessary . . . that either some part of the agent, which was formerly at rest, is now moved, and so the mutation consists in this motion; or some part, which was formerly moved, is now otherwise moved, and so also the mutation consists in this new motion; or which, being formerly moved, is now at rest, which . . . cannot come to pass without motion; and so again, mutation is motion; or lastly, it happens in some of these manners to the patient, or some of its parts; so that mutation, howsoever it be made, will consist in the motion of the parts, either of the body which is perceived, or of the sentient body, or of both.[44]

Hobbes's argument is that if A (a body) has not moved, been moved, or suffered a change in its previous motion, then A must be the same as it was; if A remains the same, then it is not changed; so, if there is no change in motion, there is no change at all. Thus, Hobbes concludes that all change is motion, and that rest cannot be the cause of anything.[45]

Although it is clear that Hobbes's argument does not demonstrate his contention that all change is motion,[46] it does clarify his fusion of causation, change, and motion. Need this connection be demonstrated? Is it demonstrable? This section of *De Corpore* is concerned with principles; the theory of causation is one of the bases of Hobbes's natural philosophy. Principles are not demonstrable. Nevertheless, there is an argument for accepting these principles: if any explanation of the world, or of the events in it, is offered, it must rely on some fundamental ordering assumptions. Hobbes's principle of causation is a relatively good ordering concept because it com-

---

[44] *De Corpore* (ix. 9), *EW* I, 126.

[45] *N.B.* that Hobbes does not attempt to derive the principle of causation from empirical evidence. Causes are antecedent events, but they are not necessarily observable events. The necessary connection of cause and effect is not the conclusion of an argument based on evidence, but part of the definition of causation. Hobbes was not asking Hume's question: How do we come to have an idea of a necessary relation of cause and effect?

[46] Brandt, pp. 279–88.

bines the principle of a sufficient reason for any occurrence
with the assumption that the occurrence and its reason can be
stated in terms of motion. The principle implies the possibility
of a universal mechanical theory of nature.

Motions and Magnitudes

In the second part of his discussion of natural philosophy
(Part III of *De Corpore*), Hobbes elaborates the theoretical
tools of explanations in terms of motions. In the final chapters
of the previous section, Hobbes had outlined a geometry of
comparison. Chapter 12, "Of Quantity," was concerned with
the ways in which size, time, number, velocity, weight, and
proportion may be measured.[47] These quantities are measured
by comparison, usually comparison with a conventional standard or with a uniform motion.

Comparison is most useful when it is combined with proportion. Chapter 13, "Of Analogism," deals with the mathematical
relations between proportionals. Lines, geometric figures,
times, and velocities may be compared by the use of analogical
calculations, e.g., the proportions of distances to constant velocities and times are exhibited by the sides and bases of similar triangles.[48]

In the last of these three preliminary chapters, Hobbes defines the basic terms of geometry (line, plane, circle, etc.). The
definitions are given in terms of motions. An exposition of
geometry itself would follow if this were not superfluous. With
Hobbes's explanation of the basic principles, one can safely go
to Euclid, Archimedes, Apollonius, and other ancient and modern writers for the rest of geometry.[49]

Part III of *De Corpore*, "Proportions of Motions and Magnitudes," is Hobbes's attempt to establish ways of measuring various possible kinds of motion. The central concept here is

---

[47] *De Corpore* (xii), *EW* I, 138–44.   [48] *Ibid.* (xiii), *EW* I, 144–76.
[49] *Ibid.* (xiv, xv. 1), *EW* I, 176–202, 204.

endeavour. Endeavor (*conatus* in Latin) is defined by Hobbes as instantaneous motion through minimal space: *"Motion made in less space and time than can be given; that is, less than can be determined or assigned by exposition or number; that is, motion made through the length of a point, and in an instant or point of time."* Resistance involves opposed endeavors. Pressure is an endeavor of one body to move another. The quantity of endeavor considered instant by instant is *impetus.* Impetus multiplied either by itself or by the magnitude of the moving body is *force.*[50] Weight is also a product of endeavor.[51]

From this beginning, Hobbes proceeds to the consideration of the relations and reactions of moving bodies under various conditions. He discusses the path and speed of a body moved by one or more movents. He describes the geometric and mathematical relations among time, velocity, and distance traveled of bodies moving at a uniform speed, and of bodies uniformly accelerated "where the impetus increaseth continually according to the proportion of the times." Hobbes does not rest at the rule which is to be applied to falling bodies; he goes on to discuss motion accelerated so that the impetus increases in proportion duplicate to the proportion of the time. Furthermore, any one who wishes to do so can work out the mathematical relations for motions accelerated in triplicate, quadruplicate, etc., proportions.[52]

Hobbes exhibits a similar abstract generality of approach in his calculations of combined motions in his various attempts to discover a geometrical method of finding a straight line equivalent to the arc of a circle (i.e., squaring the circle), and in his discussions of "simple" and "compound" motion. (In simple motion the parts of the moving body describe equal lines; simple circular motion is sieve-like, compound circular motion is top-like.) He attempts to exhaust the possible sorts of motions of bodies in contact with other bodies, of bodies

---

[50] *Ibid.* (xv. 2), *EW* I, 206–12. *Cf. ibid.* (viii. 12, 18), *EW* I, 112, 114–15. See Brandt, pp. 293 ff.
[51] *De Corpore* (xxiii. 1), *EW* I, 351.   [52] *Ibid.* (xvi. 1–5), *EW* I, 218–27.

in fluids, and of bodies striking and penetrating into, or re-
bounding from, bodies of varying resistances.[53]

Hobbes failed in his attempt to establish a set of theoretical
tools for the explanation of the world. He failed because the
problems that he set himself, the construction of a mechanics
and a statics based upon motion, were beyond his powers, and
beyond the power of the mathematical tools at his command.
His theories were not hopelessly behind those of others; the
questions he asked, the problems he concerned himself with,
were relevant and important. Some of his work, especially in
optics, seems to be (at least) competent. To solve the problems
that Hobbes raised, at least two things were required: (1) a
new mathematics, calculus; (2) greater precision in the theoretical terminology revolving around endeavor (including the
introduction of the concept of mass) and the limitation of inertia to rectilinear motion.[54]

Hobbes's treatment of the proportions of motion and magnitude is abstract and general. He does not limit his discussion of
uniformly accelerated motion to the formula which will apply
to falling bodies; he does not even mention that the formula
he is discussing applies to falling bodies. He goes right on to
describe other forms of uniformly accelerated motion. This is
perhaps the best example of the approach that characterizes
this whole section. Hobbes intends to elaborate a set of theoretical tools; he does not limit his construction to the tools that
he knows will be applied to the particular problems of the
final part of *De Corpore*.

[53] *Ibid.* (xvii–xxiv), *EW* I, 246–386. For a discussion of this part of *De Corpore*,
see Brandt, pp. 293–340.

[54] Perhaps it should be mentioned that Galileo's concepts of inertia and
mass are ambiguous and pre-modern. Hobbes's discussion of inertia represents
an advance upon Galileo's precisely because he recognized the possibility of
rectilinear inertial motion as well as circular inertial motion. See *De Corpore*
(xv. 5–7), *EW* I, 215–17. For a discussion of Galileo, and of the development
of the concepts of inertia and mass, see Dijksterhuis, especially pp. 347 ff.

Physics, or the Phenomena of Nature

The phenomena of nature are given; the appearances are not constructed, but experienced in sensation. It is the purpose of the final part of *De Corpore* to explain these phenomena, to give a possible generation of them using the theoretical principles set forth in the previous parts of *De Corpore*.[55]

The first of the phenomena to be explained is sensation itself: the mechanisms of animal and human sensation, including imagination, dreaming, pleasure and pain, appetite and aversion are all explained in terms of cause and effect, motion, or endeavor and resistance.[56]

In order to produce an explanation of what happens in the heavens and on earth—a general cosmological and physical theory—Hobbes must take a position on the problem of vacuum. Hobbes argued that there is a crucial experiment against the existence of vacuum: water will not flow out of the small holes at the bottom of a container until the mouth of the container is unstopped. If there were tiny vacuums in the air, then the pressure of the water in the container should force some water out into these spaces, but no water will flow until air is allowed to enter the container.[57] Hobbes denied that the ancient theoretical arguments for vacuum were conclusive. He believed that the experiments (including the modern experiments involving pressure, compression, the space at the top of a column of mercury in a closed tube, the effects produced by a machine that sucked air out of a cylinder) were more correctly explained without the vacuum hypothesis. Air, he argued, is composed of two sorts of bodies. It is a very thin fluid in which larger and harder particles float. What happens in the compression experiments is that the thin fluid, or ether, is forced out, for it can pass through heavier fluids like water

[55] *De Corpore* (xxv. 1), *EW* I, 388.   [56] *Ibid.* (xxv. 1–13), *EW* I, 389–410.
[57] *Ibid.* (xxvi. 2), *EW* I, 414–15.

and mercury. The remaining particles are forced closer to each other, and as their inert motions continue, there are more and more rebounds. The violent motion of these compressed particles produces the force, which, when the cock is opened, expels water that has been forced into an air-filled vessel through a one-way valve. The greater pressure in air guns is also the result of expelling ether rather than compressing air. No vacuums have actually been produced.[58]

The phenomena of planetary motion, of the orbit of the earth, the changing of the seasons, etc., can best be explained if the sun and the planets are supposed to move in a simple circular motion in a fluid medium, ether. The ether, which fills all the spaces in the universe not occupied by other bodies, is completely fluid. Some fluid-like bodies, e.g., dust and sand, are composed of, and divisible into, non-fluid parts, but ether is completely fluid; divide it any number of times and the parts will remain fluid.[59] If the sun moves with simple circular motion in such a fluid, the earth and the other planets will also be moved. The paths these planets take will be consistent with the demonstrations of Copernicus, Kepler, Galileo, and other astronomers. The earth will describe an elliptical orbit in which its axis will be kept parallel to itself. On this basis can be explained all the observed phenomena: the eccentricity of the earth's orbit, the change of seasons, the precession of the equinoxes, the motion of the moon.[60]

Simple circular motion explains the phenomena of light and gravity in addition to the cosmological phenomena. The motion of the sun against the fluid ether produces an endeavor through the ether. This endeavor is perceived as light. At the same time the motion of the medium produces heat.[61] Color is the result produced when the light-producing endeavor is resisted. A prism resists light, i.e., resists the propagation of

[58] *Ibid.* (xxvi. 3–4), *EW* I, 414–26. *Cf. Seven Philosophical Problems* (iii), *EW* VII, 17–24, *Decameron Physiologicum* (iii), *EW* VII, 89–95.
[59] *De Corpore* (xxvi. 4–5), *EW* I, 425–26.
[60] *Ibid.* (xxvi. 5–11), *EW* I, 426–44.   [61] *Ibid.* (xxvii. 2–3), *EW* I, 448–50.

motion through it; it produces a series of refractions which are observed as a spectrum.[62] The apparent size and colors of the sun, the moon, and the stars when they are observed close to the horizon are due to the same causes. Rainbows, too, as Descartes showed, are a result of reflection and refraction. Whiteness is the result of many reflections in a small space; blackness is the absence of light. Hobbes thought that black surfaces were composed of many extremely small projections which reflected light toward the surface instead of toward the observer. The reflection of the motion toward a surface also tends to heat that surface.[63]

Gravity is also subsumed under the phenomena explained by simple circular motion. The falling of bodies to the earth cannot be due to a natural appetite to return to their proper places; it must be produced by some external motion, for nothing can move itself. The earth's diurnal motion thrusts away air from its surface more easily than it thrusts away other bodies. Consequently, these other bodies fall; since they are subject to the same cause in each instant of time, they fall (as Galileo showed) with continually accelerated velocity.[64]

Having explained some phenomena by motion propagated through a medium—ether—Hobbes attempted to extend that explanation to phenomena for which it was less well adapted than for the explanation of light. Hobbes's attempt to unify his explanations of sense around a mediumistic theory were probably reinforced by the adequacy of a mediumistic explanation of sound. Sound is produced by a stroke upon the medium. This stroke is propagated through the medium to the hearer. In the case of sound, unlike light, solid bodies are more effective propagators of the motion than are thin fluids. Hobbes also gave a mediumistic explanation of odors. He did not think that they were produced by evaporation and the transmission of particles through the air, although this would not

[62] *Ibid.* (xxvii. 13), *EW* I, 459–62.   [63] *Ibid.* (xxvi. 14–16), *EW* I, 462–65.
[64] *Ibid.* (xxx. 3–5), *EW* I, 510–15.

be inconsistent with his other theories. He assimilated smelling to seeing and hearing rather than to tasting and touching.[65]

Hobbes's Science

Many of Hobbes's scientific explanations are strange. His cosmology of simple circular motion was untenable. His doctrines about gravity, magnetism, wind, temperature, are all erroneous. His mathematics were attacked by Wallis and others who were proponents of the new algebraic approach that eventually developed infinitesimal calculus. Except in the study of optics,[66] Hobbes was a second-rate practical scientist—this is clear on the basis of the vacuum argument alone. The most that can be said about his mathematics is that even if he was against the most recent developments, he was not for traditional theories, but for his own. That he never became a member of the Royal Society is an accurate indication of his separation from the scientific opinion of the day.[67]

The answer to this summary of Hobbes's mistakes in natural philosophy is not that he lived too long. Nor is it to plead that their sharp controversies carried Hobbes and the men of Gresham College further apart than was necessary.

Hobbes's importance does not lie in the practice, but in the philosophy, of science. In science, one starts with certain suppositions or assumptions. Hobbes's basic principles are clear. They are the theories of body, causation, and motion that he elaborates in *De Corpore*. Then, with these tools, one attempts to explain the observations that one makes in the world.

[65] *Ibid.* (xxix), *EW* I, 485–508.   [66] See Brandt, pp. 211 ff.

[67] I do not mean to imply that this was not partly a consequence of the reaction to his political and religious opinions. (On the reaction to Hobbes in the seventeenth century, see Mintz; Bowle.) Most of the scientists, for example Boyle and Newton, were religious men, so religious that they eschewed the term "atomism" (which had atheist implications) for "corpuscularianism." Hobbes, regarded as an atheist, i.e., a mechanical materialist, was not respectable enough for the Royal Society. (On the English opposition to all forms of atheistic materialism, see Colie, "Spinoza in England, 1665–1730," pp. 183–219, and also *Light and Enlightenment*.)

There are, therefore, two methods of philosophy; one, from the generation of things to their possible effects; and the other, from their effects or appearances to some possible generation of the same. In the former of these the truth of the first principles of our ratiocination, namely definitions, is made and constituted by ourselves, whilst we consent and agree about the appellations of things. And this part I have finished in the foregoing chapters [Parts II, III]; in which, if I am not deceived, I have affirmed nothing, saving the definitions themselves, which hath not good coherence with the definitions I have given; that is to say, which is not sufficiently demonstrated to all those, that agree with me in the use of words and appellations; for whose sake only I have written the same. I now enter upon the other part [Part IV]; which is the finding out by the appearances or effects of nature, which we know by sense, some ways and means by which they may be, I do not say they are, generated. The principles, therefore, upon which the following discourse depends, are not such as we ourselves make and pronounce in general terms, as definitions; but such as being placed in the things themselves by the Author of Nature, are by us observed in them; and we make use of them in singular and particular, not universal propositions. Nor do they impose upon us any necessity of constituting theorems; their use being only, though not without such general propositions as have been already demonstrated, to show us the possibility of some production or generation.[68]

The theories which are used to explain the world are manmade. This is so even though it is necessarily the case that these theories must be constructed out of the only material that is available for their construction: sense conceptions.

The first test of these theories must be that they be internally consistent. Hobbes states that his theory is not only internally consistent, but that it is "sufficiently demonstrated" on the basis of the definitions.

The second test of theories is that they be applied to explain the observations and the experiences that we have. Hobbes thought that it was more important to explain ordinary experiences than contrived experiments, but the experiments

[68] *De Corpore* (xxv. 1), *EW* I, 387–88.

must still be explained. He believed that his theory of gravity implied that bodies fall with less and less velocity as they are more and more remote from the equator. Whether or not this is the case is to be determined by experience.[69] Here Hobbes has devised an empirically testable inference from his theory. Hobbes's recognition of what is involved in connecting hypothesis and observation, and his application of this insight in a few cases, do not excuse his not having applied this connection more intelligently, e.g., in regard to smell, vacuum, etc., and to more cases than he did.

Simply having experiences, doing experiments, making observations, is not sufficient to construct a science. Experiences issue in singular and particular statements only—"Nor do they impose upon us any necessity of constituting theorems." But experience, combined with our general principles, gives us a possible causal explanation.

F. Brandt, in his book, *Hobbes' Mechanical Conception of Nature,* objects to Hobbes's view of science because he has no appreciation of the importance of collecting facts and of induction, and because he enunciates no principle of verification. These criticisms are based on a view of what science is and what it does that differs sharply from Hobbes's view, as well as from the views of many philosophers and scientists. Put crudely, the theory holds that (1) there is a single true theory of nature; (2) this true theory is discoverable and discovered by collecting facts and inducing the conclusions that our collections of facts imply. Hobbes certainly is opposed to this kind of "inductionism." He does not suppose that singular statements imply or lead to general theories.

Is there a true theory of nature? Even if there were, it would not be possible to establish it by inductive methods. Universal statements cannot be derived inductively from less than universal evidence. It would be superfluous to argue that anything

[69] *Ibid.,* (xxx. 4), *EW* I, 513.

less than a complete set of facts is insufficient to verify a universal statement. This kind of evidence will not be available until no future occurrences are possible. We cannot say that a general theory is verified, but only that it is being verified, that it has not yet been falsified, i.e., that the evidence that we have does not contradict, is not inconsistent with, the theory. Although Hobbes does not adopt the criterion of falsifiability, at least he does not suppose that his theory can be proved true. For the explanation of the phenomena of nature

depends upon hypotheses; which unless we know them to be true, it is impossible for us to demonstrate that those causes, which I have there [in Part IV] explicated, are the true causes of the things whose productions I have derived from them.

Nevertheless, seeing I have assumed no hypothesis, which is not both possible and easy to be comprehended; and seeing also that I have reasoned aright from those assumptions, I have withal sufficiently demonstrated that they may be the true causes; which is the end of physical contemplation. If any other man from other hypotheses shall demonstrate the same or greater things, there will be greater praise and thanks due to him than I demand for myself, provided his hypotheses be such as are conceivable.[70]

We cannot know that the hypotheses are true; as we have seen, the conclusions of science are always hypothetical.[71] Although Hobbes probably did not think it likely that anyone would produce a system as comprehensive as *De Corpore,* his statement explicitly recognizes that a system equally as good, or perhaps even better, and based on different assumptions, is possible.

How should systems be judged? One criterion is implied. It is the amount of experience that the system explains. It is certainly the intention of Hobbes in *De Corpore* to explain

[70] *Ibid.* (xxx. 15), *EW* I, 531.
[71] For another example of Hobbes's recognition of the hypothetical and tentative character of his (and all) science, see *De Corpore* (xxvi. 11), *EW* I, 444: "And, though the causes I have here supposed be not the true causes of these phenomena, yet I have demonstrated that they are sufficient to produce them, according to what I at first propounded."

as much as possible with the minimum of assumption. Simple circular motion in the fluid ethereal medium provides the causes of the sun's light and heat, and the motions of the earth. Endeavor is connected to weight, pressure, impetus, light, and animal motion. The theory of endeavor should apply to as wide a range of observations as possible, e.g., the explanation of motion would apply to a piece of the earth the size of a musket bullet as well as to the sun, earth, and moon.[72]

Secondly, Hobbes would have the assumptions possible and conceivable. Hobbes believed that his theories are possible and conceivable. As post-Newtonians we may differ from him about the possibility of simple circular motion, or disagree about his application of the criterion without rejecting the criterion itself. Hobbes employs the criterion of possible, conceivable generation against those who explain things with obscure words: "For as for those that say anything may be moved or produced by *itself,* by *species,* by *its own power,* by *substantial forms,* by *incorporeal substances,* by *instinct,* by *anti-peristasis,* by *antipathy, sympathy, occult quality,* and other empty words of schoolmen, their saying so is to no purpose." [73] A theory then should be mechanical and causal—it should tell us the motions that produce the effects; it should not be a word invented to disguise our own ignorance.

It is never possible to prove that one causal explanation provides a description of the way the phenomena were actually produced, i.e., there may always be at least one other theory consistent with the facts—or, as Hobbes puts it, "there is no effect in Nature which the Author of nature cannot bring to pass by more ways than one." [74] Scientific theories can never be certainly true. In addition to its explanatory function science should also be useful. Hobbes thought that natural philosophy should benefit human beings. The arts of measurement, of moving things, of architecture, of navigation, and of

[72] *Decameron Physiologicum* (IV), *EW* VII, 106–7.
[73] *De Corpore* (xxx. 15), *EW* I, 531.
[74] *Decameron Physiologicum* (ii), *EW* VII, 88.

geography have indeed proved beneficial to men where they have been cultivated scientifically.[75]

Science, then, deduces a useful, systematic account of the world from a set of basic principles. These principles need not be assuredly true. Hobbes regards his basic principles as suppositions. His argument for cause and effect has been examined above. It is an argument that explains the connections among his ideas. Hobbes does not claim to observe causes or their operations.

Hobbes is often said to be a materialist. It is true that his theory is based on the existence of bodies. What are we to understand by the word "body"? "It is a hard question, though most men think they can easily answer it, as that it is whatsoever they can see, feel, or take notice of by their senses. But if you will know indeed what is body, we must imagine first what there is that is not body." This latter is all our fancies. "But certainly when the sun seems to my eye no bigger than a dish, there is behind it somewhere somewhat else, I suppose a real sun, which creates those fancies, by working, one way or other, upon my eyes, and other organs of my senses, to cause that diversity of fancy." Body, then, is something that exists independently of sense, and that is, or may be, causally related to sense effects.[76]

Hobbes does not attempt to prove that there are bodies; his argument is an attempt to explain what he means by body. Of course, the absence of any argument about the existence of bodies and causes may be due to a complete lack of doubt of their existence, but to this objection Hobbes could answer that he is admittedly constructing a hypothetical system. This system depends upon definitions whose truth is constituted by him who defines them (provided that these are logically consistent, and imaginable). He does not have to demonstrate the definitions; nor can he prove them, for if he could do so this would change the

[75] *De Corpore* (i. 7), *EW* I, 7 ff.
[76] *Decameron Physiologicum* (i), *EW* VII, 78–81.

system to a necessary one. Hobbes does not anticipate Kant's attempt to formulate a necessary system of categories; and it is impossible to say whether he would have liked to do so had he thought of it.

Hobbes excluded theology, i.e., the doctrine of God, from philosophy, because philosophy deals with properties of bodies and their generation, but God is eternal, and not generated; since God cannot be divided and compounded and considered in comparison with other bodies, God falls outside the sphere of philosophy. He is referred to as the Author of Nature who constitutes the principles we observe in nature. But although Hobbes believed, or professed to believe, in a Creator, and argued that the existence of God—as a first cause—could be inferred, he did not think that any of God's characteristics or the mechanism of creation could be described. The questions that relate to this problem are precisely of the kind that, he argues, cannot be answered.

Concerning the world, as it is one aggregate of many parts, the things that fall under inquiry are but few; and those we can determine, none. Of the whole world we may inquire what is its magnitude, what its duration, and how many there be, but nothing else. For as for place and time, that is to say, magnitude and duration, they are only our own fancy of a body simply so called, that is to say, of a body indefinitely taken, as I have shown before. . . . All other phantasms are of bodies or objects, as they are distinguished from one another; as colour, the phantasm of coloured bodies; sound, of bodies that move the sense of hearing, &c. The questions concerning the magnitude of the world are whether it be finite or infinite, full or not full; concerning its duration, whether it had a beginning, or be eternal; and concerning the number, whether there be one or many; though as concerning the number, if it were of infinite magnitude, there could be no controversy at all. Also if it had a beginning, then by what cause and of what matter it was made; and again, from whence that cause and that matter had their being, will be new questions; till at last we come to one or many eternal cause or causes.

But anyone who expects Hobbes to produce arguments about whether the world is finite or infinite, whether, if finite, there is more than one, whether it is eternal or not and what its causes were, will be disappointed.

And the determination of all these things belongeth to him that professeth the universal doctrine of philosophy, in case as much could be known as can be sought. But the knowledge of what is infinite can never be attained by a finite inquirer. Whatsoever we know that are men, we learn it from our phantasms; and of infinite, whether magnitude or time, there is no phantasm at all; so that it is impossible either for a man or any other creature to have any conception of infinite. And though a man may from some effect proceed to the immediate cause thereof, and from that to a more remote cause, and so ascend continually by right ratiocination from cause to cause; yet he will not be able to proceed eternally, but wearied will at last give over, without knowing whether it were possible for him to proceed to an end or not. But whether we suppose the world to be finite or infinite, no absurdity will follow. For the same things which now appear, might appear, whether the Creator had pleased it should be finite or infinite. Besides, though from this, that nothing can move itself, it may rightly be inferred that there was some first eternal movent; yet it can never be inferred, though some used to make such inference, that that movent was eternally immoveable, but rather eternally moved. For as it is true, that nothing is moved by itself; so it is true also that nothing is moved but by that which is already moved.[77]

Therefore, these questions are to be determined by those "lawfully authorized to order the worship of God." Hobbes himself will adopt the doctrine to which he has been persuaded "by the Holy Scriptures and fame of the miracles which confirm them; and by the custom of my country, and reverence due to the laws." [78]

Although we might differ from Hobbes on the possibility of determining the age and size of the world, we would agree in not inferring them from the attributes of God. Moreover, on a few occasions when he discusses arguments from God's nature, he refuses to accept them as decisive. For example, when the first speaker, A, in *Decameron Physiologicum* argues that it is hard to believe that God did not leave a few small empty

[77] *De Corpore* (xxvi. 1), *EW* I, 411–12.   [78] *Ibid.*, p. 414.

spaces in creating such a vast work as the world, it is only after he asserts that he thinks that some proof of the existence of vacuum can be inferred from this that B counters with the statement that "there can be no place empty where He is, nor full where He is not." [79] So they pass immediately to more prosaic experiments.

Hobbes does not argue the mysteries of religion from natural reason, nor does he think that questions about the natural world can be determined by arguments drawn from religion.[80] So there are some questions which are beyond the scope of (natural) philosophy. Among these are theological questions, and some questions about the size and age of the world. All that we can infer from the Atomists' arguments about the impossibility of bodies beginning to move without vacuum—and the counter-argument that the beginning of motion is equally impossible in a vacuum—is "that motion was either coeternal, or of the same duration with that which is moved." [81] Hobbes's "suppositions for solving the phenomena of nature" do not include any suppositions about God's existence or his activities —he is not mentioned—but only suppositions about the existence and motions of bodies. The first supposition is that the world is the aggregate of all bodies, the earth, the stars, the planets, the tiny invisible atoms which are disseminated throughout the ether which fills all space; and the third supposition is that in the sun and the rest of the planets there is and always has been a simple circular motion.[82] Questions about the beginning of the world (if it had a beginning) and the nature of God lie outside Hobbes's system of natural philosophy.

The same sort of thing should be said about the basic assumptions of the system: that bodies exist; that the world operates by causes and effects. Hobbes's system is based on these assumptions, so they cannot be questioned within it. He cer-

[79] *EW* VII, 89.
[80] See *Six Lessons to the Professors of the Mathematics* (VI), *EW* VII, 348.
[81] *De Corpore* (xxvi. 3), *EW* I, 417.   [82] *Ibid.* (xxvi. 5), *EW* I, 426–27.

tainly believes that the system is a good one and that his explanation is valuable and probably true. He cannot and does not prove that the assumptions are valid in themselves. He does try to show that they are consistent with his other assumptions; that they can be understood; and that they provide an explanation of the phenomena.

Natural philosophy, then, begins with definitions (body, cause, effect, motion, space, place), proceeds from them to the general principles and axioms of the system and the consequences of these axioms, and then (with additional definitions and axioms when necessary) considers the various kinds of motion and their properties. This is the function of ratiocination;

and farther you must furnish yourself with as many experiments (which they call phenomenon) as you can. And supposing some motion for the cause of your phenomenon, try, if by evident consequence, without contradiction to any other manifest truth or experiment, you can derive the cause you seek for from your supposition.[83]

So, natural philosophy is reasoning plus experience—and, (seemingly) nothing else.

[83] *Decameron Physiologicum* (ii), *EW* VII, 88.

3

HUMAN NATURE

If men had sprung up from the earth in a night, like mushrooms or excrescences, without all sense of honour, justice, conscience, or gratitude, he could not have vilified the human nature more than he doth.

ARCHBISHOP BRAMHALL, *The Catching of Leviathan* (*EW* IV, 288)

Passions

That "man is a rational animal," that human nature is composed of two elements—reason and passion—has been the opinion of many writers and philosophers; it is also the opinion of Hobbes. This cliché becomes, in Hobbes's system, a philosophical challenge. His reason is not a faculty, but an act. More precisely, what we mean by a "faculty" is the power to do the act; reasoning is calculating the consequences of words, those "sensible marks" of our conceptions. Man is an animal that calculates with the help of arbitrary signs. It has been shown above that reasoning and speech are not natural acts, for aside from sense, imagination, and memory,

There is no other act of mans mind, that I can remember, naturally planted in him, so, as to need no other thing, to the exercise of it, but to be born a man, and live with the use of his five Senses. Those other Faculties, of which I shall speak by and by, and which seem proper to man onely, are acquired, and encreased by study and industry; and of most men learned by instruction, and discipline; and proceed all from the invention of Words, and Speech. For besides Sense, and Thoughts, and the Trayne of thoughts, the mind of man has no other motion; though by the help of Speech and Method, the same Facultyes may be improved to such a height, as to distinguish men from all other living Creatures.[1]

The development of reason is only possible because of the invention of speech "without which, there had been amongst men, neither Common-wealth, nor Society, nor Contract, nor Peace, no more than amongst Lyons, Bears, and Wolves." [2] God himself authorized speech; Adam developed as much language as he found useful.

But all this language gotten, and augmented by *Adam* and his posterity, was again lost at the tower of *Babel*, when by the hand of God, every man was stricken for his rebellion, with an oblivion of his former language. And being hereby forced to disperse themselves into severall parts of the world, it must needs be, that the diversity of Tongues that now is, proceeded by degrees from them, in such manner, as need (the mother of all inventions) taught them; and in tract of time grew every where more copious.[3]

Since the natural endowment of man does not include speech, it does not include reasoning in general terms. (Although a man may reckon without words in particular things, this can lead neither to science nor to absurdity.) So little reasoning is possible without speech that the Greeks could use the same word, *logos,* for both speech and reason; "not that they thought there was no Speech without Reason; but no Reasoning without Speech." Man is an animal very much like other animals. In animals, life is motion, and motion, life. What is called "vital" motion begins when the animal is generated, and continues until the animal dies. Respiration, circulation of the blood, digestion, excretion are all motions which are included in vital motion. Animals also have the power to reproduce their own kind—the power of generation. They are capable of

---

[1] *Leviathan* (3), p. 22.   [2] *Ibid.* (4), p. 24.   [3] *Ibid.*

other motions, of moving themselves or parts of themselves
from place to place.

It has already been shown that conception, sense, imagination, memory, etc., is motion. Some motions, unlike vital motions, can only occur after an imagination. Animal or voluntary
motion is first fancied in the mind: "And because *going, speaking,* and the like Voluntary motions, depend alwayes upon a
precedent thought of *whither, which way,* and *what;* it is evident, that the Imagination is the first internall beginning of
all Voluntary Motion." [4] Imagination itself is a motion, not
merely an incipient motion. Motions need not be visible; the
beginnings of the grosser voluntary motions are endeavors. To
be an animal, then, is to be a complex of interacting motions:
vital motion, sensation, passion, imagination, voluntary motion. These motions may be connected in various ways; usually
imagination precedes bodily motion, but in dreams this relation is reversed.[5]

Imagination, although it is the origin of voluntary motion,
is not a self-moving mover. For imagination is an effect of sensation, and sensation itself results from the contact of a sensing
organism with motion external to it. External motion, then,
produces in an organism more than one effect. It produces,
first of all, that reaction which is called sensation—sight, hearing, smell, taste, or touch. Second, when the action of the object is continued to the heart, there is an effect upon the vital
motion. The bodily activity of the organism is either stimu-
lated or impeded. A motion or endeavor that helps or rein-
forces vital motion initiates appetite, or desire, a motion or
endeavor of the organism toward the object. The "appearance"
of this motion, the internal sensation of the organism, is called
"delight" or "pleasure." When the vital motion is hindered,
an appearance of displeasure and a motion or endeavor away

[4] *Ibid.* (6), p. 39.
[5] See *Elements of Law* (I. iii. 3), pp. 8–9; *Leviathan* (2), pp. 15–16. For an
interesting discussion of Hobbes's concept of endeavor and its influence on
Leibnitz, see Watkins, *Hobbes's System of Ideas,* pp. 120–35.

from the object—aversion—are created.[6] Hobbes seems to be assimilating all appetite-pleasure and aversion-molestation to the stronger bodily reactions that men have in extreme situations: the quickened pulse, the heightened perception, the ease of action that men feel at moments of excitement; the impeded circulation of blood, the constricted feeling in the chest that men have in shock.

The reaction of the organism to external stimuli includes a sensation, an effect upon the internal non-voluntary motions of the organism, the beginning of voluntary motion—a desire or aversion, and linked to this desire or aversion, a feeling or sensation of pleasure or pain. "Pleasure therefore, (or *Delight*,) is the apparence, or sense of Good; and *Molestation* or *Displeasure*, the apparence, or sense of Evill. And consequently all Appetite, Desire, and Love, is accompanied with some Delight more or lesse; and all Hatred, and Aversion, with more or lesse Displeasure and Offence." [7]

The object of a man's desire is what he calls good; the object of his hatred or aversion, he calls evil. If he neither loves nor hates a thing he contemns it as vile or inconsiderable. But this does not mean that there are three sorts of natural objects: good things attracting men; evil things repelling men; and neutral things, neither attracting nor repelling men. Not only does the constitution of a man's body continually change so that it is almost impossible that he should always have the same desires and aversions, but also men differ from one another in what they find desirable and hateful. "For these words of Good, Evill, and Contemptible, are ever used with relation to the person that useth them: There being nothing simply and absolutely so; nor any common Rule of Good and Evill, to be taken from the nature of the objects themselves. . . ." [8] Things

---

[6] *Elements of Law* (I. vii. 1–2), pp. 28–29; *Leviathan* (6), pp. 41–42; *De Homine* (xi. 1), *LW* II, 94–95; *De Corpore* (xxv. 12), *EW* I, 406–8. See Watkins, *Hobbes's System of Ideas*, pp. 107–15.

[7] *Leviathan* (6), p. 42.

[8] *Ibid.*, p. 41. *Cf. De Homine* (xi. 4), *LW* II, 96–97: "[I]taque simpliciter bonum *dici non potest; cum quicquid bonum est, bonum sit aliquibus vel alicui.*

may be good or evil in three ways. (1) They may promise good or evil—i.e., appear *pulchrum* (fair, handsome, beautiful, gallant, comely, honorable) or *turpe* (foul, deformed, ugly, base, etc.). (2) They may be good or evil in effect—delightful or unpleasant. (3) They may be good or evil as means, useful or profitable; useless or unprofitable. Again there are three sorts of possible responses to objects: attraction, repulsion, or no motion; good, evil, and contemptible are respectively the names men call things when they produce these results.[9]

There are some desires inborn in men. These may be called appetites toward, or aversions from, something felt in their own bodies. They are mainly those which men share with other animals: appetite for food, for excretion, etc. But every appetite for a particular thing is not natural but acquired by experience. A man has no instinctual knowledge of objects which enables him to distinguish the delightful from the unpleasant, the useful from the useless, the fair from the foul, upon his first contact with them; men's desires for particular things "proceed from Experience, and triall of their effects upon themselves, or other men." [10] This is equally true of aversions; we have aversions to things which have hurt us, but we also have aversions to things whose effects we do not know.[11] Were love and hatred, delight and displeasure, appetite and aversion not susceptible of degree, an immediate instinctual response of either "yes" or "no" would be necessary. There would be no such thing as choosing the lesser of two evils, or the greater of two goods. All goods and all pleasures would be equally desirable; all pains and all evils would be equally undesirable. Furthermore, curiosity would not be possible; the untried could never cause desire (unless a theory of instinctual

---

Bona erant ab initio omnia quae creavit Deus. Quare? Quia ipsi opera sua omnia placuere." See also *Elements of Law* (I. vii. 3), p. 29: "Every man, for his own part, calleth that which pleaseth, and is delightful to himself, GOOD; and that EVIL which displeaseth him:" so that as men differ in constitution, they differ in distinguishing good and evil. Nothing is simply good. "For even the goodness which we attribute to God Almighty, is his goodness to us."

[9] *Leviathan* (6), pp. 40–41.   [10] *Ibid.*, p. 40.   [11] *Ibid.*

appetites for particular things be accepted), but must always repel. This is certainly not the case. Clearly an aversion to something known by experience to be evil must be stronger than an aversion to something whose effects are completely unknown. (The greater the certainty of the evil effect or the greater the evil of the effect, the stronger the aversion will be.) In fact, the only desire we can have for something of which we have no experience is the desire "to tast and try."

Pleasures and pains are of two sorts. The first arises "from the sense of an object Present." Pleasures and pains of sense are produced by the internal functions of the body and by sight, hearing, smell, taste and touch. The second sort of pleasure and pain arises from the expectation of good or evil consequences. These *"Pleasures of the Mind* of him that draweth those consequences" are called joy; the corresponding pains are called grief.[12]

Passions are emotions in the literal sense that they are motions that result from other motions. The basic passions are appetite (love, joy) and aversion (hate, grief). First, these passions are considered according to the opinion men have of the likelihood of attaining what they desire. Thus, if they desire, and think that their desire will be satisfied, they hope; and if they think it will not, they despair. *"Aversion,* with opinion of *Hurt* from the object, FEARE. The same, with hope of avoyding that Hurt by resistance, COURAGE." [13] Second, passions have been given different names because of the different objects loved, or hated. Desire for another's good is benevolence, good will, or charity; for riches, covetousness; for office and honors, ambition. Desire to know is called curiosity. Hobbes's catalogue of passions is long, but not as long as a modern catalogue would be if it included every philia and phobia: Anglophilia, Germanophilia, claustrophobia, acrophobia, etc. Third, the

---

[12] *Ibid.,* p. 42. According to the *Elements of Law* (I. vii. 4), p. 29, the pleasures and pains of immediate sense conception are stronger than those of the imagination, or the mind, because sense is stronger than imagination.
[13] *Leviathan* (6), p. 43.

passions are considered in combination, and finally in sequence. Contempt for trifling helps or hindrances is called magnanimity; and if this is exhibited in a dangerous situation, valor; magnanimity exhibited in the use of wealth is liberality. Glory is joy at the imagination of a man's own power; and if this is based on the experience of success in the past it is the same as *confidence* (constant hope), but if it is pure fancy—grounded in supposition, romantic daydreams, or flattery—it is called vainglory; *vain* because, unlike confidence, it does not lead to action.[14]

Sudden Glory, is the passion which maketh those *Grimaces* called LAUGHTER; and is caused either by some sudden act of their own, that pleaseth them; or by the apprehension of some deformed thing in another, by comparison whereof they suddenly applaud themselves. And it is incident most to them, that are conscious of the fewest abilities in themselves; who are forced to keep themselves in their own favour, by observing the imperfections of other men.[15]

The joy in laughter does not consist in wit or in the jest but in the comparison between another's follies, infirmities, or absurdities (or even one's own past follies) and one's own present abilities. Sudden dejection—the realization of lack of power—produces weeping,

and therefore children weep often; for seeing they think every thing ought to be given unto them which they desire, of necessity every repulse must be a sudden check of their expectation, and puts them in mind of their too much weakness to make themselves masters of all 'they look for. For the same cause women are more apt to weep than men, as being not only more accustomed to have their wills, but also to measure their power by the power and love of others that protect them.[16]

Men weep when deprived of revenge over another by his repentance and reconciliation, or, at the realization of their impotence to help those they pity. The passions that produce

[14] *Ibid.,* pp. 42–44. *Cf. Elements of Law* (I. ix. 1), pp. 36–38.
[15] *Leviathan* (6), p. 45. *Elements of Law* (I. ix. 13), pp. 41–42.
[16] *Elements of Law* (I. ix. 14), pp. 42–43. *Cf. Leviathan* (6), p. 45.

laughter and weeping—sudden glory and sudden grief—are similar. They both proceed from an evaluation of power. Those who have little power, few abilities, are more likely to be given to laughter (especially at trifles) when they realize that they compare favorably with someone else, but they are likely to weep when they are reminded of their actual weakness. "But in all cases, both Laughter, and Weeping, are sudden motions; Custome taking them both away. For no man Laughs at old jests; or Weeps for an old calamity." [17]

Life is motion; being alive is to have one desire after another. Since "appetite presupposeth a farther end, there can be no contentment but in proceeding." [18] Felicity, or happiness, is not a word that describes a condition that can be gained, or a prize that can be won and retained.

Continuall successe in obtaining those things which a man from time to time desireth, that is to say, continuall prospering, is that men call FELICITY; I mean the Felicity of this life. For there is no such thing as perpetuall Tranquility of mind, while we live here; because Life it selfe is but Motion, and can never be without Desire, nor without Feare, no more than without Sense. What kind of Felicity God hath ordained to them that devoutly honour him, a man shall no sooner know, than enjoy; being joyes, that now are as incomprehensible, as the word of Schoole-men *Beatificall Vision* is unintelligible.[19]

Presumably the only desire one could have for the next world would be to try it. Of that world we have no experience; the "life" promised in that world is so different from life in this one that we cannot even conceive of it.

Life is motion, motion from one point to another, from one desire to another, from one satisfaction to another. Happiness consists in continuing this motion successfully, without impediment. Since happiness is a process—the successive satisfaction of desires—there is always a comparative element in it. A

---

[17] *Leviathan* (6), p. 45.
[18] *Elements of Law* (I. vii. 7), p. 30. *Cf. De Homine* (xi. 12), *LW* II, 100.
[19] *Leviathan* (6), p. 48. *Cf. De Homine* (xi. 15), *LW* II, 103.

man is happier when he succeeds than before he has succeeded. When a man compares his own activities and satisfactions to those of other men, his estimate of his own happiness (and therefore his happiness itself), depends upon the relation between his success and that of others. Life may be compared to a race.

The comparison of the life of man to a race, though it holdeth not in every point, yet it holdeth so well for this our purpose, that we may thereby see and remember almost all the passions before mentioned. But this race we must suppose to have no other goal, nor other garland, than being foremost; and in it:

To endeavour, is appetite.
To be remiss, is sensuality.
To consider them behind, is glory.
To consider them before, humility.
To lose ground with looking back, vain glory.
To be holden, hatred.
To turn back, repentance.
To be in breath, hope.
To be weary, despair.
To endeavour to overtake the next, emulation.
To supplant or overthrow, envy.
To resolve to break through a stop foreseen, courage.
To break through a sudden stop, anger.
To break through with ease, magnanimity.
To lose ground by little hindrances, pusillanimity.
To fall on the sudden, is disposition to weep.
To see another fall, disposition to laugh.
To see one out-gone whom we would not, is pity.
To see one out-go we would not, is indignation.
To hold fast by another, is to love.
To carry him on that so holdeth, is charity.
To hurt one's-self for haste, is shame.
Continually to be out-gone, is misery.
Continually to out-go the next before is felicity.
And to forsake the course, is to die.[20]

Is life, the race itself, pleasant? Is all activity pleasurable? Hobbes does not say whether action is itself pleasant or un-

[20] *Elements of Law* (I. ix. 21), pp. 47–48.

pleasant. For every satisfaction energy must be expended. The expenditure of energy could be regarded as a pleasure itself. Motion occurs in a world of other motions and resistances. Action seems therefore to have an unpleasant aspect; it is an effort, a struggle, in a recalcitrant environment. Hobbes does not seem to think that activity is pleasant in itself. Should he not have asked of any activity, "Is the game worth the candle?" Struggle does not seem to make victory sweeter, for magnanimity is to get what one wants with ease.

Will

The passions of men are the motions that move them: appetite, aversion, love, hate, joy, and grief. Passion is connected with sensation or imagination; conception of something good or evil is always the beginning of endeavor. And like imagination, passion must be considered in process. Man is not, in his natural condition, in a state of rest, but rather in one of motion. Just as there is a succession of sense conceptions and imaginations in man, there is a succession of passions.

When in the mind of man, Appetites, and Aversions, Hopes, and Feares, concerning one and the same thing, arise alternately; and divers good and evil consequences of the doing, or omitting the thing propounded, come successively into our thoughts; so that sometimes we have an Appetite to it; sometimes an Aversion from it; sometimes Hope to be able to do it; sometimes Despaire, or Feare to attempt it; the whole summe of Desires, Aversions, Hopes and Feares, continued till the thing be either done, or thought impossible, is that we call DELIBERATION.[21]

Deliberation can only concern actions that are thought to be possible. Actions in the past, actions known or believed to be impossible, cannot be the subject of deliberation. Supposed power, then, is the necessary presupposition of deliberation. If I think that I can fly I can deliberate whether I shall fly. But

[21] *Leviathan* (6), p. 46; *Elements of Law* (I. xii. 1), p. 61.

if I know that I have not the power to fly then I cannot deliberate whether or not I shall fly. As long as the action remains possible, deliberation remains possible. Only future actions can be the subject of deliberation, and these only as long as there is hope to do the act, or a possibility of not doing it.

The process of deliberation does not require the possession of reason (in Hobbes's sense of calculating the consequences of general names), or speech, or science. Deliberation is a succession of appetites and aversions, involving the imagination of good or evil consequences (and the reckoning of the likelihood of their occurrence). Since this is the case, anything that has sense, imagination, and memory (and therefore prudence) applied to appetites and aversions may deliberate. Clearly, then, deliberation does not distinguish man from other animals.

The last moment in deliberation, the appetite or aversion that immediately precedes the doing or omission of an action, is what is called the *will;* "the Act, (not the faculty,) of *Willing.*" So, beasts that deliberate have will. Hobbes denies that will is a rational appetite in any sense other than the last appetite, an appetite after a deliberation. For if will were rational, there could be no unreasonable voluntary acts, whereas, as we all know, men voluntarily do the most foolish things. At any intermediate moment in deliberation, the appetite of the moment is an "inclination," or, if the deliberation is interrupted, an intention, or purpose.[22]

Will is so equivalent to appetite that every action, whether it be done from lust, or greed, or ambition, or any other appetite, or from any aversion, or from fear of the consequences of not doing the action, is voluntary. The man who throws his goods into the sea to save himself acts voluntarily; "for, there

[22] *Leviathan* (6), pp. 46–47; *Elements of Law* (I. xii. 2, 9), pp. 61–62, 63. *Cf. The Questions concerning Liberty, Necessity, and Chance* (animadversion to reply xvii), *EW* V, 234: "And it seemeth to me that a rational will, if it be not meant of a will after deliberation, whether he that deliberateth reasoneth aright or not, signifieth nothing."

is nothing there involuntary, but the hardness of the choice, which is not his action, but the action of the winds; what he himself doth, is no more against his will, than to fly from danger is against the will of him that seeth no other means to preserve himself." [23] There are involuntary "actions," e.g., a man is pushed, falls into another and hurts him. There are even some actions which Hobbes says are mixed. The example given is of a man going to prison. He has no desire to go to prison—this is involuntary. But rather than be dragged, he walks—and this is voluntary.

Since will is appetite, the causes of appetite and aversion are also the causes of will. "Appetite, fear, hope, and the rest of the passions are not called voluntary; for they proceed not from, but are the will; and the will is not voluntary. For a man can no more say he will will, than he will will will, and so make an infinite repetition of the word will; which is absurd, and insignificant." [24] Passions are motions that result from other motions. The will is not a self-moved mover. Although a man may be free to do as he will—as he is when he has the power to do what he wills, no man can be free to will what he desires, i.e., no man has a free will, because this is absurd. To have a will free from causation would be to be unmoved by desire—in short, to be dead.

Hobbes's description of the voluntary motion of animals is similar to, and connected with, his natural philosophy. The basic rules "nothing can move itself," "every effect has a cause, and both cause and effect are motions," and "only motion can be the cause of motion," are applied in both areas. In natural philosophy the concepts of motion, cause and effect, etc., are applied to explain the causes of the effects that we call physical phenomena. Natural philosophy explained how effects in one body, called sensation, are produced by reaction to motion originating in other bodies. In examining the passions, we have

[23] *Elements of Law* (I. xii. 3), p. 62. *Cf. Leviathan* (6, 21), pp. 47, 161–62.
[24] *Elements of Law* (I. xii. 5), pp. 62–63. *Cf. Leviathan* (21), p. 162; *Of Liberty and Necessity* (Ep. Ded.), *EW* IV, 240.

discovered that the appearances of sensation are not the only effects produced by the reaction of the sensing organism. In addition to sensing, the animate body is also attracted or repelled, in greater or less degree, by the external bodies which cause these motions. This attraction or repulsion is itself a motion, initially the smallest possible motion, i.e., an endeavor, and it is motion resulting from the effects upon the animal's internal vital motion produced by the motions in sensation. This helping or hindering of vital motion is felt as pleasure or pain, and the following endeavor is desire or aversion. The process is complicated insofar as the principle of inertia operates. Where imagination and memory intervene, the imagination of the consequences of a thing or an action may produce a series of endeavors resulting in an alternation of desires and aversions, hopes and fears. The final moment in this process of deliberation is the will. So, sensation is causally related to all desires and aversions—both those that are immediate and those that are the result of imagination. Desire and aversion are, in turn, causally related to the will.

However, the relation of desire and aversion to will is not simple and direct, but complicated and compound. This is partly true for animals as well as for man, at least insofar as they remember the past consequences of their actions and imagine them to be the same in the future, i.e., insofar as they have prudence. The imagination of the consequences of the action deliberated creates appetites and aversions as these consequences appear to be good or evil. (It is, of course, unlikely that one will foresee all the consequences.) Insofar as the good or evil results seem to predominate, the whole chain of consequences is called apparently good or apparently evil.[25]

This process thus involves two elements. The first is the foresight of results. The second element is the appetites and aversions invoked by imagination. Foresight consists in a series of presumptions about fact: *"it will be,* or, *it will not be; or it*

[25] *Leviathan* (6), p. 48; *Elements of Law* (I. vii. 8), p. 30.

has been, or, *has not been.*" This process is called doubt; it is parallel to deliberation. "And that which is alternate Appetite, in Deliberating concerning Good and Evil; the same is alternate Opinion, in the Enquiry of the truth of *Past,* and *Future.*" [26] Because it is a sequence of appetites about consequences, deliberation involves the formation of opinions about the likelihood of past and future facts, and the last opinion in this process is called *judgment.*

The Differences Between Men and Animals

What has been said in the preceding sections applies to animals as well as to men. The purpose of making this point is not to prove that men are the same as other animals, nor that they are completely different from animals, nor that men are half-beast and half-angel. The mechanics of sense, imagination, memory, passion, deliberation apply to men and to animals. The differences between men and other animals are minor, unless speech be considered. The effect of the addition of words, sensible marks, to man's natural powers is immense. Prudence can be improved because words act as an aid to memory. Speech allows the communication of opinions, judgments, desires, aversions, and wills. With speech, science becomes possible.

Writing and printing add a further level of complexity. Registers of facts, all sorts of histories, are possible. Books of science may be produced. There will be many books of opinions; much will be written, often in words colored by the passions of their authors, to influence men in their deliberations. In this situation, men conduct their deliberations with the opportunity of using the conclusions of other men, either of science or of prudence, as well as their own conclusions. Animals do not speak and do not participate in the conventional element of speech. The sounds and acts of men when

[26] *Leviathan* (7), p. 49.

they affect domesticated animals are natural signs to them,
rather than artificial signs as they are to other men. Men may,
in their reckonings, begin from, or take account of, the indications that they have of another man's opinions, passions, judgment, will, or counsel. When a man relies on another's pro-
nouncement in his reckoning, he *has faith in,* or *trusts,* or
believes him, i.e., (1) he doubts neither his ability to know
the truth nor his honesty in expressing it; (2) he believes
what he says. These two things are logically distinct. It is possible to believe that something Paul says is true although we
have no trust in Paul at all. But

> when wee believe any saying whatsoever it be, to be true, from
> arguments taken, not from the thing it selfe, or from the principles
> of naturall Reason, but from the Authority, and good opinion
> wee have, of him that hath sayd it; then is the speaker, or person
> we believe in, or trust in, and whose word we take, the object of
> our Faith.[27]

Such reliance on the mere undemonstrated opinion of others
in our reckonings and deliberations is a great source of error
and absurdity.[28]

It is not only the advice of the counsellors, the opinions of
the learned, the persuasions of the dogmatics that affect deliberation. Men are subject to the influence of declarations designed to influence their passions. Praise or invective may be
used to influence opinion of the goodness or badness of something. Request, promise, threat, and command are all intended
to move the person to whom they are addressed to some
action.[29]

Although language, and therefore reason (because language
makes reasoning—thinking in general terms—possible), establish the distinction between man and beast, the difference
between man and other animals is not wholly due to reason.
There is one passion that man possesses which beasts do not

[27] *Ibid.,* p. 51.   [28] *Ibid.* (5), p. 35.
[29] *Elements of Law* (I. xiii. 5–7), pp. 67–68. *Cf. Leviathan* (6), pp. 47–48.

possess at all, or only in a very slight degree. This is curiosity, the desire to know why and how. It is "a Lust of the mind, that by a perseverance of delight in the continuall and indefatigable generation of Knowledge, exceedeth the short vehemence of any carnall Pleasure." [30] When an animal sees anything new his only interest is whether it will help or hurt him, but men attempt to discover both the causes and the possible uses of everything.[31] Animals live in a world of immediate desires and satisfactions; unlike men, their curiosity extends only to immediate consequences.

Man's peculiar combination of (1) ordinary animal desires, (2) greater imagination and memory than animals have (plus improvements due to speech), and (3) curiosity about causes and effects, results in the conversion of the moderate degree of natural prudence, which animals also have (e.g., the association of a raised hand with a pain or a noise with food or feeding time), into the peculiarly human anxiety about future satisfactions which implies the seeking of means to these satisfactions and of means to secure these means, i.e., "a perpetuall and restlesse desire of Power after power, that ceaseth onely in Death." [32]

Men are more equal, more similar to each other, than we sometimes suppose.[33] Does Hobbes's theory require them to be all precisely alike? It has been argued that it does. Nominalism requires that things with the same name be similar.[34] And it seems that we must regard overt resemblance as the sort of similarity which is meant. Sets of "trade-name" products, e.g., Daimlers, Cadillacs, Hershey bars, prints from the same plate, are ideally nominalist things—stamped out from the same pattern—whereas "mammal," "weapon," and "game" are much more difficult to treat in a nominalist fashion. Men, therefore,

---

[30] *Leviathan* (6), p. 44.   [31] *Elements of Law* (I. ix. 18), pp. 45–46.
[32] *Leviathan* (11), p. 75.
[33] *Ibid.* (13), p. 94; *Elements of Law* (I. xiv. 2), p. 70.
[34] See Watkins, "Philosophy and Politics in Hobbes," pp. 142–43; *Hobbes's System of Ideas*, pp. 104–7, 147–50.

are to be regarded as engines of a similar design whose only difference is their speed of operation. Hobbes, it is concluded, cannot admit that men can be differently motivated.

This analysis is useful; it provides a philosophic ground for Hobbes's use of introspection. If men are the same then the understanding of the internal mechanism of one man is knowledge of human psychology. But the argument requires that men be much more similar than Hobbes supposed, or wanted to suppose, they were.

Names need not be imposed only in cases of overt resemblance, if this means the most obvious observable similarities. Similarity of effects on our senses—color, figure, sound, taste, smell, etc., are not the only similarities that are important. "[I]n this succession of mens thoughts, there is nothing to observe in the things they think on, but either in what they be *like one another,* or in what they be *unlike,* or *what they serve for,* or *how they serve to such a purpose.*" [35] It would be surprising if Hobbes could omit the categories of causes and effects from the sources of names, when he would not omit them from men's thoughts. The similarity in "weapons" is not in what they look like but in what men use them for; their "overt resemblance" is in their function, in the purposes for which they are used. Fancy, man's ability to construct unusual comparisons,[36] enables us to call a knife, a revolver, an airplane, or a bomb, a "weapon." Men, discovering more abstruse similarities, may say that money (or an idea, or peace) is a weapon.

Thus, mammals have similarities in physiological structure, in the ways in which they behave, in the way they reproduce and develop, which enable them to be classified under the same name in spite of their obvious differences. A classification indicates that men consider things similar in some respect—but not that there are no other ways of classifying the same set of

[35] *Leviathan* (8), p. 53.   [36] *Ibid.; Elements of Law* (I. x. 4), p. 50.

things.[37] We need not search for some property (or essence) to justify a classification. Could not Hobbes argue that the similarities discovered by the biophysical analysis of protein molecules supported the application of the same name to apparently dissimilar things? There may even be ways in which chess is more like football than it is like mathematics.

Men are affected by objects. The affections possible are desire, contempt, and aversion. Desires and aversions involve degrees of endeavor. Desired objects are "good"; those we avoid "evil." Passion, desire, aversion, joy, grief, hope, fear are all names that are applied to describe human activity. These names are all quite general and so refer to many specific and different acts. The consequence is not, as Watkins says, that Hobbes supposes that men cannot be differently motivated, but, on the contrary, that Hobbes supposes that all men are motivated—i.e., that no men are unmotivated. For to be without any desire would be to be unmotivated, and this would be to be dead. The process of motivation in men is similar, their passions are similar, but the objects of their passions are dissimilar. Introspection tells us what men are likely to be thinking, and, more importantly, how men desire, reason, think, believe, hope, and fear (i.e., what it means to do these things). The saying, *"Nosce teipsum, Read thy self,"* was meant

to teach us, that for the similitude of the thoughts, and Passions of one man, to the thoughts, and Passions of another, whosoever looketh into himself, and considereth what he doth, when he does *think, opine, reason, hope, feare,* &c, and upon what grounds; he shall thereby read and know, what are the thoughts, and Passions of all other men, upon the like occasions. I say the similitude of *Passions,* which are the same in all men, *desire, feare, hope,* &c; not the similitude of the *objects* of the Passions, which are the things *desired, feared, hoped,* &c: for these the constitution individuall, and particular education do so vary, and they are so

---

[37] Watkins' argument seems to require that a single name, or at most a restricted set of names, be applicable to each thing.

easie to be kept from our knowledge, that the characters of mans
heart, blotted and confounded as they are, with dissembling, lying,
counterfeiting, and erroneous doctrines, are legible onely to him
that searcheth hearts.[38]

The Diversification of Human Ends

Men are fundamentally similar in their physiological equipment. Although differences in size, physical strength, and operation of sense organs are not impossible and do exist, these
differences do not account for the wide variety of men's interests, abilities, and powers. Men find it much easier to agree
on the similarities or differences of shapes, colors, sounds, etc.,
than on whether something is good or evil. The underlying
cause of the important differences between men are differences
in passions. The passions differ partly because of different
bodily constitutions and partly from differences in education.
An appetite for any particular thing, as we have seen, is acquired rather than inborn, a historical fact not deducible
from scientific laws alone.

Not only do men continuously pursue the satisfaction of
one desire after another, but they also pursue one object as a
means to the next. Desire is compounded by prudence—foresight of future desires and fears—into a search for present
means to future satisfaction. So "the object of mans desire, is
not to enjoy once onely, and for one instant of time; but to
assure for ever, the way of his future desire." Felicity thus
becomes the acquisition of power as well as the satisfaction of
desire.

So that in the first place, I put for a generall inclination of all
mankind, a perpetuall and restlesse desire of Power after power,
that ceaseth only in Death. And the cause of this, is not always
that a man hopes for a more intensive delight, than he has already
attained to; or that he cannot be content with a moderate power:

---

[38] *Leviathan* (Introduction), p. 9.

but because he cannot assure the power and means to live well, which he hath present, without the acquisition of more.[39]

Present satisfaction is the effect of past power; future satisfaction is the effect of present and future power, and in order to safeguard present power, more power must be acquired.[40]

To say that men desire power is not to say that they all desire the same thing, for power is as generic a word as desire is. What is power? It is anything that may be used as a means to an end. It includes what depends immediately on a man's original endowments, what can be developed from them, and any external things which can be acquired or used. Power includes everything that is used as a means to some further end—and anything that attracts the help of others: personal strength, beauty, eloquence, success (good fortune, or God's pardon), any quality that makes a man loved or feared, nobility (where privileged), the assistance of other men (family, friends, the powerful, a faction), prudence, wisdom, riches (with liberality; unused riches would not be power, although reputed riches might be), the sciences, and arts of public use. To be reputed to possess any of these powers is also power. Some powers (beauty, strength) are entirely or mainly dependent on natural

[39] *Leviathan* (11), p. 75. Cf. *Elements of Law* (I. vii. 6–7), pp. 29–30; *De Homine* (xi. 15), *LW* II, 103.

[40] Strauss, *The Political Philosophy of Hobbes,* pp. 8–10, argues that Hobbesian man's infinite desire is not mechanistic but spontaneous: "Hobbes bases the proposition that life is limitless appetite mechanistically on the assumption that appetite is only an automatic consequence of perception, but also on the incompatible assumption that appetite is essentially spontaneous." On the second theory, appetite is infinite in itself; on the first, each desire arises as a reaction to external impressions—infinite desire can only be the result of infinite impressions.

Can the limitless infinity of desire be derived from the mechanistic infinity of one desire after another? I believe that it can. Mechanistic desire is for one object or satisfaction after another. This desire is common to men and animals. Man's desire for immediate ends is transformed by imagination and curiosity into the desire for power (the means to future ends). Desire for immediate satisfactions is infinite only in the sense that it proceeds infinitely from one object to the next but each satisfaction is limited—one can only eat or drink a certain amount. The desire for power is unlimited—infinite in a different sense because it can never be satisfied; for power is whatever may be of use and power can only be assured by more power.

endowment, some are abilities developed by experience or method (eloquence, prudence, science, arts), some are what Aristotle would have called external goods (riches, success, reputation, friends). Many of these forms of power can be acquired by the use of other forms of power, and used in turn to acquire more power. "For the nature of Power, is in this point, like to Fame, increasing as it proceeds; or like the motion of heavy bodies, which the further they go, make still the more hast." [41]

The worth or value of a man is the price that another would give for the use of his power; a man's value "therefore is not absolute; but a thing dependant on the need and judgment of another." Good soldiers are valuable in war; good judges are valuable in times of peace. Although the buyer (as in other things) determines the price—a man's "true Value is no more than it is esteemed by others"—yet the seller, each man, rates himself usually as highly as he can. "To Value a man at a high rate, is to *Honour* him; at a low rate, is to *Dishonour* him. But high, and low, in this case, is to be understood by comparison to the rate that each man setteth on himselfe." [42]

Actions—and words—indicate opinions of a person's value. To honor a person is to indicate by words or actions that he is powerful. To request aid, to treat with deference or respect, to obey, to ask an opinion, to agree in opinion, to imitate, to

[41] *Leviathan* (10), p. 66.

[42] *Ibid.*, p. 67. *Cf. Elements of Law* (I. viii. 5), pp. 34–35. I am not sure that these passages support C. B. Macpherson's inference of a competitive market in power. (See pp. 34–46, 61–68.) (1) Hobbes is (at least) unclear about whether there is a market valuation of the price of an individual, or merely the valuation of the single buyer. Is it a market price that would be paid, or what the buyer will pay? (Individual contractual bargains do not make a market.) (2) The market view is not strengthened by Hobbes's definition of high and low valuing—honoring and dishonoring. The comparison is not to the market rate of value but to the individual's self-valuation. (3) Hobbes distinguishes worthiness from worth. "WORTHINESSE . . . consisteth in a particular power, or ability for that, whereof [a man] is said to be worthy: which particular ability, is usually named FITNESSE, or *Aptitude.*" *Leviathan* (10), p. 74. Both worthiness, and worth are different from merit, which involves a right to the thing merited. (4) One of the functions of the sovereign is to establish a public valuation of men, thus reducing the "market" aspect of honor and power. *Ibid.*, p. 68.

attempt to secure protection and good will by gifts or flattery, to honor those he honors, to do to another what he takes to be honor, or what is made so by law or custom—are all signs of an opinion of another's power, and indications of the love or fear of the one who honors. To dishonor is to indicate not dislike but contempt, i.e., an opinion that a person has little or no power, and is neither loved nor feared.

Similarly, all signs that a man has power are honorable. To be the object of the respect, love, or fear of many, to be obeyed, to accomplish great things, are honorable; as are dominion, victory, wealth, resolution, gravity, great desires, liberality, courage, magnanimity, hope. These latter are all honorable signs of confidence in one's own power. Indications that one is, or thinks oneself, weak are dishonorable.[43]

Honor and dishonor are connected with shame rather than guilt. "Nor does it alter the case of Honour, whether an action (so it be great and difficult, and consequently a signe of much power,) be just or unjust: for Honour consisteth onely in the opinion of Power." [44] The Greeks honored their gods by attributing unjust and unclean acts to them. The pirate, the highwayman, the outlaw are still honored in popular literature and folk myth, although the theme of power to do as one wants, regardless of law or authority, is often gilded over with higher motives. To be honored is to receive recognition of one's power, real or supposed; it is to be reminded by others that one has power, to be confirmed by external acts in the consciousness of power. But it is not the only confirmation possible, since success in obtaining what one desires—results in action, in money, in knowledge—helps to confirm these feelings.

All men seek power, but they do not all seek the same kind of power. Some seek riches; others honor; still others knowledge, or one of the other sorts of power. The differences of

[43] *Leviathan* (10), pp. 68–72. *Elements of Law* (I. viii. 5–6), pp. 34–36.
[44] *Leviathan* (10), p. 71.

men's desires are partly inherent, partly the result of custom
and education; they arise in part "from the difference of the
knowledge, or opinion each one has of the causes, which produce the effect desired." [45] The relation between passion, experience, and opinion is one that is complicated by the continual interaction of these factors. Intellectual ability, a good
wit as opposed to a dull or stupid one, involves quicker imagination and a steadier direction to some end, i.e., to the satisfaction of some desire.

And this difference of quicknesse, is caused by the difference of
mens passions; that love and dislike, some one thing, some another:
and therefore some mens thoughts run one way, some another;
and are held to, and observe differently the things that passe
through their imagination.[46]

The differences among men are developments of their passions (as modified by their other passions, their opinions, their
knowledge, and their experience). Delight in sensual pleasures
must tend to exclude to some extent delight in the imaginations which would lead to glory, honor, riches, or knowledge.[47]
Conversely, desire for riches, honor, knowledge, or other power
must involve preferring other delights, either future or imagined, to immediate sensual delight. Men chasing authority
or wealth are curious only to the point of discovering whether
something can be used for their ends or not.[48] Curiosity, the
peculiarly human passion, causes a lessening of "another passion, which in beastes is commonly prædominant, namely, a
ravenous qualitie, which in man is called *avarice*. The desire
of knowledge and desire of needlesse riches are incompatible,
and destructive one of another." [49]

The combination of basic passions, opinions, and experience
creates a process in which each of these elements is influenced
and developed by the feedback from the others. This process
is present to some extent in all animals, but because of man's

[45] *Ibid.* (11), p. 75. *Cf. ibid.* (8), p. 56.　　[46] *Ibid.* (8), p. 53.
[47] *Elements of Law* (I. x. 3–4), pp. 49–50.　　[48] *Ibid.* (I. ix. 18), p. 46.
[49] *A Minute or first Draught of the Optiques* (Ded.), *EW* VII, 467.

imagination, his greater memory, his curiosity, and his invention of speech, its consequences are more marked in man than in any other animal. Just as the development of language creates the possibilities of science and absurdity, the development of human nature creates the possibilities of civility and of barbarism.

Human Behavior

A voluntary action is an action initiated in an act of willing by an animal or by a human being. But, having a will is itself the final moment in a process of deliberation. This process begins with some sensation or imagination and proceeds through a series of moments of either desire or aversion (which may be joined with judgments about the probability of achieving some good or avoiding some evil).

In Hobbes's philosophy passion is not a term of art; Hobbes does not attempt to derive the passions from a single source. There are several ways in which passion may be analyzed, several facets of passion which may be considered. The first of these is desire or aversion, itself the first endeavor of the subject of the passion. This is accompanied by the second element, the subject's sense of good and evil, i.e., pleasure and pain. The third is the object of the passion, the good that is to be acquired, or the evil that is to be avoided. Some passions are distinguished by opinion rather than desire—not the opinion that something is good or bad—for every desire implies an opinion that what is desired is beneficial (to have, or to enjoy, or to use) and every aversion contains an opinion that what it is desired to avoid is, in some way, harmful—but rather an opinion about the probabilities of acquiring the good or avoiding the evil by adopting one line of action or another. Finally, combinations of these various categories must be considered. Not all combinations are possible; not all possible combinations have names, e.g., the passion felt by the safe observers of other men in danger is a mixture of delight and pity.[50] Desire for an object combined with the opinion that it is only obtainable by a course leading to undesired consequences is a conceivable, perhaps even familiar, passion which seems to have no name.

Common passions usually receive names, especially when those names can carry an overtone of disapproval. Of the desires for power, wealth, satisfaction, and knowledge, i.e., the passions of ambition, avarice, greed, and curiosity, only the last, probably the least common of the four, carries no pejorative judgment.[51]

No matter what these passions are called, all men must have some desires. Having desires, and realizing that they will have future desires, must lead men from any temporary rest in present satisfaction to a continual striving for power after power: first for the power to satisfy a future desire and then for power to safeguard that power, and so on. . . . In this situation, how will men act? Or, to ask the same question, what are the consequences of their passions? What are their ethics? [52]

One reading of Hobbes's philosophy describes the morality of Hobbesian man as a conflict between vanity and fear.[53] Vainglory, or vanity, becomes the sum and substance of natural appetite; vanity is the cause of man's continual striving for precedence, and the satisfaction of vanity becomes his main purpose. As vanity is a natural appetite, so fear becomes either the substitute for natural reason, or its source. Hobbes denies that reason can control the appetites; reason has become nothing more than a scout for the passions. Hobbes has deposed reason from its traditional supremacy, a supremacy which it had held on the authority of Plato and Aristotle. So, the argument continues, some passion must be found to counteract the natural tendency of vanity. Vanity can only be limited when

[50] *Elements of Law* (I. ix. 13, 19), pp. 41, 46.
[51] Men's passions often color their descriptions of the passions of other men. See *Leviathan* (4, 11), pp. 31–32, 79; *Elements of Law* (I. v. 14), pp. 23–24.
[52] *Leviathan* (9, Table), p. 65.
[53] See Strauss, *The Political Philosophy of Hobbes*, pp. 15–21.

a man attempts to realize his vain dreams of glory in the real world. In making demands for recognition from other similar creatures, the naturally vain man puts himself into real conflict with the natural vanity of others. The vain man demands from others a recognition of his power, his precedence, that cannot be given because it contradicts their natural vanity. The demand provokes a refusal which is itself a counter-demand for recognition. Each, then, has been insulted. Only revenge upon the other can preserve his vanity. Vain men must provoke each other to a battle in which the stakes at the beginning are honor, revenge, and triumph for the victor, defeat and subjection for the vanquished. But the conflict is real and not illusory; in the struggle, bodily damage is inflicted, "or, more accurately, physical pain, arouses a fear for life." [54] Fear tempers anger and transforms the desire for revenge into hatred. "The aim of the hater is no longer triumph over the enemy, but his death." [55] The stakes of the battle have become life or death. The naturally vain man has stumbled on the danger of death, or, more precisely, he had not foreseen the danger of violent death; his vanity is tamed by the fear of death. (Bodily pain, on this account, seems to stimulate an imagination of death. Is pain a touch of death? A partial death?) Fear brings reason in train suggesting means of avoiding violent death. *Timor mortis principium sapientiae!* This explains why fear does not appear in Hobbes's description of life as a race.[56] Fear, which moderates the race, "is for that very reason exalted above the passions, and, therefore, replaces reason." [57]

This reading appears to be one which would satisfy most of the demands we should make of an interpretation of Hobbes's view of human nature. It is one that traces the causes of men's actions back to passions. It provides a motive—vanity—that leads to human conflict, and a second motive—fear—that leads to a mitigation of this conflict. It goes further and explains

---

[54] *Ibid.*, p. 20.   [55] *Ibid.*, pp. 20–21.   [56] See above, p. 56.
[57] Strauss, *The Political Philosophy of Hobbes*, p. 150n1.

how the consequences of vanity in conduct lead to the discovery of fear, and the consequences of fear change the ways
human beings conduct themselves. The ways men act, their
mores, are properly seen to be the consequences of their passions.

But, upon re-examination, this view must be discarded as
only apparently satisfying. Vanity cannot fulfill the requirements forced upon it here. It cannot provide the motivation
for the activities of natural men. Vanity is truly vainglorying.
Glorying is vain (rather than valid) not because it does not
assure success (for even true knowledge of one's own power
leads only to a better judgment about the chances of success),
but because it does not lead to action at all. Vanity is vainglory because it is satisfied with its own dream of power. Nar-
cissistically, it feeds upon its own image, contents itself with
its own illusions, pleases itself with romances. Those whose
glory rests on a false supposition of their power may act and
fail, but vainglorious men do not act. They certainly daydream,
they probably boast, they may even show off. They avoid action
because it can result in nothing but the revealing of their
defects. Vainglory is exhibited by the fly on the axletree, "saying to himself, What a dust do I raise!" [58] Other vainglorious
men, estimating their power from flattery or good fortune
instead of from true knowledge of themselves, are inclined to
engage rashly. This sort is no more likely to engage in a struggle than the first type, for when danger approaches they retire
if they can.[59]

The naturally vain men that we supposed to be jolted from
their dream-world when they sought outside confirmation for
their dreams are not very likely on Hobbes's view of vanity.
The dream-world satisfies their vanity; they do not enter a
struggle for power or honor. If they meet each other by chance,
they will engage only in a boasting contest, a contest in which

[58] *Elements of Law* (I. ix. i), p. 37. *Cf. Leviathan* (6), p. 44; *De Cive* (i. 2),
EW II, 4.
[59] *Leviathan* (11), pp. 77–78.

neither will be in any danger. When they part, each will esteem the other somewhat, but himself more—both for associating with the great and for winning the argument. The one thing that they will be most anxious to avoid is any sort of real struggle, any test that would reveal their actual prowess.

Strauss's view does more than overestimate the power of vanity; it overestimates the value of fear. Fear for Hobbes is something more than aversion; it is aversion to an expected pain. The mental sequence in fear is not sensation/aversion, but sensation/imagination of future consequences/aversion.[60] The scheme that has been presented above may escape from the error of relying on the sensation of physical pain as a direct stimulus of fear, or it may plausibly assert that physical pain not only initiates aversion but the imagination of that much greater calamity, violent death. But even the granting of such a concession will not save this argument, for it is inadequate for another reason. It has given an account of natural passion (vanity) in which the satisfaction of vanity is accomplished in the imagination. All natural imagination is pleasurable, and, since the vain man lives his life in imagination, his is a life of joy. That is to say that the first step in the argument has been carefully to eliminate sense pleasures and pains, and grief, i.e., painful imaginations, from human experience. The second step is then to introduce "real," i.e., sensible, pain, which is made the source of fear. Thus fear becomes more "real" than other imaginations because it is the only imagination that is allowed to have a sensible origin. Being more real—in fact the only real imagination—it alone can be the source of reason.[61] No wonder fear is alleged to be necessarily absent from the race. For the race is now not a real race but a dream race.

But this account of fear is certainly mistaken. All imagina-

[60] *Elements of Law* (I. vii. 2), pp. 28–29; *Leviathan* (6), pp. 42–43.

[61] That this is the basis of Strauss's interpretation of Hobbes is clear from his "On the Basis of Hobbes's Political Philosophy," pp. 170–96. (This article, which is a review of Raymond Polin's *Philosophie et Politique chez Thomas Hobbes*, appeared originally in French in *Critique*, X [1954], 338–62.) See Appendix 1.

tions are connected, as we have seen, to sense. On this view there could be no such thing as joy or glory or confidence— the imagination of one's own power grounded on past experience—for all these are nothing other than vanity.[62] (Remembering that experience is the only testimony that we have for matters of fact.) It seems to intimate that actual sensible pleasure is not experienced. Finally, it has completely eliminated the possibility of a vain fear—a fear based on an incorrect opinion of one's own power. Hobbes explicitly recognizes vain fear. Fear is not such a good thing that there cannot be too much of it. Its excess, like excessive vainglory or pride, becomes rage or fury. Excessive and causeless fear is melancholy. Another sort of excessive fear is panic terror.[63]

But the similarity of life to a race should not be pressed too far. A race is a simplified model of human activity; one of the simplifications it imposes is the restriction of all activity to continuous movement in a single, desired direction, viz., toward the finish line. Thus the race, by its very assumptions, imposes upon activity the motion appropriate to desire and tends to exclude the motions appropriate to fear or aversion, i.e., movement away from something. In the race, aversion and fear could only appear in a modified form—as hanging back, hesitation, or despair.

Since all correct imaginations are not fearful, and all fearful imaginations are not correct, reason is not the result of fear alone. Thoughts act as scouts and spies for all the passions and not for fear alone. Thought discovers the means to satisfy ambition, avarice, greed, pride, and curiosity as well as ways to avoid the fearful. Because thought depends on desire, a great passion for something is a necessary motive for great fancy or good judgment. The indifferent man, he who has no great

---

[62] *Leviathan* (6), p. 44; *Elements of Law* (I. ix. 1), pp. 36–37.

[63] *Leviathan* (6, 8), pp. 44, 57. *Cf. Elements of Law* (I. ix. 2), p. 38, and (I. x. 11), pp. 52–53: "[T]here be other examples of madness, and the degrees thereof, proceeding from too much vain fear and dejection: as in those melancholy men that have imagined themselves brittle as glass, or have had some other like imagination; and degrees hereof are all those exorbitant and causeless fears, which we commonly observe in melancholy persons."

passion for anything, but only moderate passions, is not reasonable, but dull. On the other hand, having the same passion for everything produces giddiness. Nevertheless, strong passion is dangerous, for to have an extraordinarily strong and vehement passion for something, to be obsessed with something, is madness.[64] Although passion that overruns all calculations is undesirable, passions are necessary, and strong passions are valuable; a healthy fear, though not the source of reason, may be a valuable and necessary stimulus to its application.

Another reading of Hobbes's view of human nature asserts that men are all fundamentally similar machines whose only differences are in the speeds at which they operate.[65] It has been argued that this is far too simple a view of Hobbesian man, for speed of operation is only one of the differences between men; quickness of motion is itself partly a cause of differences between men, but it is also, at least in part, an effect of other differences, viz., fundamental passions, opinions, and experience.

If we begin from this more complicated picture of man, we may still say that most men, perhaps all men, are driven to seek power after power, although not necessarily the same power. But even though this is the way that men are, it does not follow that they must necessarily, always and everywhere, all act in the same way, for they may be moved by different passions, they may have been affected by different experiences, they may have different opinions about the best way to satisfy their desires; to account for men's actions we must consider not only their passions, but also their previous experience and their opinions about the best way to achieve their ends, i.e., their evaluation of the situation in which they are acting. Because the determination of human *mores* depends on more than one factor, the resulting modes of human behavior are extremely varied. Fear, it is true, does sometimes dispose men to seek security in submission to a common power. But fear may motivate a

[64] *Leviathan* (8), p. 57.
[65] Watkins, "Philosophy and Politics in Hobbes," pp. 125–46. See above, pp. 63–64.

man, not to seek the aid of others, but to anticipate the attack of an enemy by attacking him first.[66] Determination of the choice between mutual security and preventive war is not one that depends on a difference of passion, fear being present in both cases, but one that depends on an estimate of the best means of avoiding the danger feared.

Although competition for power "enclineth to Contention, Enmity, and War," [67] there is one form of contention that is beneficial to the contenders. To receive benefits from someone we think an equal or inferior (as well as from a superior) inclines to love, provided there is a hope of requiting these benefits. This obliges the receiver to mutual aid "from whence proceedeth an Emulation of who shall exceed in benefiting; the most noble and profitable contention possible; wherein the victor is pleased with his victory, and the other revenged by confessing it." [68] But the proviso of possible requital is crucial here, for if requital is impossible the result is hate and not love.

Since passions and opinions lead to various ways of acting, it is important to determine what patterns of behavior are most likely to occur. Ordinarily, a man must desire power. Even if a man would be content with moderate power, he must seek to secure that power. Security, however, is impossible as long as men have conflicting unrestrained desires, especially since the extent of other men's desires is unpredictable; it is impossible to know that another man is rational, that he does not take pleasure in contemplating his own power, his conquests, his precedence over others. In his pursuit of happiness (satisfactions, power, security, and precedence), each man is gnawed by anxiety for the future. The best security would be the aid of others, but to gain that aid, a man must associate with others. To be with others without a society is dangerous, for they, or one of them, may despoil him, or hurt him, or kill him. To be alive is a necessary prerequisite to any further satis-

[66] *Leviathan* (11, 13), pp. 77, 95.　　　[67] *Ibid.* (11), p. 75.　　　[68] *Ibid.*, p. 77.

faction; conservation of one's life, if not the greatest good, is a primary good. Safety could be achieved by being one step ahead of everyone else, by attempting to conquer or kill others before they could do the same. But this is not a satisfactory solution, for no man can expect to be continually successful in such an enterprise. The only solution is to form a society either by dint of conquest or by mutual agreement.

Here is the pattern of human behavior which seems most important for Hobbes. Man is an animal with both desires and fears greatly expanded by his peculiar mental equipment. He is an animal that desires the presence of other men but to whom the presence of other men is both distressing and dangerous. In order to satisfy his desires and calm his fears, he must find a way to live with others. Society is possible if men can use desire and fear—especially fear—to create a situation in which men can be fairly secure with each other.

But if this pattern of human life and human motivation dominates Hobbes's writings, a second pattern of human character has frequently been discovered in them: the pattern of aristocratic behavior.[69] The aristocratic man, or the magnanimous man, disdains to owe his life or his contentment to underhanded or shameful or fraudulent acts. Here we have a pride which, according to Oakeshott, is not Satanic, but moral— *sancta superbia.* A man of this character desires power and fears death as other men do, but he puts honor above life. There are some sorts of life so shameful and so dishonorable that they are not worth living. Such a man would not depend on the flattery of others for his good opinion of himself. His is a well-deserved confidence in his own abilities. His *justa sui estimatio* does not lead him to contempt for others and unnecessary conflict with them. He endeavors peace no less than they do, but he does not do so primarily because of his fear of war, for he possesses the virtues most likely to be useful in war—courage, fortitude, and a correct estimate of his own abilities. He en-

[69] See Appendix 2.

deavors peace because he condemns as petty the actions that
lead to war. His concern for his honor leads him to keep his
word.[70] He is not cruel because he is not unreasonably afraid.[71]
He will not stoop to deceit, dishonesty, trickery, injustice, in-
equity, revenge, and ingratitude. He will not be petty. Hobbes
describes him as just or righteous. His just intention is not the
result of fear. "That which gives to humane Actions the relish
of Justice, is a certain Noblenesse or Gallantnesse of courage,
(rarely found,) by which a man scorns to be beholding for the
contentment of his life, to fraud, or breach of promise." [72]

This sort of man, the magnanimous man, is the diametrical
opposite of the pusillanimous or vainglorious man.[73] He is not
a boaster but a doer; he does not need to seek the approval or
flattery of others, for he will rely for his success on his own
power. Perhaps he is a bit more independent of other men
than most are. Although he does not seek approval, he will
probably receive it, for he will be helpful, straightforward, and
honest in his dealings with others; he will not anger easily,
for this is a mark of vainglory, neither will he be quarrelsome
or boastful. Certain of his own sufficiency, he will not hesitate
to extend a helping hand to others. So, he will probably be
respected and honored.

This magnanimous sort of man is more self-sufficient than
the fearful man. It is not that he is a Stoic wise man, bereft of
both desires and satisfactions, for he is not without desires,
nor without satisfactions, nor without pains. In a way his self-
sufficiency results from his self-centeredness. He finds his main
satisfactions and disappointments in his own conduct and not
in the imposition of his personality upon the world. Pride here
is still a passion to be God-like, but it has become a passion to
imitate God rather than a desire to be God. The consequence
of selfishness here is self-knowledge and self-respect.

[70] *Leviathan* (14), p. 108.
[71] *Ibid.* (15), p. 117. Cf. *De Cive* (iii. 10–12), *EW* II, 37–38.
[72] *Leviathan* (15), p. 114.   [73] *Elements of Law* (I. ix. 20), p. 47.

The pattern of conduct of the so-called "gallant man" or "man of pride" is possible, in Hobbes's account of human behavior, in two different ways.

(1) The morality of gallantry is possible if a man has accepted some code of moral values in which keeping one's word, being generous, and acting according to the virtue of justice are placed higher in the scale of values than life. The acceptance of such a code of values is possible if a man would (or if he believes that he would) find his life insupportably painful otherwise. His pleasure in living depends on his self-image, or upon his reputation with others, or upon his eventual fame, or upon some higher code of sanctions that he believes in.

(2) The morality of gallantry is also possible upon the ordinary principles of second-order power-seeking provided that this way of acting is believed to be the most effective way of acquiring power. Since gallant conduct indicates the possession of power (i.e., if a man can be indifferent to small or mean helps, he shows that he has so much power that he does not need them), it is likely to impress other men, thereby gaining their respect. Respect for power is honor. Honor is itself a form of power; it may be used to increase power.

In a state of nature, gallant conduct might fail to increase a man's power. The second sort of gallant man, the man whose gallantry is merely prudential, would be forced to adopt a different way of acting if gallantry failed. The first sort of gallant man may die preferring gallantry to life.

If this model of human conduct does appear in Hobbes's writings, why does he not develop it more forcefully? The most obvious reason is the one that he himself gives when discussing the two passions which can move men to keep their word.

And those are either a Feare of the consequence of breaking their word; or a Glory, or Pride in appearing not to need to break it. This later is a Generosity too rarely found to be presumed on, especially in the pursuers of Wealth, Command, or sensuall Pleasure; which are the greatest part of Mankind. The Passion to be reckoned upon, is Fear.[74]

Magnanimous men, men of good will, are rare. The problem of human conduct must be solved for most men, and for them the passion to be reckoned on is fear.

Are there any other patterns of human conduct? Hobbes does suggest, I think, at least one more such pattern. It is exhibited by the curious man, the man who seeks knowledge rather than wealth, command, or pleasure. Curiosity is a peculiarly human passion, present in all men to some degree, but not equally present in all men. To the curious man, the acquisition of knowledge is the greatest pleasure, a pleasure for which the seekers of wealth or power, "which in respect of knowledge are but sensuality," have no time.[75]

Desire, to know why, and how, [is] CURIOSITY; such as is in no living creature but *Man:* so that Man is distinguished, not onely by his Reason; but also by this singular Passion from other *Animals;* in whom the appetite of food, and other pleasures of Sense, by prædominance, take away the care of knowing causes; which is a Lust of the mind, that by a perseverance of delight in the continuall and indefatigable generation of Knowledge, exceedeth the short vehemence of any carnall Pleasure.[76]

Such a life, then, would be the most pleasurable of all because the pleasures of knowledge are more within human power and less ephemeral than other pleasures. Significantly it is curiosity that leads to other peculiarly human characteristics: care for the future, religion, and science. The desire to know should lead a man to be peaceful, for it implies a desire for leisure, and consequently the desire to be protected. The scientist or philosopher will be inclined to obey a common power. Furthermore, knowledge about causes reduces ignorance and credulity; it should produce a true knowledge of causes both natural and

[74] *Leviathan* (14), p. 108.   [75] *Elements of Law* (I. ix. 18), pp. 45–46.
[76] *Leviathan* (6), p. 44. *Cf. ibid.* (8), p. 56, and *A Minute or first Draught of the Optiques* (Ded.), *EW* VII, 467.

political, and therefore disinclination to obey private men in religion or politics.[77] But this pattern of human life must be even rarer than the pattern of magnanimity; most men are curious only insofar as it concerns their immediate benefit or distress. It is doubtful that the curious man can exist at all in that miserable condition of men known as the state of nature.

[77] *Leviathan* (11), p. 76, 78–81.

4

THE NATURAL

CONDITION

Let us return again to the state of nature, and consider men as if but even now sprung out of the earth, and suddenly, like mushrooms, come to full maturity, without all kind of engagement to each other.

De Cive (viii. 1), *EW* II, 108–9

The State of Nature

In order to construct political science, the knowledge of human organization, we must begin, as we began in the construction of natural science, with its constitutive causes.

For everything is best understood by its constitutive causes. For as in a watch, or some such small engine, the matter, figure, and motion of the wheels cannot well be known, except it be taken insunder and viewed in parts; so to make a more curious search into the rights of states and duties of subjects, it is necessary, I say, not to take them insunder, but yet that they be so considered as if they were dissolved; that is, that we rightly understand what the quality of human nature is, in what matters it is, in what not, fit to make up a civil government, and how men must be agreed amongst themselves that intend to grow up into a well-grounded state.[1]

[1] *De Cive* (Preface), *EW* II, xiv.

Like the investigation of nature, the investigation of society begins with its imaginary dissolution or annihilation. So the constitutive causes of human order must be derived from the way human beings would conduct themselves in a situation in which no order existed. This situation is what Hobbes calls the "natural condition of mankind" or "the state of nature." The way that men conduct themselves, as we have seen, depends upon their passions and their opinions or knowledge about the consequences of various possible courses of action.

It has already been shown that the desires of a rational, i.e., calculating, being are in principle unlimited. The desire for simple but continual satisfactions, for felicity, is transformed by prudence (care for the future and the ability to project the conceptions of cause and effect from the past into the future with the presumption that this projection is valid) into the desire to gain present means of future satisfactions. The desire for satisfaction has become the desire for power, and this implies the desire for more power, for the power necessary to assure the possession of present power. Power, it will be remembered, includes command, honor, wealth, and knowledge. Each individual man begins with his natural appetite for what he senses or imagines to be good and his natural aversion to whatever he senses or imagines to be evil. Good and evil are not objective and unchanging qualities of things but the subjective description of the apparent beneficial or harmful effects of things, this description being ultimately based upon the effects that these things have upon vital motion, either immediately or as the result of a chain of consequences. Whatever helps vital motion is good and what hinders it is evil. So, the transformation of first-order desires (for satisfaction) into second-order desires (for power) changes the objects of desire into the means of acquiring future satisfaction, and the means to acquire and preserve those means. And disinclination to immediate dissatisfaction and sorrow becomes aversion from what will produce future dissatisfaction and sorrow, and from whatever leads to what will produce these things. Life itself is motion—from desire to desire—a perpetual and restless desire of power after power. "For there is no such *Finis ultimus,* (utmost ayme,) nor *Summum Bonum,* (greatest Good,) as is spoken of in the Books of the old Morall Philosophers."[2] Life and desire come to their end together; only the dead are without desire. When the desires are no longer in motion, when the vital motion has stopped, then is man in repose, at rest, and then do we correctly say *requiescat in pace.*

Men's first-order appetites are for things that help their vital motion, and their second-order appetites are for things that they believe will help vital motion, or will be the means of acquiring these helps. Each man's aversions are to what hinders his vital motion, to what he believes will hinder it, and to what will be the means of bringing these hindrances upon himself. Men seek to preserve life, and acquire satisfactions and the means to satisfactions, and they seek to avoid death, dissatisfaction, sorrow and those things that lead to them. So each man desires *bonum sibi,* his own good, which is continual life and satisfaction and power; and each desires to avoid evils to himself, but especially the greatest of evils—his death.

[N]ecessity of nature maketh men to will and desire *bonum sibi,* that which is good for themselves, and to avoid that which is hurtful; but most of all that terrible enemy of nature, death, from whom we expect both the loss of all power, and also the greatest of bodily pains in the losing.[3]

The situation in which men by nature find themselves is one in which they are all equal, or at least, they must consider themselves as equal. For although there are differences among them in strength and intelligence, "the difference between man, and man, is not so considerable, as that one man can thereupon

[2] *Leviathan* (11), p. 75.
[3] *Elements of Law* (I. xiv. 6), p. 71. Hobbes means each man's preservation of his own life and not all men's (collective) preservation of their lives; see *Leviathan* (14), pp. 99, 101, and *De Homine* (xi. 6), *LW* II, 98.

claim to himselfe any benefit, to which another may not pretend, as well as he." [4] Men are to be considered equal for three reasons: (1) They are relatively equal in strength, i.e., equally vulnerable to being killed and equally able to kill. (2) They are relatively equal in wisdom; prudence is equally bestowed by equal time, and science is so much of a rarity that it need not be considered. Men think their own wits as good as any others', and few are foolish enough to prefer being governed by another to governing themselves. (3) Furthermore, if any man claim superiority on the basis of wisdom (or any other quality), since there is neither an agreed standard of value nor an agreed judge, should anyone else deny this superiority or claim equality, the only way to decide the question would be by battle.[5]

The consequence of natural equality is an equal hope in each man to attain his ends. Since desire in any man is in principle unlimited (even though it need not be unlimited in fact), and since all men have equal hopes to attain their ends, whenever two men happen to desire the same thing that they cannot both enjoy, they become enemies. In their competition to satisfy their desires, they endeavor to destroy or subdue each other.[6] Moreover, since no man has any special privileges over other men in the state of nature, both men may act within their rights. By the right of nature, the liberty that each man has to use his own power to preserve his own nature, each man may do anything that he actually (honestly) believes to be the best means to his own preservation.[7] In this situation, just as there can be no limit to desire, there can be no limit to right.

[4] *Leviathan* (13), p. 94; *Elements of Law* (I. xiv. 2), p. 70; *De Cive* (i. 3), *EW* II, 6–7.

[5] In a fight, those who have been alleged to be naturally superior, viz., the wise, by such philosophers as Aristotle, "do [not] alwaies, or often, or almost at any time, get the Victory." *Leviathan* (15), p. 118; *De Cive* (iii. 13), *EW* II, 38–39; *Elements of Law* (I. xvii. 1), pp. 87–88.

[6] *Leviathan* (13), p. 95. According to *De Cive* (i. 6), *EW* II, 8, conflict of appetites is the most frequent reason why men desire to hurt others.

[7] *De Cive* (i. 10), *EW* II, 9–11; *Leviathan* (14), p. 99. See Warrender, *The Political Philosophy of Hobbes*, pp. 18–26, 49, 59–60.

There is nothing which a man may not use as a help in preserving his life against his enemies; "It followeth, that in such a condition, every man has a Right to every thing; even to one anothers body." [8]

The right of nature—the right that all men have to all things—should not be regarded as an absolute and unlimited right. Hobbes does overstate the situation somewhat. The actual situation is that each man has a right to his own preservation and to everything he believes to be a necessary means to this end. Since each is the judge of the necessity of the means, and since there is, in principle, no limit to what may be desired as necessary means of preserving life and to securing the means of preserving life, it follows that any man may have a right to anything. A man's right is limited only by what he believes he needs.

Each man's natural right expands to encompass whatever he thinks he needs for his own preservation, and contracts to exclude what he thinks he does not need. A man may believe, perhaps unreasonably, that he needs control over everything; he may believe that any frustration of his desire would endanger his life; or, in the most limited case, he may believe that he needs some particular thing. If all men were possessed of their maximum natural right, then all men would be in contention with all other men for all things at all times—a maximal state of nature. But even if men only desired and believed they needed what was actually necessary to preserve themselves (a situation which may safely be regarded as counterfactual), then, assuming only that goods are scarce and men's knowledge of others' desires and needs is imperfect, the state of nature would still be a state of insecurity and contention. In such a

---

[8] *Leviathan* (14), p. 99. A marginal note (which seems to be in Hobbes's hand) in the presentation copy of *Leviathan,* British Museum, Egerton MSS, 1910 (at p. 95) reads: "Nature alloweth a mans security which there is in no civil state, to murder and subdue all that he thinks can hurt him." *Cf. Elements of Law* (I. xiv. 10), p. 72; *Leviathan* (28), p. 239.

state of nature, although A and B do not necessarily have a right to the same thing, they may have. B's right does not exclude A's right; in a state of nature no man can acquire an exclusive right to anything. A may claim what B currently has, for in the state of nature, though there may be possession and enjoyment of goods, there is "no Propriety, no Dominion, no *Mine* and *Thine* distinct; but onely that to be every mans, that he can get; and for so long, as he can keep it." [9] To acquire a right to any thing, or to do any action, a man need only judge that it is necessary to his preservation. If, as Hobbes sometimes suggests, mere desire indicates a belief that the thing desired is necessary to preservation, then every man has a right to whatever he desires.[10]

Since in the state of nature a man who possesses anything may expect that someone will come and desire what he possesses, and that this invader may have as much right to the good as the occupier, no man can enjoy anything in security.

And from hence it comes to passe, that where an Invader hath no more to feare, than an other mans single power; if one plant, sow, build, or possesse a convenient Seat, others may probably be expected to come prepared with forces united, to dispossesse and deprive him, not only of the fruit of his labour, but also of his life, or liberty. And the Invader again is in like danger of another.[11]

So every one who possesses anything of value must fear that he will be attacked by someone else who wants this thing. Clearly, his best course of action is "Anticipation; that is, by force, or wiles, to master the persons of all men he can, so long, till he see no other power great enough to endanger him: And this is no more than his own conservation requireth, and

[9] *Leviathan* (13), p. 98.
[10] *De Cive* (i. 10), *EW* II, 10: "[W]hatsoever a man would, it therefore seems good to him because he wills it, and either it really doth, or at least seems to him to contribute towards his preservation."
[11] *Leviathan* (13), p. 95. The state of nature does not preclude temporary cooperation of the sort described here.

is generally allowed." [12] In the state of nature, other men cannot be assumed to have a reasonable opinion of what sort of security their preservation actually requires. They must be assumed to have the unlimited desire that it is in principle possible for them to have, and their desire is not only for things, but for glory (the feeling of power over other men) and for honor (the recognition of their power, even when they are in fact equal or inferior). This not only adds a third factor (glory) to the causes of conflict already mentioned (competition and diffidence) but it also must increase the amount of security that men, who would otherwise be satisfied with moderate power, reasonably believe to be necessary for their preservation. "And by consequence, such augmentation of dominion over men, being necessary to a mans conservation, it ought to be allowed him." [13]

The consequence drawn in *De Cive* is even more explicit. (1) In danger one has a right to protect oneself according to one's own will (the right of nature). (2) Equality leads to danger (as has been shown above); it follows that if anyone has another person in his power he has a right to take caution against that person's becoming an equal and therefore a danger; i.e., *a sure and irresistible power confers the right of dominion and ruling over those who cannot resist.*[14] It is true that this sort of power is unlikely to be gained in the state of nature, and if gained it is unlikely to be kept, for the state of nature is a state of equality and uncertainty in which the resort to violence must always be expected, i.e., the state of nature is a state of war. It is a period of time in which men

---

[12] *Ibid.; Elements of Law* (I. xiv. 3–12), pp. 70–73.

[13] *Leviathan* (13), p. 95. The same set of causes for conflict in the state of nature are set forth in all three versions of this argument: (a) divisive appetite: *Elements of Law* (I. xiv. 5), p. 71; *De Cive* (i. 6), *EW* II, 8; *Leviathan* (13), p. 95; (b) fear or diffidence: *Elements of Law* (I. xiv. 3), pp. 70–71; *De Cive* (i. 3–4), *EW* II, 6–7; *Leviathan* (13), p. 95; (c) glory or precedence: *Elements of Law* (I. xiv. 4), p. 71; *De Cive* (i. 4–5), *EW* II, 7–8; *Leviathan* (13), pp. 95–96.

[14] *De Cive* (i. 14), *EW* II, 13; *Elements of Law* (I. xiv. 13), pp. 73–74. God's power (if there is an omnipotent God) is the greatest but not the only such power possible in a state of nature. A man might have sure and irresistible power for a time over a prisoner, a wounded or sleeping man, or a child.

have declared (by words or deeds) that they have the will to contend by force.[15] The maximum state of nature is the maximum state of war, i.e., the war of all against all. In this situation, a man must presume that everyone is his enemy and that at least some of these enemies will believe that everything they want is necessary to their preservation. Thus he has a maximum natural "right to all things, that is to say, to do whatsoever he listeth to whom he listeth, to possess, use, and enjoy all things he will and can." [16] Under these circumstances his actual power cannot be greater than his right—for everything here can be useful to him in his struggle. (Whether or not his right is complemented by an obligation on the part of others to obey is another question.) Clearly, a man may secure his own safety by taking caution for the future. If he were afraid of any man in his power, he would be justified in killing or imprisoning him. Under certain conditions, which could only be satisfied by the establishment of some sort of social bond between them, the conqueror could reasonably allow his prisoner to live and to live without being shackled in irons.[17]

Whatsoever, therefore is consequent to a time of Warre, where every man is Enemy to every man; the same is consequent to the time, wherein men live without other security, than what their own strength, and their own invention shall furnish them withall. In such condition, there is no place for Industry; because the fruit thereof is uncertain: and consequently no Culture of the Earth; no Navigation, nor use of the commodities that may be imported by Sea; no commodious Building; no Instruments of moving, and removing such things as require much force; no Knowledge of the face of the Earth; no account of Time; no Arts; no Letters; no Society; and which is worst of all, continuall feare, and danger of violent death; And the life of man, solitary, poore, nasty, brutish, and short.[18]

[15] *Leviathan* (13), p. 96; *Elements of Law* (I. xiv. 11), pp. 72–73; *De Cive* (i. 12), *EW* II, 11.

[16] *Elements of Law* (I. xiv. 10), p. 72. Cf. *De Cive* (i. 10), *EW* II, 11.

[17] In the state of nature, a man may kill any man or beast that is dangerous to him, and save any man or beast useful to him. *De Cive* (viii. 10), *EW* II, 113–14; *Elements of Law* (II. iii. 9), pp. 130–31; *Leviathan* (28), p. 239.

[18] *Leviathan* (13), pp. 96–97.

Isn't this model of human life untrue? It is no more untrue and no less scientific than Galileo's law of falling bodies. No earthly body had ever been observed in frictionless free fall. Hobbes's explicit answer to the objection is that the (scientific) inference from the passions is confirmed by experience. Perhaps there has never been any general state of nature, but there are four areas of experience that the concept explains:

(1) The conduct of men in settled states. They arm themselves for journeys, lock their doors, safeguard their valuables. They do this even though they are protected by public security forces. (If anyone believes this is no longer true since the establishment of a preventative police, let him consider the situation in which police protection breaks down.)

(2) The situation where the only social organization is on a very small scale, e.g., that of the family, the extended family, or the tribe (including the ancient Germans as well as seventeenth-century American Indians).

(3) The situation in which a society degenerates into civil war.

(4) The condition of sovereign states in international relations at all times.[19]

In the natural condition, and especially the maximum state of war, the cardinal virtues are force and fraud; the maxim of conduct (both one's own and what one expects from others) is *homo homini lupus*.

And thus much for the ill condition, which man by meer Nature is actually placed in; though with a possibility to come out of it, consisting partly in the Passions, partly in his Reason.

The Passions that encline men to Peace, are Feare of Death; Desire of such things as are necessary to commodious living; and a Hope by their Industry to obtain them. And Reason suggesteth convenient Articles of Peace, upon which men may be drawn to agreement.[20]

These articles are the laws of nature.

[19] *Ibid.*, pp. 97–98; *Elements of Law* (I. xiv. 12), p. 73. *Cf. De Cive* (i. 13), *EW* II, 12. See Polin's description of the state of nature as a (Weberian) ideal type which has a real application, pp. 88–89.

[20] *Leviathan* (13), p. 98.

The Laws of Nature

The right of nature is the liberty each man has to use any means he thinks necessary to preserve himself. In the maximum state of war, this right is a right to all things. But, since the state of nature is a state of insecurity and violence, the purpose of each man to preserve himself is frustrated. The actual preservation of many men, perhaps even in time, of all men, is frustrated by exercise of the right of each to preserve himself.

Yet cannot men expect any lasting preservation, continuing thus in the state of nature, that is, of war, by reason of that equality of power, and other human faculties they are endued withal. Wherefore to seek peace, where there is any hopes of obtaining it, and where there is none, to enquire out for auxiliaries of war, is the dictate of right reason, that is, the law of nature.[21]

Right reasoning is a correct deduction by any individual man of what he must do and not do toward others in order to preserve himself. The whole breach of the laws of nature consists in the folly of those who do not see what duties they must necessarily perform to secure their own conservation.[22]

The laws of nature, then, may be considered as a set of reasonable precepts for the guidance of men toward what they desire to obtain, namely, their own good, which in this case is their own preservation. Hobbes's most explicit formulation of the definition of a natural law is that in *Leviathan*.

A Law Of Nature, (*Lex Naturalis*,) is a Precept, or generall Rule, found out by Reason, by which a man is forbidden to do, that, which is destructive of his life, or taketh away the means of preserving the same; and to omit, that, by which he thinketh it may be best preserved.[23]

In this sense, the laws of nature are a formulation of the best means to the end of each man who desires to preserve

[21] *De Cive* (i. 15), *EW* II, 13.   [22] *Ibid.* (ii. 1), *EW* II, 16n.
[23] *Leviathan* (14), p. 99. *N.B.* that this is a definition rather than a rule. *Cf.* *Elements of Law* (I. xv. 1), p. 75.

himself. They are not categorical imperatives but hypothetical imperatives: if you wish to preserve yourself, do this.

The first and fundamental law of nature, the law from which the other special laws of nature are derived, is: *"That every man, ought to endeavour Peace, as farre as he has hope of obtaining it; and when he can not obtain it, that he may seek, and use, all helps and advantages of Warre."* [24] A man should seek peace, while he hopes to obtain it. *Seek peace* is not a categorical duty, for it is a duty that depends upon a man's own judgment of the situation in which he is acting. If seeking peace seems to be a hopeless quest, then he may use any convenient means to preserve himself. He may turn to war; Hobbes does not say he must turn to war.[25]

The second law of nature is derived from the fundamental law. Since the maximum right of nature is a cause of conflict, endeavoring peace implies: *"That a man be willing, when others are so too, as farre-forth, as for Peace, and defence of himselfe he shall think it necessary, to lay down this right to all things; and be contented with so much liberty against other men, as he would allow other men against himselfe."* The maximum state of nature, in which everyone has a right of doing whatever he likes, is a state of war. "But if other men will not lay down their Right, as well as he; then there is no Reason for any one, to divest himselfe of his: For that were to expose himselfe to Prey, (which no man is bound to) rather than to dispose himselfe to Peace." [26] One can have no sufficient reason to give up a right if one receives no benefit in return.

Laying down a right is accomplished in one of two ways: by renouncing it or by transferring it. If John Doe renounces his right to x, he does not give any specific person a new right to x. He stands aside; he divests himself of the liberty of hindering

[24] *Leviathan* (14), p. 100; *De Cive* (ii. 2), *EW* II, 16–17.
[25] If any weight can be placed on this point it means that preserving oneself is neither an absolute natural necessity nor a moral duty.
[26] *Leviathan* (14), p. 100; *De Cive* (ii. 3), *EW* II, 17; *Elements of Law* (I. xv. 2), p. 75.

anyone else. Either no one acquires any new right from the renunciation because no one's right is thereby increased, or anyone with a right benefits somewhat because an impediment to the use of that right has been removed.

Transferring a right differs from renouncing it.

(1) Unlike renunciations transfers must be made to some specific person. (I, John Doe, do give my right to Richard Roe.)

(2) The person (Richard Roe) to whom the right is transferred must accept it. No right is transferred to a person who does not declare his acceptance in some way, either in person or through an intermediary. Thus, no rights can be transferred directly to an absentee, to God, or to any living creature whose will to accept we have no sufficient means of establishing.[27]

(3) The extent of the right transferred depends upon the situation:

(a) In the state of nature, Richard Roe has a right to the thing before the transfer of right. His right is not increased by the transfer.

(b) Under other conditions, John Doe can transfer to Richard Roe no greater right than he himself has.

(c) In all cases, John Doe only benefits Richard Roe by transferring his right to him and by agreeing not to hinder his attempt to exercise his right. John Doe does not agree not to hinder other people in their attempts to exercise their rights, if any, to the thing, for he intends the benefit of his transfer to come to one person; consequently, if the transfer is not accomplished, e.g., if Richard Roe refuses to accept the right, John Doe retains his original right; the transfer does not become a renunciation.

(d) The first transfer of right voids any subsequent transfer of the same right. Rights are like things: if John Doe gives his apple to Richard Roe at 4 p.m. he cannot give the same apple to William Smith at 5 p.m. John Doe no longer has it to give.

---

[27] *Leviathan* (14), pp. 100–1, 106; *De Cive* (ii. 4–5, 12), *EW* II, 17–18, 22; *Elements of Law* (I. xv. 3–4, 11), pp. 75–76, 78–79.

All transfers and renunciations are motivated; they are voluntary acts; like all voluntary acts their aim is to secure some good for the actor. Consequently there are some rights which cannot be abandoned or transferred. What I shall call "the basic right of self-preservation" is such a right. This is the right to defend oneself against forceful assault with intent to kill. This right of resistance extends to situations in which it is not possible to tell whether the attackers intend death or "serious bodily harm" (and to situations in which the assaulted believes that death or serious harm, although unintended, is likely to occur).

The basic right of self-preservation includes the right to resist imprisonment and chains. There is no benefit in suffering these things. Self-accusation without a previous pardon cannot be obligatory because it leads to punishment, i.e., death, wounds, or imprisonment.

The basic right to preserve oneself cannot be understood to be transferred or abandoned.[28] There seem to be several sets of reasons for this position. The first depends on the purpose of voluntary action. Since all voluntary actions (and hence all conveyances of right) aim at the actor's own good, and basically therefore at his own preservation, he cannot be understood to give up his right to his fundamental purpose. He cannot transfer a right to frustrate his end. The reason Hobbes generally gives is that man naturally and necessarily chooses the lesser evil instead of the greater. He chooses danger of death in resisting over what he believes is certain death.[29] This does not mean that no one can kill himself, nor does it mean that everyone will in fact resist attack. What cannot be given up voluntarily is not life itself but one's right to make one's own choice at the crucial moment. Even if John "has transferred" to Richard the right to kill John, John would not be wrong in resisting. Hobbes seems to believe that no one could feel himself obliged not to resist, but not that anyone was obliged to resist.

The basic right of self-preservation cannot be validly trans-

---

[28] *Leviathan* (14), pp. 101–2. *Cf. De Cive* (ii. 17–19), *EW* II, 24–26; *Elements of Law* (I. xv. 3–4, 14), pp. 75–76, 80.
[29] *Leviathan* (14), pp. 107–8.

ferred since such a transfer frustrates the premises of voluntary action. Furthermore, if we have any knowledge of human nature we would not expect the obligation to be kept. And no one could feel that he had no right to break it. A promise that is not a promise, that cannot be relied on, and that cannot in conscience oblige, must be considered no promise at all.

There are two possible modes of conveying rights: contract and gift.[30] A contract involves a mutual transfer of rights and a mutual exchange of benefits. Since there are two elements here: (a) the right to the thing or benefit and (b) the thing or benefit itself, there are several kinds of contracts. (1) In the simplest kind the right and the thing are transferred at the same time—exchange of goods, buying or selling in a market. (2) In the second type of contract one or both parties contract now to perform in the future, i.e., they transfer the rights to things that will be delivered at some determinate time in the future (e.g., A sells his cow to B; A is to deliver his cow in a week and B is to pay in monthly installments). The contractor who does not perform immediately is trusted to perform later, "and then the Contract on his part, is called Pact, or Covenant: Or both parts may contract now, to performe hereafter: in which cases, he that is to performe in time to come, being trusted, his performance is called *Keeping of Promise,* or Faith; and the fayling of performance (if it be voluntary) *Violation of Faith."* [31]

Contracts may be *express* or *inferred.* Express contracts involve words like "I give," "I have given," or "I will give." Contracts may be inferred from whatever words or silence, action or inaction indicate the will of the contractor, e.g., if B accepts a thing from A on credit. A contract is "implied in fact" when one party silently and passively, but knowingly, accepts the benefits conferred upon him by another.

When an obligation has been created by a contract, there

[30] The three conditions noted above apply to all transfers, both by contract and by gift.
[31] *Leviathan* (14), p. 102; *De Cive* (ii. 9–10), *EW* II, 20–21; *Elements of Law* (I. xv. 8–9), pp. 77–78.

are two ways in which the obligation may be discharged and liberty regained. The first is by performing the obligation. By performing A does what he has covenanted to do. Since he promised to do no more his obligation ceases and he is free. Discharge by performance extends to the attempt by A to perform to the best of his ability. Presumably if he has done as much as he can, he cannot reasonably be asked to do more. He is not required to do what is impossible. The second method of discharge is forgiveness. When B forgives A his obligation to do x he retransfers the right to A; it is, in effect, a gift. 'No one can covenant with himself, for he can always forgive himself.[32]

Gift does not involve a mutual transfer of right.

When the transferring of Right, is not mutuall; but one of the parties transferreth, in hope to gain thereby friendship, or service from another, or from his friends; or in hope to gain the reputation of Charity, or Magnanimity; or to deliver his mind from the pain of compassion; or in hope of reward in heaven; This is not Contract, but GIFT, FREE-GIFT, GRACE: which words signifie one and the same thing.[33]

Hobbes has accepted the distinction made by English common law between contracts and mere promises. In a contract there must be consideration—a benefit given in exchange for a benefit received. The benefit given cannot be so insubstantial as affection, friendship, etc. The parallel doctrine of *causa* in continental law recognized some of these things as valid benefits. Unlike a contract, in which covenants, promises of future benefits, may be exchanged, a gift must be actually given; promises are not gifts. A bare promise, words of the future alone, leaves the promisor in the process of deliberation; it does not convey the right.

Since the law of nature requires that men divest themselves of rights, it was necessary to describe the possible ways in which

[32] *Leviathan* (14), pp. 106–7; *De Cive* (ii. 15), *EW* II, 23; *Elements of Law* (I. xv. 12), p. 79.
[33] *Leviathan* (14), pp. 102–3; *De Cive* (ii. 8), *EW* II, 19–20; *Elements of Law* (I. xv. 7), p. 77.

they can achieve this: abandonment, and conveyance to another by gift or in exchange for something. But this knowledge is insufficient to remove men from their condition of misery and war. In the state of nature, contracts and gifts are possible —and in both these cases, by accepting a benefit a man obliges himself to benefit his benefactor, either generally or by performing his specific covenant. But, although these obligations are possible in the state of nature, each man remains his own judge; each retains the right to decide that the conditions under which the contract was made no longer exist; like sovereign states, they are bound *rebus sic stantibus.* The absence of an external tribunal does not affect contracts of barter, for even though each party is likely to suspect the other party of attempting to cheat or of planning an attack, the actual exchange of things may be accomplished. Reciprocal covenants become very precarious because each party must wonder whether the other will perform. Each must suspect that by performing first he will betray himself into the other's hands. Hobbes says that such contracts are of no effect, but all that he can logically claim is that either party, suspicious as he must be, is not only free but also very likely to judge (on the basis of almost any of the other's actions) that the other party intends not to perform. Of course, when one party has performed he has conferred a benefit upon the other, who by accepting it has obliged himself to reciprocate.[34]

Can rational tactics for the state of nature be extrapolated from this account? If a man were sure of another's friendship, he should maintain it by continually performing covenants, by giving benefits, and by reciprocating such benefits as he received. If he were sure of enmity, he should resort to the tactics of war. But if, as would usually be the case, he were unsure of the way to act, his most rational course of action would be to apply the principles of game theory, randomly to vary his per-

[34] *Leviathan* (14), pp. 104–5; *De Cive* (ii. 11), *EW* II, 21; *Elements of Law* (I. xv. 10), p. 78.

formances and non-performances so that no one could be sure whether he would perform or not perform on any given occasion. Clearly no one will covenant with a man who never performs; clearly one who always performs leaves himself open to the passions of others. So rational activity in the state of nature is to act so that no one will be certain what that action will be; rational activity in the state of nature creates uncertainty and insecurity, a state of war in which the resort to force must always be expected.

The purpose of the laws of nature is to provide a rational method for preserving oneself. This aim is to be accomplished by seeking peace, and if peace is to be achieved everyone must divest himself (by renunciation or transfer by contract or gift) of most of his natural right. Since covenants are necessary to achieve peace it follows that the third law of nature is *"That men performe their Covenants made:* without which, Covenants are in vain, and but Empty words; and the Right of all men to all things remaining, wee are still in the condition of Warre."[35] The performing of a covenant is a just action, not performing is unjust. An unjust act, then, can only occur when a person has transferred a right, obliging himself not to do what he could rightfully have done, and then acts against this obligation. Injury can only be done to some individual person to whom a right has been passed:

And therefore many times the injury is received by one man, when the dammage redoundeth to another. As when the Master commandeth his servant to give mony to a stranger; if it be not done, the Injury is done to the Master, whom he had before Covenanted to obey; but the dammage redoundeth to the stranger, to whom he had no Obligation; and therefore could not Injure him.[36]

A person can harm himself or another person, but he can only injure someone to whom he is obliged by covenant. Since no one can covenant effectively with himself, no one can injure

[35] *Leviathan* (15), p. 110. *Cf. De Cive* (iii. 1), *EW* II, 29–30; *Elements of Law* (I. xvi. 1), p. 82.
[36] *Leviathan* (15), pp. 114–15.

(although he may damage) himself. Similarly, nothing done to a man according to his own will signified to the doer injures him. Hobbes regards B, acting with A's permission, as equivalent, for these purposes, to A acting; and A cannot injure himself.[37]

The laws of nature bind to an endeavor to fulfill the laws, not to a specific performance in every action. They are rules for men's intentions and manners. Therefore, by distinguishing between the justice of actions and the justice or righteousness of the actor's intention, four situations are possible: (1) a righteous man performing a just action; (2) an unrighteous man performing a just action; (3) a righteous man performing an unjust action; (4) an unrighteous man performing an unjust action. In situation (1) the actor both performs his covenant and keeps the third law of nature. In situation (4) the actor both breaks his covenant and violates the law of nature. In situation (3) the actor breaks his covenant but he does not intend to violate the law which commands the performance of covenant. In situation (2) although the act conforms to the law, the actor's intention does not.

For there is an *oderunt peccare* in the unjust, as well as in the just, but from different causes; for the unjust man who abstaineth from injuries for fear of punishment, declareth plainly that the justice of his actions dependeth upon civil constitution, from whence punishments proceed; which would otherwise in the estate of nature be unjust, according to the fountain from whence they spring.[38]

Since justice is the performing of covenants which a man himself has made, rather than acting according to a natural order, justice cannot be used as a principle of judgment about the terms of a contract or the distribution of goods. The "just

[37] *Ibid.*, p. 115. In the state of nature, it is no injury to a man to kill him, or hurt him, or enslave him, but it would be an injury to break a covenant with him.
[38] *Elements of Law* (I. xvi. 4), p. 83. *Cf. Leviathan* (15), pp. 114–15; *De Cive* (iii. 5), *EW* II, 32–33.

price" is the price agreed upon in the contract. It is not unjust to sell dearer than we buy. "The value of all things contracted for, is measured by the Appetite of the Contractors: and therefore the just value, is that which they be contented to give." [39]

Hobbes denies that commutative and distributive justice have been distinguished correctly. Commutative justice is contractual justice—each party accepting the good exchanged. By distributive justice the Aristotelians mean the distribution of benefits in proportion to merit. "Distributive justice" requires that there be a natural and obligatory order of merit according to which benefits may be distributed.[40] But there is no natural order. In the state of nature, all men are, or are presumed to be, equal. We are not obliged to give equally to all; we are only obliged to fulfill our covenants and beyond that we have liberty to do as we please. It is just to give a man what we have covenanted to give him, but to give a gift (a benefit which we are not obliged by contract to give) is neither just nor unjust. Every man is at liberty to dispose of his own according to his own will. It would not have been unjust for the owner of the vineyard to have given someone who had not worked at all as much as he gave those who had worked all day.[41]

In the state of nature, covenants which societies enforce may easily become invalid, and covenants which societies forbid, or refuse to enforce, are permitted, e.g., agreements extorted from captives are valid.[42] Civil societies exist to protect men from fear and from being terrorized by other men. A successful society monopolizes the use of coercion and the motive of fear, and so does not and cannot allow private men to extort benefits by using those means.

To act benevolently in return for benefits given is the fourth law of nature. Accepting a gift creates an obligation in the recipient to do good to the donor. In some cases, this may be only

[39] *Leviathan* (15), p. 115.

[40] See Greenleaf, pp. 14–17, for an exposition of what he calls the "political theory of order."

[41] See Matt. 20:1–16.

[42] *Leviathan* (14), p. 107; *De Cive* (ii. 16), *EW* II, 23–24; *Elements of Law* (I. xv. 13), pp. 79–80.

to be thankful. If men were to act ungratefully and meanly, there could be no beginning of trust, confidence, or friendship among them.[43]

In addition to unjust and ungrateful actions, there are other acts that provoke war and promote enmity among men. They are forbidden in a group of laws of nature differing from the third and fourth laws in that they do not involve the creation of a specific obligation to a determinate person, but relate to a general ordering of conduct. "A fifth Law of Nature, is COMPLEASANCE; that is to say, *That every man strive to accommodate himselfe to the rest."* [44] Men are presumed to be striving for the necessities of life; conflict may be inevitable if this is truly the case. But if anyone is contending to get or keep more than what is necessary then he is irrationally prolonging the conflict—irrationally because he is risking his existence for something that is superfluous to his existence.

"That upon caution of the Future time, a man ought to pardon the offences past of them that repenting, desire it," and *"That in Revenges,* (that is, retribution of Evil for Evil,) *Men look not at the greatnesse of the evill past, but the greatnesse of the good to follow"* are the next two laws of nature.[45] Pardon is giving peace; if we refuse to grant peace to those who want peace (the repentant) when we are secured (by taking caution), then we must be prolonging a war when this is no longer necessary. Revenge is a triumph, sweet because it is a triumph over those who have formerly gloried over the now triumphant. But revenge is an end which is not a means to any future good; it may inspire hatred and a desire for revenge in return, i.e., revenge promotes hostility. Revenge then must be restricted to punishment which attempts to deter others or correct the offender.

Since contumely, pride, and arrogance hinder peace and

[43] *Leviathan* (15), p. 116; *De Cive* (vii. 8), *EW* II, 35; *Elements of Law* (I. xvi. 6–7), pp. 84–85.
[44] *Leviathan* (15), p. 116; *De Cive* (iii. 9), *EW* II, 36; *Elements of Law* (I. xvi. 8), p. 85.
[45] *Leviathan* (15), p. 117; *De Cive* (iii. 10–11), *EW* II, 37–38; *Elements of Law* (I. xvi. 9–10), pp. 85–86.

promote war, the eighth, ninth, and tenth precepts are directed against these causes of conflict: (8) *"That no man by deed, word, countenance, or gesture, declare Hatred, or Contempt of another"*; (9) *"That every man acknowledge other for his Equall by Nature"*; (10) *"That at the Entrance into conditions of Peace, no man require to reserve to himselfe any Right, which he is not content should be reserved to every one of the rest."* [46] Unlike the eighth law, which is designed to reduce hostility, the acknowledging of equality is not a counsel of perfection. It is a logical necessity. Not only are men naturally equal—there are no standards determining men's values in the state of nature and no natural superiors and inferiors based on differences of intelligence (as in Aristotle)—but even if men were not equal, *"yet because men that think themselves equall, will not enter into conditions of Peace, but upon Equall termes, such equalitie must be admitted."* [47] The tenth maxim merely extends this equality into the conditions of the covenant.

The third group of laws provides some of the mechanisms necessary for peace, and deals with the conditions under which these mechanisms may operate. In order to deal with controversies so as to settle them peacefully and without resorting to violence and so maintaining a state of war, it is necessary *"That they that are at controversie, submit their Right to the judgement of an Arbitrator."* (16) [48] Even if everyone intended to obey the laws of nature, i.e., if everyone had a good will, controversies could still arise, both on questions of fact and on questions of right. To settle these questions the parties must agree to submit to another's judgment. Since such a submission would be disastrous were the judge prejudiced in favor of one party, it follows that *"if a man be trusted to judge be-*

---

[46] *Leviathan* (15), pp. 117–18; *De Cive* (iii. 12–14), *EW* II, 38–40; *Elements of Law* (I. xvi. 11, xvii. 1–2), pp. 86, 87–89.

[47] *Leviathan* (15), p. 118.

[48] *Ibid.*, p. 120; *De Cive* (iii. 20), *EW* II, 41–42; *Elements of Law* (I. xvii. 6), pp. 90–91.

tween man and man, it is a precept of the Law of Nature [11th] *that he deale Equally between them."* [49] Since men are presumed to do all things for their own benefit, no man is to judge his own case (17th) or any case in which some greater benefit (profit, honor, or pleasure) would result to him from the success of one party rather than from that of the other (18th).[50] Where one party is the judge, there the other may also judge, but this is the situation that we wish to avoid. In the case where the judge benefits, the judge is bribed, perhaps unavoidably, but bribed nevertheless. Where there is a cause of partiality we cannot be satisfied that the parties have been equally treated. For we either suspect that the judge has favored his prejudice, or alternatively, that he has dealt harshly in overcompensating for his prejudice. In the earlier versions Hobbes even included a provision that the judge makes no contract with either or both parties—even to judge justly. For, he argued, such an agreement would imply that the party has a right to judge whether the judge's decision is just; consequently the controversy would not be settled by the arbitration.[51] This emphasizes the point that when a party agrees to submit to arbitration he agrees to accept the result of that arbitration. In deciding questions of fact, the judge is to hear witnesses in addition to the parties. (19) [52]

These rules concerning arbitration may help to prevent the outbreak of hostilities. But they may be used to settle conflicts in progress only if the parties concerned can be convinced to agree to arbitrate. War, like motion, continues until some means can be found to stop it. The annihilation of one side is possible, but unless this occurs there will have to be an agreed peace. This means that the parties will have to negotiate with

[49] *Leviathan* (15), p. 119; *De Cive* (iii. 15), *EW* II, 40; cf. *Elements of Law* (I. xvii. 7), p. 91.
[50] *Leviathan* (15), p. 120; *De Cive* (iii. 21–22, 24), *EW* II, 42, 43–44; *Elements of Law* (I. xvii. 7), p. 91.
[51] See *De Cive* (iii. 24), *EW* II, 43–44; *Elements of Law* (I. xvii. 7), p. 91.
[52] *Leviathan* (15), p. 120; *De Cive* (iii. 23), *EW* II, 43; the witness provision is absent from the *Elements of Law*.

each other. But negotiations cannot be undertaken without mediators, either neutrals or enemies meeting to talk. Someone must go from one side to the other—or at least to a neutral spot. So, "It is also a Law of Nature, *That all men that mediate Peace, be allowed safe Conduct."* (15) [53]

The last part of this group of laws is concerned with the rules for dividing goods. These rules follow from the eleventh rule which enjoins equity, i.e., equal distribution to each man of what in reason belongs to him. If a thing cannot be divided, then it is to be enjoyed in common; either without any limit, if there is enough, or equally among those with right (12). If it can neither be divided nor used in common, then either the whole right, or else, if the use is made alternate, the first possession, is to be determined by lot (13). Lot is either arbitrary—a method established by the competitors—or natural, i.e., primogeniture or first seizure (14).[54] In these regulations Hobbes seems to be at least as concerned with equality as he is with the establishment of private property.

There may be other laws of nature. Hobbes includes a further one in his "Review and Conclusion," i.e., *"That every man is bound by Nature, as much as in him lieth, to protect in Warre, the Authority, by which he is himself protected in time of peace."* [55] This addition emphasizes a point that might have been deduced from some of the previous laws, but it does not increase a man's actual duties in civil society. The timorous civilian is still only bound to fight when the defense of the commonwealth requires the help of all able to bear arms; "because otherwise the Institution of the Common-wealth, which they have not the purpose, or courage to preserve, was in vain." [56]

[53] *Leviathan* (15), p. 119; *De Cive* (iii. 19), *EW* II, 41; *Elements of Law* (I. xvi. 13), p. 87.
[54] *Leviathan* (15), p. 119; *De Cive* (iii. 16–18), *EW* II, 40–41; *Elements of Law* (I. xvii. 3–5), pp. 89–90.
[55] *Leviathan* (Review and Conclusion), p. 548; cf. *Leviathan* (26), p. 210: "And it is a Dictate of Natural Reason, and consequently an evident Law of Nature, that no man ought to weaken that power, the protection whereof he hath himself demanded, or wittingly received against others."
[56] *Leviathan* (21), p. 168.

Hobbes suggests that there are, in addition to the rules which apply to the conduct of one man to another, further laws of nature which prescribe how a man should treat himself. Among these are rules about drunkenness and other sorts of intemperance—a rule actually stated in *De Cive*.[57] If it were necessary, these rules could be listed. Drunkenness and gluttony would be forbidden because they hinder the use of reason as well as because they are destructive of other natural faculties, e.g., health and strength of body. Presumably rules about health would fall under this category. Keep fit. Drink milk every day. Eat a balanced diet. Hobbes would no doubt have recommended walking, tennis, singing, and other forms of exercise, activities he himself engaged in, as means to the maintenance of health and strength.[58] Perhaps these laws of nature would include such maxims as "Do not swim until an hour after eating," and "Don't swallow poison." Although these rules presumably would be binding in the state of nature, unlike the other laws of nature (with which Hobbes is primarily concerned) they are not pertinent to the purpose of guiding men in their relations to their fellows.[59]

The Status of the Laws of Nature

The laws of nature have been discovered to be a set of rules prescribing the means to be followed in the pursuit of peace. Peace itself is a means to self-preservation.

These dictates of Reason, men use to call by the name of Lawes; but improperly: for they are but Conclusions, or Theoremes concerning what conduceth to the conservation and defence of themselves; whereas Law, properly is the word of him, that by right hath command over others. But yet if we consider the same Theo-

[57] *De Cive* (iii. 25), *EW* II, 44; *Leviathan* (15), p. 120; *Elements of Law* (I. xvii. 14), p. 94.
[58] See Aubrey, I, 351: "Besides his dayly walking, he did twice or thrice a yeare play at tennis (at about 75 he did it); then went to bed there and was well rubbed. This he did believe would make him live two or three yeares the longer." See also *ibid.*, pp. 347, 350.
[59] See Appendix 3.

remes, as delivered in the word of God, that by right commandeth all things; then are they properly called Lawes.[60]

As they have been considered above, it is not correct to call these rational conclusions about conservation and defense "laws." They exhibit the characteristics of scientific conclusions; they are immutable and eternal, they tell us nothing about the existence of facts, they are hypothetical and not absolute.[61] Unless these rules are followed, there can be no peace (the best means of preserving ourselves), i.e., if there is to be peace, then we must follow the laws of nature. If these rules are not followed, then war will be the result. Since war cannot be a means of preserving life, and peace cannot be a means of destroying it,[62] these rules are logical and not merely prudential. (This does not mean that defense may not be a means of preserving life, and failure to protect oneself a means of losing it. Nor does it tell us when we should fight and when we should surrender, for this choice depends on our estimate of the situation and of our adversaries.) The laws of nature are not impractical. They tell us that certain things are causally related to war and others to peace. Knowing this we know how to act to get and preserve peace and we know what sort of actions lead to the destruction of peace or the promotion of war. Furthermore, we know that some kinds of actions, e.g., cruel ones, are useless in promoting peace by either victory or negotiation.

The knowledge of the laws of nature is the true moral philosophy. Men differ on what is good and evil not only to sense but also to reason. Their immediate judgments, appetites, and actions in the state of nature, in which each man is judge of good and evil, frustrate the implied purpose of acting, i.e., to continue one's existence, by creating a situation of war in

[60] *Leviathan* (15), pp. 122–23. *Cf. De Cive* (iii. 33), *EW* II, 49–50; *Elements of Law* (I. xvii. 12, xviii. 1), pp. 93, 95.

[61] *Leviathan* (7, 15), pp. 49–50, 122. See Watkins, *Hobbes's System of Ideas*, pp. 82–85.

[62] *Ibid.* (15), p. 122.

which existence becomes precarious. Peace is therefore rationally good—because it is a necessary means to assure one's continued existence. It must follow that the means to peace are good, and their contraries evil.[63] These are moral goods and evils, because they deal with the conduct of human beings—with men's manners. A review of the laws of nature shows that some (but not all) of them prescribe virtues and forbid vices: justice, gratitude, sociability, forgiveness, equality, modesty or humility, equity, temperance, and courage are prescribed; injustice, stubbornness, cruelty, contumely, pride, arrogance, and favoritism are forbidden. "The sum of virtue is to be sociable with them that will be sociable, and formidable to them that will not. And the same is the sum of the law of nature." [64]

The laws of nature are also divine laws. It is only in this sense that they can be called laws at all. For they are not laws in respect of nature but of God, the author of nature.[65] There are two senses in which this is true; the laws of nature are divine natural laws and divine positive laws.

The fact that the laws of nature are divine natural laws adds precisely nothing to our knowledge of these laws or to our obligation to follow them. They are discovered by reasoning—"the light of nature." By natural reason, man is drawn from a consideration of an effect, to seek the cause, and then the cause of that cause. Although men cannot trace this series of causes back to its beginning, for it is so long a chain that they cannot help but give up before they have reached their goal, yet they can infer that there must have been one first cause.[66] That which is conceived as a first cause cannot have a cause; this would not only

---

[63] *De Cive* (iii. 31–32), *EW* II, 47–49; *Elements of Law* (I. xvii. 14), pp. 93–94; *Leviathan* (15), p. 122.

[64] *Elements of Law* (I. xvii. 15), p. 95.

[65] *Elements of Law* (I. xviii. 1), p. 95; *De Cive* (iv. 1), *EW* II, 50–51; *Leviathan* (30), p. 273.

[66] *De Corpore* (xxvi. 1), *EW* I, 412. Although the *Elements of Law* (I. xi. 2), pp. 53–54, asserts the possibility of actually tracing the chain of causes to a first cause, the position taken in *Leviathan* (11, 12), pp 80–81, 83, i.e., a profound search into causes inclines the inquirer to believe in God, is consistent with (and may imply) the position taken in *De Corpore*.

involve us in an infinite regress, but would also mean that it was not a first cause. That for which we can imagine no cause or beginning, we call eternal. So "there must be, (as even the Heathen Philosophers confessed) one First Mover; that is, a First, and an Eternall cause of all things; which is that which men mean by the name of God." [67] Hobbes admits that not many men make the profound study of natural science required to reach this conclusion. Most men, anxious about what will happen to them, and supposing causes without distinguishing immediate causes from remote causes, imagine invisible agents as suggested either by their own fancy, or by other men whom they believe to be wise and good. In their fear and solicitude for their own good, these men, unlike the philosophers, are hindered in their search for causes; they end by the "feigning of as many Gods, as there be men that feigne them." [68]

Reason has led us to the conclusion that there is a first and eternal cause of all things, God. Although we can infer that God is, we can conceive no idea of him in our minds. Therefore, we cannot describe his attributes. There is one more thing that we know about God; God is a cause. It follows that he is or has power, and to this power we can imagine no limits. This power is the cause of a world so large that we are not certain whether it is finite or infinite. God is an omnipotent first cause, King of all that is, for everything is subject to his power.

Whether men will or not, they must be subject alwayes to the Divine Power. By denying the Existence, or Providence of God, men may shake off their Ease, but not their Yoke. But to call this Power of God, which extendeth it selfe not onely to Man, but also to Beasts, and Plants, and Bodies inanimate, by the name of King-dome, is but a metaphoricall use of the word. For he onely is properly said to Raigne, that governs his Subjects, by his Word, and by promise of Rewards to those that obey it, and by threatning them with Punishment that obey it not. Subjects therefore in the King-dome of God, are not Bodies Inanimate, nor creatures Irrationall; because they understand no Precepts as his: Nor Atheists; nor they

[67] *Leviathan* (12), p. 83.   [68] *Ibid.*

that believe not that God has any care of the actions of mankind; because they acknowledge no Word for his, nor have hope of his rewards, or fear of his threatnings. They therefore that believe there is a God that governeth the world, and hath given Præcepts, and propounded Rewards, and Punishments to Mankind, are Gods Subjects; all the rest, are to be understood as Enemies.[69]

God rules his subjects by his words. These words must be known if they are to be laws. If God were a man, these laws would have to be publicly promulgated. Not being a man, God has three ways of declaring laws instead of one: by natural reason, by revelation, and by the voice of some man. So Hobbes says that there is a triple word of God: rational, sensible, and prophetic; and a corresponding triple hearing of his word: by reason, by sense supernatural, and by faith (through our natural senses). In fact, no universal laws are given (solely) by revelation; revelation is the way in which God issues his orders to individual men to do various things. So, from God's threefold word there arises but a twofold kingdom. In his natural kingdom God governs, by the natural dictates of reason, those men who acknowledge his providence. In his prophetic kingdom God chose to govern, as a peculiar nation, the Jews. In his prophetic kingdom God does not act as a ruler by nature but as a ruler by the consent and covenant of his subjects whom he governs by positive laws delivered by prophets.[70] So the laws of nature, when delivered by authoritative prophecy in this particular civil society, are positive laws. The existence of God's prophetic kingdom explains how and when "natural" laws became divine positive laws, but it does not tell us if the precepts of natural reason may properly be called laws apart from this kingdom.

We have now ascertained that the laws of nature are laws that are known by natural reason alone when conceived as the laws of God's natural kingdom. The right by which God rules

[69] *Ibid.* (31), pp. 274-75. *Cf. De Cive* (xv. 2), *EW* II, 204-5.
[70] *Leviathan* (31, 35), pp. 275, 314-17. *Cf. ibid.* (26), pp. 219-20.

in this kingdom is his natural right. Dominion over men, as has been shown, would by right belong to anyone whose power was so great that he could not be resisted.[71] God's right is neither derived from men's consents or covenants, nor is it dependent upon his having created them or upon their gratitude for the benefits God has given them, but it is the effect of God's omnipotence.[72] God's right to afflict men for their sins at his own pleasure is derived from his power. But God's natural right does not imply a corresponding duty on the part of men to obey.[73] To put it another way, although God's power extends to all men, not all men are God's subjects in his natural kingdom. For example, atheists are not subjects but enemies. God's subjects in his natural kingdom are only those men who acknowledge his power. Conscious of their own weakness in respect to the divine power, they realize that they "cannot not obey" (*non potest non obedire*):

From this last kind of [natural] obligation, that is to say, from fear or conscience of our own weakness in respect of the divine power, it comes to pass that we are obliged to obey God in his natural kingdom; reason dictating to all, acknowledging the divine power and providence [*dictante scilicet ratione omnibus Dei potentiam et providentiam agnoscentibus*], that there is no kicking against the pricks.[74]

Man's natural obligation to God, as distinguished from any covenanted obligation, is derived from an act of man's mind, his submission when he understands and acknowledges God's power and providence.

It would be wrong to conclude that Hobbes, having started from a conception of God as a first cause, has arrived at the conception of God as revealed in Christianity, a God of love and mercy, ordaining rewards and punishments after this life for those who believe in him and consequently endeavor to

[71] See above, p. 90.
[72] *Leviathan* (31), p. 276; *De Cive* (xv. 5), *EW* II, 206–7.
[73] See Warrender, *The Political Philosophy of Hobbes*, pp. 18–26.
[74] *De Cive* (xv. 7), *EW* II, 209; *LW* II, 336–37. See Appendix 4.

keep his commandments. I should like to suggest that what the rational realize when they admit their weakness in the face of God's power, is not that there is a Christian God who has provided for a final reckoning, but that there is a God who is an eternal, omnipotent first cause. This God has caused a world in which there are necessary links between causes and effects, links which men cannot break. It is not by chance, nor by the favors of Fortune that goods and evils come to men; these are consequences which are not accidental but necessary. What men realize is something they already knew—that just as in the physical world every event is linked in a chain of necessary effects and causes, so in the world of human behavior every action results from prior causes, and produces further consequences. Where the consequences are desired, they are called "ends" or "goods," and the actions necessary to produce them, "means." Thus, they realize that some actions necessarily produce results they wish to avoid, while the results they wish to obtain are the consequences of other actions. They have discovered that the laws of nature are necessary means to the establishment of peace; the necessity of these means has, as it were, been built into the world by God.

If the preceding argument is correct, then it can hardly be said that the laws of nature are more obligatory as divine commands than they are as rational precepts. Their directive force remains what it was: they are means to a desired end. If it could be shown (a) that Hobbes thought that reason could establish that God had provided rewards for obeying the laws of nature, and punishments for disobeying them, in another life; or (b) that the end of following the laws of nature was salvation; or (c) that what Hobbes means by self-preservation is something other than the preservation of a man's life in this world—then my interpretation must fall. None of these points can be established.

Although men may believe that there is a life after death, and punishments and rewards provided in it, this is not a matter of natural knowledge, but of "faith supernatural." In denying that breaking agreements may be conducive to salvation, Hobbes denies that there is any natural knowledge of a higher law, or higher sanctions, than the law of nature. Some men

will not have the Law of Nature, to be those Rules which conduce to the preservation of mans life on earth; but to the attaining of an eternall felicity after death; to which they think the breach of Covenant may conduce; and consequently be just and reasonable. . . . But *because there is no naturall knowledge of mans estate after death,* much lesse of the reward that is then to be given to breach of Faith; but onely a beliefe grounded upon other mens saying, that they know it supernaturally, or that they know those, that knew them, that knew others, that knew it supernaturally; Breach of Faith cannot be called a Precept of Reason, or Nature.[75]

Reason cannot establish the laws of nature as means to an end beyond this life because there is no natural knowledge of any such end. Present belief in rewards and punishments in another life is a matter of faith. Believers may be expected to act in accordance with their beliefs. Hobbes, as a self-confessed Christian believer, is quite prepared to say what a Christian should believe and what he should do, but he does not think that Christianity is a purely rational religion. Christian faith is not the same as natural reason. The laws of nature are universal laws; they do not apply only to Christian believers, nor are their sanctions limited to believers. He argues that injustice, the breaking of covenant, can never be beneficial even if it leads to sovereign power. Why cannot injustice be beneficial, conducing to a man's own good? Surely, it must conduce sometimes to some man's ends. "This specious reasoning is neverthelesse false."[76] Let us suppose a situation in which there is a valid obligation—either where there is a power which will enforce performance, or else, in the state of nature, where one party has already performed. It is never unreasonable to perform; when

[75] Italics added. *Leviathan* (15), p. 113.   [76] *Ibid.,* p. 112.

a man does something that tends toward his own destruction, it does not make his action wise or reasonable if something he could not foresee happens to turn that action to his benefit. In the state of nature, no one can be sure of his preservation without help from confederates. No one who declares he thinks it reasonable to deceive those who help him can expect any help from others.

He therefore that breaketh his Covenant, and consequently declareth that he thinks he may with reason do so, cannot be received into any Society, that unite themselves for Peace and Defence, but by the errour of them that receive him; nor when he is received, be retayned in it, without seeing the danger of their errour; which errours a man cannot reasonably reckon upon as the means of his security: and therefore if he be left, or cast out of Society, he perisheth; and if he live in Society, it is by the errours of other men, which he could not foresee, nor reckon upon; and consequently against the reason of his preservation; and so, as all men that contribute not to his destruction, forbear him onely out of ignorance of what is good for themselves.[77]

No one who thinks that he is right in breaking his contractual obligations to others can expect anyone to treat him (except by accident, mistake, stupidity, or ignorance) as anything but an enemy. As for attaining sovereignty by an act of rebellion, success cannot be reasonably expected. And even if such an unjust act were successful in gaining sovereignty, its purpose would be frustrated because it would teach others to do the same.

As for attaining salvation by injustice, Hobbes thinks it a frivolous possibility, for the only conceivable way of attaining salvation is not by breaking but by keeping covenants.[78] Since attaining salvation is not a natural end of mankind, but the

[77] *Ibid.*, pp. 112–13.
[78] *Ibid.*, p. 113. Since Hobbes gives no reason for assuring the reader that it is not imaginable that eternal felicity can be gained by injustice, the reader must judge whether, as Warrender asserts (*The Political Philosophy of Hobbes*, p. 276), "It is evident that only the last of these reasons is conclusive; the rest is merely cautionary advice to those who might think that rebellion is too easy of success, and embark upon it without adequately weighing the chances."

end of only some men, e.g., Christians, Hobbes has asserted the compatibility of faith and reason (he has yet to prove it).

This discussion of injustice indicates that Hobbes conceived the sanctions for the breach of natural law to be neither punishments in another world nor extraordinary events in this one, but rather the natural effects of the actions performed. Breaches of natural law are naturally punished by the consequences of these acts.

> There is no action of man in this life, that is not the beginning of so long a chayn of Consequences, as no humane Providence, is high enough, to give a man a prospect to the end. And in this Chayn, there are linked together both pleasing and unpleasing events; in such manner, as he that will do any thing for his pleasure, must engage himselfe to suffer all the pains annexed to it; and these pains, are the Naturall Punishments of those actions, which are the beginning of more Harme than Good. And hereby it comes to passe, that Intemperance, is naturally punished with Diseases; Rashnesse, with Mischances; Injustice, with the Violence of Enemies; Pride, with Ruine; Cowardise, with Oppression; Negligent government of Princes, with Rebellion; and Rebellion, with Slaughter. For seeing Punishments are consequent to the breach of Lawes; Naturall Punishments must be naturally consequent to the breach of the Lawes of Nature; and therfore follow them as their naturall, not arbitrary effects.[79]

The sanctions for the laws of nature need not be punishments in another life, for this is a world in which effects follow necessarily from antecedent causes.

Self-preservation is the end to which the laws of nature are the means. But what is the precise nature of this end? Self-preservation is the obverse of Hobbes's negative expression, the avoidance of death. Is the death to be feared and avoided merely a natural death? Or is it a shameful, dishonorable death that men should avoid? Is it not the death at the end of this life that is to be feared, but rather an eternal death?[80]

[79] *Leviathan* (31), p. 284; *cf. ibid.* (6), p. 48; *De Cive* (iii. 32), *EW* II, 49.
[80] See Warrender, *The Political Philosophy of Hobbes*, pp. 272–77, 287–98; and Oakeshott, "The Moral Life in the Writings of Thomas Hobbes," *Rationalism in Politics*, pp. 273–94.

Each of these possibilities has much to recommend it; each generates a distinct view of moral conduct; and each may be supported by passages in Hobbes's works. If (to take Mr. Warrender's position first) the aim of human conduct is to avoid ultimate death and attain eternal salvation, then a second and higher sort of conduct may be opposed to conduct based on merely earthly prudence. Since this conduct would be directed to man's greatest good and avoidance of man's greatest evil, it may be said to be truly moral and not merely self-interested. At the least, a higher sort of self-interest is involved. There would then be three classes of action:

(1) Actual conduct. A man does those actions that he believes to be in his best interest. What he does, of course, will be the result of his actual deliberation. The accuracy of his reckoning of the consequences of the actions he considers is limited by the extent of his knowledge. In this class of action there are then two sub-classes: (a) conduct resulting from inadequate deliberation; (b) prudent conduct: conduct resulting from adequate deliberation, i.e., taking account of all the individual knows.

(2) Most prudent conduct: the action that a man would do given his particular values, (a) if he had complete knowledge and (b) if he exercised adequate deliberation.

(3) Conduct tending to salvation. This is a special sub-class of most prudent conduct—consisting of the actions which a man who takes salvation as his greatest good would do if he had complete knowledge and exercised adequate deliberation.[81]

Only actions in the third class of conduct can be said to be morally obligatory. It is a class of conduct which is prudent and self-interested, it is true, but prudence and self-interest here are directed toward something truly good.[82] This conduct is moral conduct not only because it is oriented toward the good

---

[81] Warrender, *The Political Philosophy of Hobbes,* pp. 282–83.
[82] *Ibid.,* pp. 295 ff.

but also because it is conduct which has for its foundation a choice among values. No one is obliged to choose salvation, although it may be the case that anyone who reasons correctly and deliberates adequately will do so. The atheist is, as Hobbes says, not unjust, but foolish. (He is a fool because he has not reasoned correctly that there is a God.)

This interpretation provides us with the grounds of moral obligation in obedience to God's commands, the laws of nature. All other obligations, no matter how they have been incurred, derive their force from these foundations, and the irreducible minimum of natural right (that natural right which Hobbes says cannot be alienated) can be shown to operate as "validating conditions of obligation." [83] This interpretation does more than find a consistent theory of obligation within Hobbes's system; it shows that Hobbes was not a disguised atheist, for there is no atheism in his system to disguise. The contemporary accusation of atheism is due to Hobbes's argument that duty, religion, moral obligation, and obedience to the civil law are entirely consistent except in the special case of those who are called to preach to infidels.[84] The consistency of duty, religion, moral obligations and lawful conduct is greatest in a Christian commonwealth. Insofar as these spheres overlap they are identical. Usually the civil law is not coextensive with moral obligation; most states allow the citizen some areas of conduct in which law does not prescribe how he shall act; e.g., gratitude, though it is a principle of the law of nature, is rarely enforced by civil law.

This theory explains the presence in Hobbes's works of passages which emphasize the importance of considering divine rewards and punishments, e.g.,

Every man by nature (without discipline) does in all his actions look upon, as far as he can see, the benefit that shall redound to

[83] In Warrender's terminology, the validating conditions of obligation are the conditions under which obligations become effective, e.g., if madmen have no obligations, then sanity is a "validating condition of obligation." See *The Political Philosophy of Hobbes*, pp. 21–29.

[84] *Leviathan* (42, 43), pp. 388–90, 469–71.

himself from his obedience. He reads that covetousness is the root of all evil; but he thinks, and sometimes finds, it is the root of his estate. And so in other cases, the Scripture says one thing, and they think another, weighing the commodities or incommodities of this present life only, which are in their sight, never putting into the scales the good and evil of the life to come, which they see not.[85]

But, in spite of its attraction, this theory involves several difficulties. First, it requires that there be a legislator God, presumably Christian, knowable by natural reason. It also requires that the rewards for obedience to his laws and the sanctions for disobedience to his laws be knowable without promulgation. Neither of these requirements is consistent with Hobbes's philosophy. There is no knowledge of rewards and punishments beyond this life, although men may come by faith to believe in these rewards and punishments.

No doubt, Hobbes, as a professing Christian writing to influence Christians, identified the God of natural reason and the God of Christian faith. From his own point of view, that faith was not and could not be contrary to reason and experience, he was entitled to do this.[86] Nevertheless, the God discoverable by reason is an omnipotent first cause and not a legislator of a set of moral rules. Such a first cause is discoverable by reason only on the scientific premise that this is a world of cause and effect. The precepts of reason are laws in two different ways. (1) They are laws if we regard the world as a necessary sequence of causes and effects, and if, having realized this, we

[85] *Behemoth* (Dialogue 1), p. 54. See Warrender, *The Political Philosophy of Hobbes*, p. 276. *N.B.*, Hobbes is describing a Christian's duty according to the Scriptures rather than man's duty according to the laws of nature.

[86] *Leviathan* (32), p. 286: "Nevertheless [in interpreting revelation] we are not to renounce our Senses, and Experience; nor (that which is the undoubted Word of God) our naturall Reason. For they are the talents which he hath put into our hands to negotiate, till the coming again of our blessed Saviour; and therefore not to be folded up in the Napkin of an Implicit Faith, but employed in the purchase of Justice, Peace, and true Religion. For though there be many things in Gods Word above Reason; that is to say, which cannot by naturall reason be either demonstrated, or confuted; yet there is nothing contrary to it; but when it seemeth so, the fault is either in our unskilfull Interpretation, or erroneous Ratiocination."

acknowledge the existence of God as a first cause. Thus, we submit to God and recognize the causal order as a lawful order. In this case, the laws of nature are laws in the same sense that we call the principles of physics "laws." And we know that we cannot avoid their operation, just as we cannot avoid the operation of the law of gravity. Although these laws cannot be broken, they can be used to effect desired consequences. (2) They are laws (as Hobbes says) as they are promulgated in Scripture. Scripture is law to those who belong to a kingdom in which it has been made law, or to those who have accepted it as law. In this case, the laws of nature are not natural law but positive law, although the content of the laws is unchanged.

> But those which we call the laws of nature, (since they are nothing else but certain conclusions, understood by reason, of things to be done and omitted; but a law, to speak properly and accurately, is the speech of him who by right commands somewhat to others to be done or omitted), are not in propriety of speech laws, as they proceed from nature. Yet, as they are delivered by God in holy Scriptures, . . . they are most properly called by the name of laws: for the sacred Scripture is the speech of God commanding over all things by greatest right.[87]

A second serious disadvantage of this view is that it regards men as being under the same set of moral obligations at all times, although these obligations are only effective under certain validating conditions. But Hobbes regards men as free from moral bonds as long as they retain the right to make their own decisions. The state of nature is intolerable because the right of nature and the laws of nature are interpreted by each individual man; no man can be sure about any other man's rationality—either his knowledge of the laws of nature, or his assessment of the circumstances, or his judgment of what conduct is appropriate. Hobbes attempts to show that if all conduct were regulated only by the private conscience and reason of each man, this would be a beastly and immoral world. The

[87] *De Cive* (iii. 33), *EW* II, 49–50.

right of private judgment creates a situation that frustrates moral action—and even worse, this situation tends to contradict the fundamental assumption of any human action, that it must be done by a living person. Hobbes's main concern is with the fundamental rules and the mechanics of creating, from the situation of maximum freedom, maximum uncertainty, and minimum obligation, a system of objective, enforced obligations.

Because Warrender's interpretation regards the laws of nature as universal, eternal, and categorical (in spite of the fact that Hobbes thought that universal propositions could only be eternal because they were scientific and therefore hypothetical), it exaggerates the agreement among men about good and evil. Here men agree in regarding death as their greatest evil and preservation as their greatest good, and, if they have reasoned correctly, death here means eternal death, and preservation, salvation. But men do not agree in regarding death as their greatest evil; each man regards his own death as the greatest evil that can befall him. A man has no categorical duty to protect another's life,[88] and the dangers of the state of nature partly result from the fact that each man is regarded as a potential enemy whose death may therefore be beneficial. In the state of nature A thinks A's death evil but he may well think B's death good. If death means eternal destruction, there seems to be no reason why anyone else's destruction should seem evil (apart from relatives, friends, and other interested parties).

If men do not agree about what is evil, they agree still less about what is good. This theory requires that there be a *summum bonum,* salvation or conservation, an end for which we strive in this life. But Hobbes denies that there is such a thing in this life. Felicity is not progressing toward salvation nor conserving oneself; it is satisfying desire. Hobbes's argument that men can agree that peace is a good and therefore that the

[88] As he would have according to Locke; see Locke, *Second Treatise,* chap. ii, sec. 4; Laslett ed., p. 289.

means to peace are good is based on the premise that to conserve himself, each must realize that peace is the best means. Conserving oneself is important because it is a primary good—without life, no other goods are possible.[89] Men need not agree on ultimate ends, but life is a necessary means, a *sine qua non* of attaining any end; since peace is the best means to assure life, everyone who cares to stay alive ought to seek peace, and desire the performance of the laws of nature, the means to peace.

If salvation and eternal death must be rejected as natural human ends, the questions of what death men wish to avoid, and why they wish to avoid it, are raised again. Men could have a duty to avoid death, i.e., a duty to preserve their lives. A law of nature, after all, is a rule by which a man is forbidden to do that which is destructive of his life, his own nature.[90] But this would make self-preservation both a natural right and a duty, contrary to Hobbes's distinction of right and obligation. (Natural right is the liberty to use one's own power for the preservation of one's nature.) Although Hobbes talks of obligation and liberty being inconsistent in the same matter, natural right could mean the right to the end, while a natural law—the precept supplied by the individual's reason—could determine the means to be used in any particular situation. Still, the first and fundamental law of nature is not *preserve yourself,* but *seek peace,* and this seems to support the contention that self-preservation is not a duty.

Hobbes often seems to regard self-preservation as a natural necessity. Man naturally chooses the lesser evil of danger in resisting force than the greater evil of certain and present death.[91] Although the law calls suicide a felony, Hobbes does not see

[89] *De Homine* (xi. 6), *LW* II, 98. *"Bonorum autem primum est sua cuique conservatio."*
[90] *Leviathan* (14), p. 99.
[91] *Ibid.,* pp. 107–8, 101–2; *De Cive* (ii. 18), *EW* II, 25–26.

how any man can bear *animum felleum,* or so much malice towards himself, as to hurt himself voluntarily, much less to kill himself. For naturally and necessarily the intention of every man aimeth at somewhat which is good to himself, and tendeth to his preservation. And therefore, methinks, if he kill himself, it is to be presumed that he is not *compos mentis,* but by some inward torment or apprehension of somewhat worse than death, distracted.[92]

Men can kill themselves not because they bear malice toward themselves, but because they believe that there is something worse than death. The presumption must be that suicides are in fact insane. Their insanity is not an established fact but a legal presumption.

Any man who believes that there is something worse than death (e.g., eternal torment) will act accordingly when he is faced with the dilemma of choosing between it and death.[93] Some men will use violence, and consequently die, for a trifle, to revenge an insult.[94] Other men are proud enough to refuse to rely on shameful means even to preserve their lives.[95] Christian pastors become "secondary" martyrs because of their belief and their responsibility to other believers.[96] The avoidance of death does not seem to be an absolute natural necessity. Hobbes sometimes suggests that it may be possible to regard death as an end of one's troubles and pains. Although death, and especially death with torment, is the principal evil; yet "the sorrows of life may be so great, that, unless the end of these is foreseen to be near, death may be numbered among goods." [97]

Preserving one's existence is something less than an unavoidable necessity. But it is so close to being naturally necessary, that, except in the case of those who are insane, or tormented without hope of relief, or convinced that life under some circumstances is worse than death, or who believe in a higher

---

[92] *Dialogue of the Common Laws, EW* VI, 88.   [93] *Leviathan* (38), p. 345.
[94] *Ibid.* (13), p. 96; *cf. ibid:* (18), p. 139.   [95] *Ibid.* (15), p. 114.
[96] *Ibid.* (42), pp. 388–90.   [97] *De Homine* (xi. 6), *LW* II, 98.

self-preservation, we may presume that a man will act to preserve his own existence if he realizes that it is threatened. This
presumption is not based on a panic terror of death, but on
fear—an aversion to something because we imagine it it be
harmful.

> And forasmuch as necessity of nature maketh men to will and
> desire *bonum sibi,* that which is good for themselves, and to avoid
> that which is hurtful; but most of all that terrible enemy of nature,
> death, from whom we expect both the loss of all power, and also
> the greatest of bodily pains in the losing; it is not against reason
> that a man doth all he can to preserve his own body and limbs,
> both from death and pain.[98]

This is what is meant by natural right.

Men cannot live forever; Hobbes did not suppose that they
could. What men desire to do is "[to live] out the time, which
Nature ordinarily alloweth men to live." [99] This is presumed
to be every man's fundamental minimum purpose; the use of
the means he thinks fit for this end is a man's natural right
(although it is not a right that excludes other men's having
conflicting rights or that imposes a duty on anyone to respect
it). The end of all transfers of rights is "nothing else but the
security of a mans person, in his life, and in the means of so
preserving life, as not to be weary of it." [100]

Men are creatures set in motion at their generation. They
operate in a world of things that sometimes helps and sometimes hinders that motion. The friction involved in life eventually extinguishes that motion. Men act to put off that extinction as long as possible. Perhaps the worst thing—and the
most painful—is to be extinguished while the force of this
motion is still strong. To die a violent and painful death is an
evil that men desire to avoid. A quiet and peaceful death at the
end of a period in which the pulse of life has become slower
and weaker is preferable.

The greatest danger that life will be prematurely cut off

[98] *Elements of Law* (I. xiv. 6), p. 71.   [99] *Leviathan* (14), p. 100.
[100] *Ibid.,* p. 102.

exists when one is most in danger of death at the hands of other men—i.e., in the state of nature.[101] The laws of nature that Hobbes discusses provide a means of eliminating this danger; they provide for the conservation of men by prescribing the means of minimizing discord. They are scientific rules for dealing with this danger. But these are not the only laws of nature; other laws of nature deal with dangers to the individual from other sources.[102] Precepts may be formulated to cover, e.g., health. New scientific laws of nature may be discovered—like the connection between cigarette smoking and lung cancer. Hobbes himself acted according to this interpretation of the laws of nature. He took exercise at tennis or walking, followed by a rubdown, because he believed this would prolong his life two or three years; he sang in bed to improve his lungs, and sought thereby to prolong his life; he was rarely drunk, and would not take wine regularly because it would eventually muddle his wits.[103] Men desire their own well-being; consequently they must desire life and health, and security of these for the future.[104] Furthermore, men have a natural right to the means of life, including food, air, and medicine.[105]

The laws of nature concerning conduct toward other men are not difficult to discover. They are all reducible to a simple rule of thumb: *Quod tibi fieri non vis, alteri ne feceris*—Do not that to another, which thou would not have done to thyself.[106] Nevertheless no one can be sure that another will act according to this rule. For in the state of nature the laws of nature concerning the conduct of men toward each other bind *in foro interno* but not *in foro externo*. In the state of nature

[101] I emphasize premature death rather than (its special case) violent death (see Strauss, *The Political Philosophy of Hobbes*, pp. 16–17) or shameful death (see Oakeshott, "The Moral Life in the Writings of Thomas Hobbes," *Rationalism in Politics*, p. 254).

[102] See above, p. 107.   [103] See Aubrey, I, 347, 350–52.

[104] *De Homine* (xi. 6), *LW* II, 98.

[105] See *Leviathan* (21), p. 167; *ibid.* (27), p. 232; *Elements of Law* (I. xvii. 2), p. 88.

[106] *De Cive* (iii. 26), *EW* II, 44–45; *Leviathan* (15), p. 121; *Elements of Law* (I. xvii. 9), p. 92.

one need only follow these precepts of reason while it is safe
to do so. One who is keeping the laws of nature endeavors to
conduct himself according to them—he desires that keeping
them should be the case, but he is only bound to actual specific
performance of the laws of nature when he will not endanger
himself thereby. So, in the state of nature these rules are precepts for men's intentions and not precepts for men's actions.
Just as the laws may be fulfilled in intention without being
obeyed in action, they may be (apparently) kept in action while
being broken in intention. A man who intends hostility may be
afraid to act according to his intention; or he may accidentally
keep the law; or act according to it to trick another into laying
himself open to attack.[107]

It is impossible to tell whether any action is right or wrong,
just or unjust, moral or immoral in the state of nature. There
are no objective standards of actions in this situation, only the
standard of conscience. Each man is himself the judge of his
actions, and if he conscientiously believes that they are right
there is no man who can challenge this belief, and establish
the contrary against the actor's own judgment. In the state of
nature, every man is his own judge, and his own moral authority. Each man is his own interpreter of the right of nature and
laws of nature, and his own religious authority, for in the
state of nature his own belief in invisible powers is each man's
religion.[108]

Since in any particular case we cannot tell who is rational and
who is not, nor can we tell whether a man believes himself
conscientiously bound in this case, or, if he does not believe
himself bound, whether he fears that his gods will punish him,
or that human beings will retaliate, the state of nature is a
state of insecurity and war. To change this, we need not supply
everyone with a good will, we need not make everyone aware
of his rational self-interest in obeying the laws of nature; it is

[107] *Leviathan* (15), pp. 121–22; *De Cive* (iii. 27–29), *EW* II, 45–47; *Elements of
Law* (I. xvii. 10), pp. 92–93.
[108] *Leviathan* (11, 12, 14), pp. 81, 82 ff., 108.

not necessary that men actually be rational; it is only necessary that they act as if they were. The solution to the moral problem is political, i.e., it is to establish a power on earth that men will be forced to obey. This power will provide known and determinate laws, standards of conduct with penalties annexed to their breach, sufficient security that men will (for the most part) act according to these laws.

Since the laws of nature are contrary to our passions, or at least to some of them, most men, desiring their immediate profit, will neither obey these laws nor keep their word.[109] But some motives may be conducive to peace. These motives are pride (appearing not to need to break one's word) and fear. This sort of pride is too rare to provide a basis for society, and so the passion to be reckoned on is fear, fear of the power of invisible spirits, or of other men. "Of these two, though the former be the greater Power, yet the feare of the latter is commonly the greater Feare." [110] Covenants will not suffice to create a secure situation, for,

Covenants, without the Sword, are but Words, and of no strength to secure a man at all. Therefore notwithstanding the Lawes of Nature, (which every one hath then kept, when he has the will to keep them, when he can do it safely,) if there be no Power erected, or not great enough for our security; every man will, and may lawfully rely on his own strength and art, for caution against all other men.[111]

The laws of nature are effective in the state of nature only when the actor (a) knows the laws of nature, i.e., he is rational and has discovered them, and (b) feels he is secure in following them, i.e., he feels bound to follow them in this case. This is such a precarious situation that Hobbes thought it necessary that men create a situation in which no one can reasonably claim to be insecure, and everyone has a will to keep the laws because:

[109] *Ibid.* (17), p. 128; *De Cive* (iii. 27, v. 1–2), *EW* II, 45–46, 63–64; *Elements of Law* (I. xix. 1), pp. 99–100.
[110] *Leviathan* (14), p. 108.
[111] *Ibid.* (17), p. 128.

(a) they are promulgated to all by their senses—they do not have to reason them out; and

(b) private assessment of the situation is limited—a visible source of laws and punishments is established so that men's wills can be influenced by a visible human power. What is necessary is not that all men should hold the same values and have the same purposes, but that, whatever their values and their purposes, they should all be subject to the same law, a human law known to all (because publicly promulgated), and effective (because publicly enforced by human authority).

How, then, can so necessary an authority be created?

5

CONSTRUCTION
OF A
SOCIAL ORDER

When first from Earth crawl'd forth each Man and Brute,
Mankind, like them as wretched and as mute,
With Nails and Fists for Dens and Acorns fought,
And then with Clubs and Arms, by Custom taught:
Till Names to Things were by Degrees assign'd,
And Language form'd, that Index of the Mind.
Then soon they learn'd from Rapine to refrain,
Cities to fortify, and Laws ordain,
Adulterers, Thieves, and Robbers to restrain.

HORACE, *Satires* I. iii. 99–106

The Necessity of a Social Contract

In a pure state of nature, each man must be regarded as an
individual bound by no ties to any other individual. Each is
to be held to be the equal of any other. In this situation each
man is his own defender and preserver, his own moralist, and
his own high priest. His own belief about the existence of
invisible spirits is his religion; his own belief about whether
an action is right or wrong, i.e., his conscience, is his morality.

Having incurred no obligations, he is free to do as he wills insofar as he has the power. He acts with right even when he attempts to secure himself by anticipation, i.e., by attacking and killing or subduing another before he has been attacked by him.[1]

There may be spots of security within the state of nature. Over a period of time, it is possible that men could come to aid one another. They could build up situations in which they had obligations to others by covenants, or by gratitude for past help. Human beings who have no societies excèpt for small families may be considered to be in an incomplete state of nature. They do have social arrangements, but not very extensive ones. Clearly, men who are thrown into the state of nature as a result of the collapse of a civil society in war or revolution will not lack some of the trappings of their previous civility. Independent societies, also, are in a state of nature toward each other; pacts, alliances, economic ties, and international conventions notwithstanding. But it is only for individuals and small groups that life is "solitary, poor, nasty, brutish, and short" in the state of nature.

Life is mean in the state of nature, not only because there is no friendly fellowship among men, but also because there is little or no cooperation among men. The improvement of the practical arts and the development of the liberal arts occur only in a civil society. Life is short and insecure in the state of nature because it is a state of war. Untimely death is likely, not because men are always engaged in hostilities in the state of nature but because the threat of a resort to force is constantly present. The motives that drive men to fight are varied. Conflict occurs because the state of nature is a state of scarcity.

---

[1] This is a right contrary to the traditional natural law duty not to harm others. By nature, there is not only a duty to do good and avoid evil, but a natural inclination to good, including a good life in society. See St. Thomas Aquinas, *Summa Theologica* I–II, Qu. 94, Art. 2; Hugo Grotius, *De Jure Belli ac Pacis*, Prolegomena, Sections 5–9. *Cf.* S. Pufendorf, *De Jure Naturae et Gentium*, II. ii. 2–3, II. iii. 15–18, II. v. 6–8, where Pufendorf specifically opposes Hobbes's views and carefully restricts any right to attack in self-defense.

It is not a state of plenty, as Locke was to claim,[2] for such a condition would only be possible where nature was cultivated, improved by human artifice. For such natural goods as there are in the state of nature there is continuous and bitter competition because there is no natural limit to the desires of men. If some men invade others' possessions from their need (or their desire) for something, others invade to gain power and precedence, and still others because of diffidence—their fearful expectations concerning the conduct of other men. Profit, glory, and security are the goals that cause strife in the state of nature.

Even though their passions lead men into conflict, they also motivate men to seek a way out of that conflict. Realizing that war frustrates their ability to achieve their desires, and, even worse, threatens their continued existence (the basic condition of having desires), men realize that, in order to preserve themselves, they must have peace. And peace is something more than a truce between battles. They work out the laws of nature which are convenient articles for establishing a peace—rational precepts concerning the conduct of men to one another which are necessary means to peace, and which may be summarized in a simple rule of thumb: "Do not that to another which you would not have done to you." These causal relations may even be regarded as moral rules promulgated by a God discoverable by reason and sanctioned by rewards and punishments discoverable by reasoning about causes and effects. This God is the cause of all causes and these rewards and punishments are consequences linked to the laws of nature by causal chains.

Whatever interpretation of the laws of nature (regarded as divine natural laws) is adopted, and whatever sort of God is held to be discoverable by nature (even if it is held that Hobbes was in fact disguising his atheism by professing to be a believer), Hobbes's point remains the same: no man is under a law who has not put himself under it by his own act. This is part of his more general principle of obligation, i.e., that all

[2] Locke, *Second Treatise,* chap. v, sec. 31; Laslett ed., p. 308.

obligations are self-imposed. Although it is permissible to speak of being obliged according to the laws of physics, this is a metaphorical usage, and not the sort of obligation that is important in human conduct. "Physical obligation" is perfectly compatible with liberty. The stone follows the laws of physics when it falls freely, as animals do when they move their limbs.

Of course, both physical consequences and the expectation of these consequences may influence human behavior. One doesn't step off a one-hundred-foot-high cliff, because one knows the consequence of doing so. A threat to throw a person off such a cliff might very well influence that person's conduct. The point to notice about these physical laws is that the consequences of the behavior follow whether the laws are known and accepted or not. One need not know the laws of falling bodies in order to be subject to those laws. But if one does not know these laws (in some form), they cannot influence one's behavior. When we voluntarily avoid stepping off the cliff because we do not relish the consequences of a fall, we know the law, we believe that it holds, and in a sense, we are "obliged" by it. The "obligation" is conditional; it depends upon our desires. If one wished to commit suicide, he would not feel obliged to refrain from leaping over the edge.

These "laws" are regularities that cannot be abrogated, although they may be formulated incorrectly. Crude formulations may be replaced by formulae at once more precise and more elegant. These laws may be manipulated (but not violated) for human purposes. Precision and elegance of formulation enlarge the power and subtlety of the possible manipulations; the mathematics of falling bodies makes possible more precise use of artillery.

If these natural regularities apply whether they are known or not, how can a man be obliged to obey them only by his own act? In the sense of physical necessity, surely no one has a choice. Nevertheless there is another sense in which these laws oblige only by a man's own act: it is by his own discovery of their existence and their necessity that he realizes that he is bound to respect them in the sense of taking account of them in his deliberations. He is then obliged by his own acceptance of the existence and necessity of these laws, and this can only occur if he knows them. His power to disregard them and suffer the consequences still exists, but if he does not like the consequences, he is obliged to act so as to avoid them.

It has been suggested above that the precepts discovered by reason as convenient articles of peace are laws of nature in this sense. This is why "men may shake off their Ease, but not their Yoke." [3] They can regard the universe as governed by chance or by the whims of men or spirits. They may think that some are favored of the gods and that there are no unavoidable consequences of human conduct. They may regard the world as irregular, and events as unpredictable not because of the limits of human knowledge of causes but because the world is inherently disorderly. Such a belief destroys ease by destroying the possibility of knowledge; it increases fear and anxiety. It does not affect the inexorable operation of causes and effects, but it does affect human conduct insofar as it is not based on the recognition of that operation. When a man recognizes that there is an order in the world that is more than chance, when he sees this order as regular—recognizing rules and laws and regarding himself as bound by these *regulae* and subject to their author—then he has subjected himself in a way in which he was not subject before. This is even more clearly the case if the rules involved are rules concerning human conduct. These influence a man's action only as he knows them and regards himself as bound to follow them.

The laws of nature are "laws" only to men who believe that there is a God who has given these laws and propounded rewards and punishments. God's subjects include the reasoners who have come to this conclusion about the existing world, as well as those who believe in some revealed truth. These men

---

[3] *Leviathan* (31), p. 274.

have subjected themselves, and obliged themselves to follow these laws. Although God's right is not derived from their submission, their obligation is. Atheists, and others who have not submitted, are not subjects but enemies of God.[4]

This position scandalized Hobbes's contemporaries because it denied that all men are obliged to obey God. For if they were obliged to obey God, atheists would not be enemies of God but rebels against him. If men are obliged to obey God apart from their acceptance of this obligation, if men are morally obliged by God's commands although they have not accepted this obligation, if the laws of nature as God's commands are the ground of all other obligation,[5] then the sin of the atheist would not be imprudence but unjust rebellion. The atheist's argument is *"that he never submitted his will to God's will, not conceiving him so much as to have any being: and granting that his opinion were erroneous, and therefore also a sin, yet were it to be numbered among those of imprudence or ignorance, which by right cannot be punished."* [6] Hobbes admits that this argument is correct up to the assertion of the atheist that he cannot rightly be punished. Although the sin is imprudence, the atheist is rightly "punished," not as a subject but as an enemy. Hobbes's whole argument, defended in the second edition of *De Cive* (1647) in a footnote in which he declares that he could find no law that the atheist has unjustly broken, is based on the premise that no one is obliged who has not submitted his will, "there being no Obligation on any man, which ariseth not from some Act of his own." [7]

Obligation to obey the law of nature depends upon the acceptance of the laws of nature as obliging. But, even if one could be sure that everyone knew the laws of nature and had accepted them as obliging (conditions which do not exist), this

4 *Ibid.,* p. 275. See above, pp. 110–12.
5 See Warrender, *The Political Philosophy of Hobbes,* pp. 81–85, 97–100, 285–98; and Hood, pp. 22–40.
6 *De Cive* (xiv. 19), *EW* II, 198.   7 *Leviathan* (21), p. 166.

would not suffice to establish peace. Even if everyone in the
state of nature were endeavoring to keep the laws of nature,
each man would still be following only his own individual
interpretation of those laws. No one is obliged to the laws of
nature in the state of nature except by his own conscience; no
one is bound to accept another's interpretation of those laws.
Each man has a right (part of his natural right) to judge for
himself between right and wrong and to judge another's judgment right or wrong when it concerns him. The morality of
the state of nature is the morality of private individual conscience. The rules of right and wrong are conscientious and no
one is bound but by his own conscience.

Hobbes held that the state of conduct wholly according to
private conscience and private reason was a state of war. Every
man being his own moral authority means that every man has
his own morality—or at least his own interpretation of morality. Morality thus far involves only how one treats other human
beings; it is general and indeterminate, rather than specified
in duties owed and determinate about the persons to whom
these duties are owed. There are ways of accepting determinate
obligations in the state of nature, both specific and general
obligations. The rule for determinately obliging oneself (i.e.,
obliging oneself to A and to no one else) is that one man accepts a determinate obligation to another man when he accepts
a benefit of some sort from him. If he has made no specific
agreement with his benefactor, the benefit he accepted is called
a gift and he has a determinate obligation to his benefactor to
benefit him in some (unspecified) way. If they have made a
specific agreement, a contract, then he owes a specific duty to
a determinate person. The third and fourth laws of nature
provide the form that these obligations take, but they do not
themselves make any determinate or specific obligations. They
provide the ways for obliging oneself, but not the obligations.
True obligations must be determinate; one cannot be obliged
to someone unknown. Before one can violate the third law

of nature one must have a specific and determinate obligation; before one can violate the fourth law of nature one must have accepted a determinate (though unspecified) obligation.

Both of these ways of translating rights or accepting obligations involve something more than bare promise. A gift is an actual giving of the thing—and this not done by a mere promise to give it. The distinction is clear, although there may be difficulties in deciding whether John Doe gave his horse to Richard Roe or only promised to give it. (The practical and legal difficulty is likely to be due to Doe's ambiguous words, or his own conflicting desires to give the horse to Roe and keep it himself.) A contract is also something more than a set of mutual promises, even if it is a contract of mutual covenants, i.e., one in which both parties are trusted. A covenant or pact does include a promise, the promise to perform, but it also includes a transfer of the right to that performance (and not a promise of that transfer). In the state of nature, contracts of mutual covenants are precarious. At times Hobbes says that they are invalid,[8] but strictly speaking he was wrong to speak as if they were void *ab initio*. His argument that they are invalid is simply that they are voidable by either party upon any reasonable suspicion (i.e., one that arises after the contract has been made) that the other party does not intend to perform.[9] The first performer has no guarantee that the other party will carry out his part of the bargain, even though the obligation of the second to perform would be clear. After a man has accepted a benefit for which he has contracted, he no longer has the excuse for not performing that he had when he was uncertain about whether he ever would actually receive that benefit. But the first performance is unlikely to occur in the state of nature. Men are wary in the state of nature; any con-

[8] *Ibid.* (15), p. 110.
[9] *De Cive* (ii. 11), *EW* II, 21. Cf. *Leviathan* (14), p. 105; *Elements of Law* (I. xv. 10), p. 78, where Hobbes seems to suggest that there is always a reasonable suspicion of the other party's non-performance in the state of nature.

tracts of mutual covenants that they make then are very likely to become void, even if they are not invalid.

Neither the laws of nature alone, nor the laws of nature reinforced with determinate agreements, are sufficient to remove men from the state of nature. The laws of nature alone are insufficient because every man is still possessed of his natural right to make his own decisions. Furthermore, some sort of security is necessary before the laws of nature can be observed in practice.[10] Clearly this sort of security is not provided by a group of men agreeing to help each other. Even if we suppose that there are enough men to provide the sort of mutual assistance that is necessary, a truly secure peace is not established. As long as each man retains his right to decide for himself according to his own judgment, the temporary peace is always apt to break down. As long as they unanimously agree they may indeed be safe and strong, but as soon as they disagree among themselves their unstable peace dissolves and with it their slight security.

For if we could suppose a great Multitude of men to consent in the observation of Justice, and other Lawes of Nature, without a common Power to keep them all in awe; we might as well suppose all Man-kind to do the same; and then there neither would be, nor need to be any Civill Government, or Common-wealth at all; because there would be Peace without subjection.[11]

Contracts to keep the peace will not help them, for those contracts would involve mutual covenants. The performance of those covenants would be continual and therefore the covenants, if not void *ab initio,* could be voided at any time by anyone who suspected that someone else was not going to continue performing. Here we have the situation of insecurity continued; each man scrutinizing the actions of his fellows,

[10] *Leviathan* (17), p. 128; *De Cive* (v. 3), *EW* II, 64–65; *Elements of Law* (I. xix. 1), pp. 99–100.
[11] *Leviathan* (17), pp. 129–30; *De Cive* (v. 4), *EW* II, 65–66; *Elements of Law* (I. xix. 4), pp. 101–2.

gnawed by anxiety that someone will make a prey of him. (It can even be argued that the more stable a consensus became, the more tempting and the more profitable a violation of the peace would become.)

The solution to the problem of insecurity is to form a union that does not depend on men's continuing to assent to the actions of the group. What men do is to incorporate themselves into a political society. They cannot become a single living creature—a real natural unity—but they can become a single feigned or artificial unity.[12]

Men in the state of nature are a multitude, a collection of particular individuals. This collection does not naturally form a harmonious group; men are not by nature political. Unlike bees and ants, they have individual wills for individual goods that conflict with the common good. They do not agree naturally, but disagree and originate other disagreements by discussion; men only agree by covenant. They think and act in ways different from the ways of animals; they contend for precedence.[13]

Societies of men are artificially constructed by men. Knowledge of the natural laws is necessary to such a society, but it is not sufficient to construct it. Even the supposition that all men have good wills would not be a sufficient basis for a society. A limited unity based on universal consent in a particular action does not convert a multitude into a body politic.

Hobbes's problem is to construct a society from a collection of individuals. The device that reduces the many to a unity is to make them a single person—an artificial person. Such a thing is like a natural human being in that it has a way of deliberating, a way of reaching a decision, and therefore a will. It has a way of making its decisions known, a voice. It must also have a way of acting, a way of making its determinations

[12] *Ibid.*, pp. 131–32; *De Cive* (v. 6–7), *EW* II, 68; *Elements of Law* (I. xix. 6–7), p. 103.
[13] *Leviathan* (17), pp. 130–31; *De Cive* (v. 5), *EW* II, 66–68; *Elements of Law* (I. xix. 5), pp. 102–3.

obeyed by its members. If it is to be a society, it must have power.

Universal consent to some course of action in a crisis does not suffice to establish a commonwealth. Those who have consented may come to dissent, destroying their precarious unanimity (concord) and reducing themselves once more to a state of war.[14] Concord is precarious both *de jure* and *de facto*. It is in fact precarious because diverse opinions about ends or means are likely to spring up when the burden of crisis is lifted. This return to normal disagreement revives the state of nature because it has never legally been destroyed. Concord is the agreement of many men; "When the wills of many concur to some one and the same action, or effect, this concourse of their wills is called CONSENT." [15] Here each individual in the multitude retains his right to decide his own course of action. His right to judge the wisdom of an action continues; his right to reconsider is preserved; he may resume his deliberations. That each consents implies that each retains his right to change his will in the future. The concord of a multitude of individual wills implies the right of each individual to dissent and his right to withdraw from the common enterprise.

A body politic, or commonwealth, exists when several men have authorized a representative person to act for them "in those things which concern the Common Peace and Safetie." To this person they "submit their Wills, every one to his Will, and their Judgements, to his Judgment." This authorization and submission create a new legal situation; the members of the society have done what mere promises to live together in peace could not do: They have erected "a Common Power, to keep them in awe, and to direct their actions to the Common Benefit." [16] To construct a commonwealth men must transfer rights and impose upon themselves obligations. They must

---

[14] *Elements of Law* (I. xix. 4), pp. 101–2; *De Cive* (v. 4), *EW* II, 65–66; *Leviathan* (17), p. 129.
[15] *Elements of Law* (I. xii. 7), p. 63.
[16] *Leviathan* (17), p. 131.

establish a society with the right to make regulations for the common peace and benefit. They must take upon themselves the obligation to obey these regulations. The method by which those rights can be transferred and these obligations imposed is covenant.

Contractarian Thought

Covenant is the most explicit way of constructing a precise obligation of one person to another. The promisor knows the terms of the agreement—the stipulations, and the person to whom he is obliged. It is, as Hobbes points out, a relation between two persons, one promising and the other accepting the promise. Formal agreements construct obligations between two independent parties. Consequently, not only the obligations but the limits of those obligations may be stipulated. Covenant or contract is a convenient model for constructing limited or conditional obligations.

It is convenient in a second way. It allows the question of moral philosophy to be set aside or at least to be set back one step. It is no longer necessary to inquire into the moral obligations of the subject or of the ruler. God's word, the teachings of religion, the obligations of natural law, the conclusions of moral philosophy, are no longer relevant. The question becomes a legal one: what are the terms of the agreement? Until the validity of an agreement is challenged, the prior question "What sort of stipulations are allowable in agreements?" need not be asked.

Social contracts may be distinguished into two types: the pact of association, and the pact of government.[17] The pact of

---

[17] See S. Pufendorf, VII. ii. 7-8. Pufendorf argues that there is a pact of association (an agreement to form a society), followed by a decree that specifies the form of government, followed in turn by a pact of government (a submission by the subjects to the rulers in return for their engagement to care for the common peace and security). *Cf.* J.-J. Rousseau, *Contrat Social*, who accepts the pact of association (I. vi) but denies the pact of government (III. xvi). For

government is a pact between the prince and the people. The people transfers power to the prince and the prince in return promises to rule justly. Violation of its obligation by either party creates a right to redress. Support for this account of the origin and limits of the authority of government could be derived from three distinct sources. The first of these is Ulpian's famous text from the Pandects, which implied that the powers exercised by the prince had been conferred upon him by the people: *"Quod principi placuit, legis habet vigorem: utpote cum lege regia, quae de imperio eius lata est, populus ei et in eum omne suum imperium et potestam conferat."* [What pleases the prince has the force of a law, for by a Lex Regia, passed concerning his authority, the people confer upon him all its authority and power.] [18] If the transfer of power to the prince were conditional or revocable (the text does not say that the people had transferred its power absolutely and irrevocably), then this text could be used to assert the ultimate sovereignty of the people. Although the people's power is usually dormant, it is revived or evoked by the tyranny of the prince.[19]

Second, the coronation ceremony was regarded as incorporating a contract between the king and the people. In this ceremony the king promised to govern justly, and he confirmed to the people their customary liberties; the people then consented to obey him—consenting to his election as king.[20]

The third source of a governmental contract was the Bible —God's Holy Writ. The Hebrews had chosen their kings (and

---

general discussions of the development of contractarian thought, see Gierke, *Political Theories of the Middle Age*, pp. 37–48, 87–100; Gierke, *Natural Law and the Theory of Society, 1500–1800*, pp. 35–79; Gough, pp. 33–118.

[18] *Digest* i. 4. 1.   [19] See Lewy, pp. 45–47, 66–81; Hamilton, pp. 59–67.

[20] For an example of the coronation oath taken by the King of England (in this case, James I), see Prothero, pp. 391–92. For some examples of the argument that the coronation oath involves a contract, see: Laski, pp. 148–49, 174–76; Sidney, pp. 322–29; Tyrrell, pp. 505–9. *Cf.* Filmer's argument against the coronation oath contract theory, pp. 103–5. On the transmission of French monarchomachic and contractual thought to England, see Salmon, pp. 39–57.

had from time to time deposed them). The powers of the rulers could be regarded as limited; at least there had been opposition to the acts of rulers, opposition by holy prophets, sacred priests, and righteous men—opposition approved and sanctified by God.[21]

When the governments in France and in England accepted the theory of absolute monarchy (kingship by divine right), and adopted policies intended to strengthen the king's position (policies whose aims were uniformity of religion, greater financial resources for the crown by means of royal imposition, diminution of the political influence of the magnates and towns upon the policies of the central government and restriction of their local independence), those who were opposed to these policies discovered contractarian arguments to explain their position and to justify their opposition.

The *Vindiciae Contra Tyrannos,* a Huguenot pamphlet of the sixteenth century frequently reissued in English during the seventeenth century,[22] illustrates the use of the contract of government. The argument of the *Vindiciae* combines religious and political opposition to the king just as it fuses biblical, historical, and legal arguments. God alone rules in his own right; kings are his vassals. The king, as God's vassal, promises to obey God's law and command according to it. No subject is bound to obey the king's laws (the law of a vassal) when they conflict with the laws of the liege lord. But not only does the king promise to obey God and preserve the church, the people also promise God, as sureties to the contract, that they will obey God and preserve the church among them. Therefore the people—i.e., the inferior magistrates having authority from the people, viz., *parlements,* estates, and local officers—have a duty to God to resist forcefully, if it is appropriate, a king who infringes God's law or ruins his Church. The *Vindiciae* justifies

[21] Many of the works cited in the previous footnote use sacred as well as profane history; see, for example, Laski, pp. 118 ff., 174–76.

[22] Laski records editions in 1581, 1589, 1622, 1631, 1648, 1660, and 1689. *Ibid.,* p. 60.

constitutional resistance as well as religious resistance. The king becomes king, not at the death of his predecessor [23] but at his coronation. In this contract between king and people, the people stipulate and the king promises that he will govern justly and according to the laws. The people then promise to obey as long as he does so. The king has an absolute obligation, the people a conditional one. The king's power is limited and derivative; he is bound to laws which he may not change. The king is neither owner nor usufructuary of the kingdom; he is an administrator. Even if these obligations are not expressly made, they exist naturally, tacitly, implicitly.

The limitation of the king's power is based on an agreement between the king, people, and God, and a second agreement between the king and the people. Both agreements imply that the people is a corporate body—a society—and not a collection of individuals. This theory assumes the existence of an organized society. It does not justify the existence of government or society; it merely justifies limits to the authority of a government. These limits are established by an agreement between the parties to a contract. Political obligation and political authority are the result of an agreement between a corporation and a prospective ruler—two independent parties. Political obligations are reduced to contractual obligations (or at least quasi-contractual obligations); the contract is the constitution of the country; it specifies the terms upon which the governors and the governed have agreed. Violation of any of the clauses of the agreement releases the other party from its obligations. And if the *Vindiciae* be admitted as the model of such a system, then the rights and the duties of the ruler are to be strictly construed, and his powers narrowly interpreted.

The governmental pact is designed to justify limits upon the authority of a government. The bounds of the powers granted to a government are stipulated in a contract; actions outside

[23] Contrary to "Le roi est mort, vive le roi." The king never dies; see Kantorowicz, pp. 7–23, 314 ff.

those limits are *ultra vires*. Such actions may be rightly opposed.

To base the limits to a government's authority upon an agreement with the people implies that the people is already a corporate body capable of making agreements. It is not supposed or asserted that there is an agreement with any single subject-citizen. It is the subjects as a community—a society—a single corporate body—that have made the agreement.

But what is it that makes a collection of human beings into an organized group? Society may exist by nature as an outgrowth of the family. The family is not a product of human choice, human agreement, or human reasoning; it is man's natural condition. Patriarchalism was one variant of this theory in the seventeenth century. The natural authority, or the authority appointed by God, is the father. The authority over a group of fathers is the patriarch, the father of the fathers of families, or the person who has inherited the patriarch's position. Carrying this argument through to the next stage of social organization eliminates the governmental contract. As Filmer argued, the king or ruler is properly the inheritor of the rights of the father over a large group of people.[24] The powers of rulers are justified because the rulers are rulers by nature, or alternatively are appointed by God. The limits to their authority can only be limits imposed by natural or divine law, not limits imposed by human agreements. This theory then leads to a royalist rather than a resistance theory.

The great "politique" Jean Bodin had already tried to discover a way to combine natural and divine authority, violence, and consent to build a political theory justifying the powers of government and limits to those powers. Bodin, following Aristotle, holds that the family is natural. The father is the natural ruler of the family and of the household. The household is not a political community; it is nevertheless the model of right order in the commonwealth, and "not only the true source and origin of the commonwealth but also its principal constitu-

[24] Filmer, pp. 60–61.

ent." [25] "A commonwealth may be defined as the rightly ordered government of a number of families, and of those things which are their common concern, by a sovereign power." [26] A commonwealth is a community of families and communities (there must be at least three households in any community), a community distinguished from other communities because it is ordered by a sovereign power. The members of each household are the subjects of the commonwealth; heads of households are its citizens, free subjects who owe obedience to the sovereign power.[27]

Although life in a commonwealth is not contrary to human nature, the commonwealth is not a natural association in the sense that the family is. Bodin appears to believe that families have always existed; before there were states each head of a family was an independent sovereign. Conflicts ensued. The victors became the subjects of their chosen leaders, who retained their authority; the defeated became slaves. "Reason and common sense alike point to the conclusion that the origin and foundation of commonwealths was in force and violence." [28]

In spite of its assumption that the family is a natural social unit, this account, like Hobbes's commonwealth by acquisition, emphasizes the artificial origin of the state in conquest. However, Bodin not only fails to analyze this development but he also gives another account of the development of societies which is both more confusing and more Aristotelian. Families, growing larger, expanded to become hamlets and villages. These gradually grew into separate towns; since there were neither laws, nor magistrates, nor sovereign rulers, disputes about property and water rights led to conflict.

This led to the towns first surrounding themselves with ditches and then walls, and to men associating together, some for the defence of their homes and families, others to attack those in possession, and rob, despoil, and destroy them. . . . This license and impunity

[25] Bodin, *Six Books of the Commonwealth*, p. 6.   [26] *Ibid.*, p. 1.
[27] *Ibid.*, pp. 7, 18–19.   [28] *Ibid.*, p. 19.

in preying upon one another compelled men, who knew neither rulers nor magistrates, to join together as friends for mutual defence one against another, and institute communities and brotherhoods.[29]

Communities existed before rulers and sovereigns. When they were harassed by their enemies, "gatherings of the tribes met and chose a leader, whom God had inspired, to whom they gave sovereign authority." [30] In this case sovereignty originates in consent. Bodin sometimes seems to imply that the community is sovereign. It may appoint a magistrate as its 'agent, limiting his powers in extent or duration. But it may renounce all its sovereign power and invest it in the magistrate, thus following the example of the Roman grant of *imperium* as Bodin interprets it.[31]

Sovereignty is absolute and perpetual power.[32] The powers of the sovereign are extensive. His rightful commands are law, "binding on all his subjects in general and on each in particular." [33] To make law he needs no one's consent. He is bound neither to his previous enactments, nor to existing laws, nor to custom, which binds during his good pleasure.

All the other attributes and rights of sovereignty are included in this power of making and unmaking law, so that strictly speaking this is the unique attribute of sovereign power. It includes all other rights of sovereignty, that is to say of making peace and war, of hearing appeals from the sentences of all courts whatsoever, of appointing and dismissing the great officers of state; of taxing, or granting privileges of exemption to all subjects, of appreciating or depreciating the value and weight of the coinage, of receiving oaths of fidelity from subjects and liege-vassals alike, without exception of any other to whom faith is due.[34]

Nevertheless, absolute and perpetual power is not power without limit in time and extent. "Perpetual" power exists in a monarch who rules for life (provided this power is not revocable), as well as in hereditary monarchies (in which power is

[29] *Ibid.,* p. 97.   [30] *Ibid.,* p. 98.   [31] *Ibid.,* pp. 26–27.   [32] *Ibid.,* p. 25.
[33] *Ibid.,* p. 43.   [34] *Ibid.,* p. 44.

vested in the king and heirs of his body), and in the truly perpetual, undying because corporate, forms of government: aristocracy and democracy (*communitas non moritur*).[35]

Although sovereign power is absolute it is not unlimited, but only as much power as any human may possess. Although a sovereign is not subject to the commands of another (he is not bound to the laws of his predecessors, to his own precedents, his own laws, or to the customs of the country), he is subject to divine and natural laws "and cannot contravene them without treason and rebellion against God." [36] God has established sovereign princes as his lieutenants to command the rest of mankind; no one on earth after God is greater; they are subject to no other authority.[37]

In spite of this position, there are two other general limitations on the powers of princes in addition to their obligations to respect divine and natural laws:

(1) They are bound by their covenants and agreements, even those they make with their subjects;

(2) They are bound by the constitutional laws of the kingdom.

Such limitations on the powers of the government should be expected in a book called *Les six livres de la république*. The title indicates Bodin's intention to write a substitute for Cicero's partially lost *De Re Publica;* the state described in the six books devoted to the discussion of the best constitution is the state for which the laws, consistent with natural law, prescribed in Cicero's *De Legibus,* are suitable.[38]

---

[35] *Ibid.,* pp. 7, 26.   [36] *Ibid.,* p. 29.   [37] *Ibid.,* p. 40.

[38] Until the recovery in 1820 of a large part of Cicero's *De Re Publica,* very little of that work was known. See *De Re Publica and De Legibus,* with a translation by C. W. Keyes (Cambridge, Harvard University Press, 1959), pp. 9 ff. Apart from the "Dream of Scipio," the main source of knowledge about the *De Re Publica* was St. Augustine's discussion of Cicero's definition of a commonwealth in the *De Civitate Dei.*

My suggestion of a connection between the lost *De Re Publica* and Jean Bodin's *Six Books of the Commonwealth* is supported by the following evidence: (1) The similarity between the titles. Bodin could have known that Cicero had devoted six books to this subject from *De Legibus* I. vi. 20. (2) Bodin was a humanist who proposed to develop a universal law. Like Cicero (*De Legibus*

But if there are no natural aristocrats, no natural rulers,[39] if neither fathers, nor warriors, nor thinkers are by nature designated as rulers, and if no one has been appointed by God to rule, how can a number of men form a society? How can subordination exist? Every organized collection of human beings, every group, must have some way of coordinating and directing the activities of its members. Groups, that is, can exist only where there is cooperation, several members working together (on one task or dividing the work to be done among them). Cooperation involves coordination, i.e., common direction, and therefore government—someone to settle disputes, and give signals and probably to assign or reassign tasks and give directions.[40]

But how, in the absence of naturally or supernaturally designated directors, is a collection of human beings to become a group? Where can they discover a leader? How can these individuals proceed to form a group or society?

If there is no given order, they must make an order for themselves. If there is no natural superior to lead them, they must appoint someone to lead them by agreement among themselves.

The alternative to the theory that society is natural is the theory that society is conventional: that society is not of divine or natural construction but merely something that men have made for themselves. This seems to be the position that was held by the Sophists. At least it is the position that Plato ascribes to Callicles in the *Gorgias* and to Glaucon in the *Republic*. Callicles asserts that laws and conventions were made by the weak to protect themselves from the strong; [41] Glaucon

I. iv. 14), Bodin criticized contemporary legal writers for their trivial concerns. See Bodin, *Method for the Easy Comprehension of History*, pp. 1–8. See also Franklin, pp. 59–79. (3) Bodin could have known Cicero's definition of a commonwealth from St. Augustine, *De Civitate Dei* II. 21. Furthermore Bodin reasserts the very element in Cicero's definition, the element of justice, that Augustine criticizes and drops from his own definition (XIX. 21–24). See Bodin, *Six Books of the Commonwealth*, pp. 1 ff.
[39] *Leviathan* (15), pp. 117–18.
[40] See St. Thomas Aquinas, *De Regimine Principum*, chap. 1; and de Jouvenel, pp. 109–17.
[41] *Gorgias*, 483 ff.

states that men have agreed not to do wrong to others in order to avoid suffering wrong.[42] Law, justice, and society are, according to this account, the results of human agreements, i.e., conventional rather than natural. Societies are not natural to humans as herds are to sheep, schools to fish, hives to bees. Society is not necessarily contrary to human nature, but it is at most a second nature, an artifice to which men become habituated.

Plato does not discuss the kind of agreement that would be adequate to construct a society. Nor, as far as I know, did the Sophists or the Epicureans specify the kind of agreement that is involved. Democritus, Antiphon, Epicurus, and Lucretius all regarded justice and society as conventional, and consequently based on some sort of human agreements. These theories, or rather the fragments of them, may be regarded as social contract theories because they do emphasize the conventional origin of justice and society. But none of these authors (in some cases in the fragments we have of their works) gives a full account of a social contract; the most we have is the mention of leagues, agreements, alliances, or conventions.[43]

Those who adopted this line of argument in the Middle Ages and afterwards could and did interpret the *lex regia* passage as describing a contract of government.[44] The power of the prince is derived from the consent of the people—and by enactment they gave him all their power and authority.

They could also rely upon biblical authority. The Israelites had not been satisfied with the rule of judges; they demanded a king to reign over them, like other nations.[45] The inspired choice of Saul by the prophet Samuel, followed by the people's acclamation of the king that they had demanded, could be used as an authoritative example of popular control over governors and forms of government.

[42] *Republic*, 359.
[43] See Havelock, pp. 148–50, 271 ff.; and Barker, pp. 178–79, 182.
[44] Gierke, *Political Theories of the Middle Age*, pp. 42–46; Carlyle and Carlyle, II, 56–75.
[45] I Sam. 8:7, 8:9–22.

To the Presbyterian, searching the Old Testament for models of correct Christian conduct, an earlier covenant might appear more relevant. The covenant between God and his people in which they accepted him as their God and he accepted them as his people could be regarded as the way for a nation to dedicate itself to the service of God. The National Covenant of the Scots (1638) to defend the true religion, their liberties and laws, was the dedication of the nation, by covenant, to God's service.[46] The biblical model in this case was reinforced by the tradition of banding—the making of agreements for protection and assistance.[47]

But the covenant of the Scots was no social covenant, and the model of the covenant with God—although influential in the seventeenth century and part of the explanation of the general understanding and acceptance of the language of contract in political and constitutional discussion—did not provide an explanation of the formation of society. However, there was a more radical form of contract theory developed by the Congregationalists.

Congregationalism, separatist and non-separatist, was in agreement with Presbyterianism on many points. It was part of the movement to reform the Church of England—the Puritan movement—and (although some could not wait for the Church to reform itself, having demanded a "reformation without tarrying for any," proceeded to reform themselves outside, separated from, the Church of England) the extent of the differences within the Puritan movement was not revealed until Parliamentary victory in the Civil War created the possibility of a new church settlement.[48]

The Puritans were agreed, following Calvin, that Christ had set men free from the bondage of the law. No things external

[46] See Gardiner, *History of England*, VIII, 329–34; Wedgwood, pp. 197–99 For the full text of the Covenant, see Gardiner, *Constitutional Documents of the Puritan Revolution, 1628–1660*, pp. 54–64.
[47] See Burrell, pp. 338–50.
[48] See Haller, *The Rise of Puritanism*, especially pp. 173–225.

to the soul of the believer could have any effect on his salvation. Furthermore, this liberty of the Christian implied that all believing Christians were equal before God. All men were equal because they all sprang from a single root, Adam; as a consequence of Adam's sin, all men were born into sin; consequently, all were equally incapable of righteousness, of fulfilling the law. All men are totally depraved. All could be justly damned. But God in his mercy has separated by his choice some to be regenerated and saved. This "saving remnant" may be regarded as a spiritual aristocracy in relation to the rest of mankind, but they, in turn, are equal among themselves. All Christians are equally kings and priests. Nevertheless, for present purposes—living a Christian life, glorifying God—some external discipline is necessary, both in Church and State.

The Congregationalists rejected the Presbyterian church discipline. They could not accept (as a permanent settlement) a church that included both the regenerate and the unregenerate, a church that required all to conform to its discipline. The Christian must be free to reject all externals incompatible with his conscience. Nevertheless, all admitted that Christians were required to obey their governments as long as their obedience did not conflict with obedience to God. God's commands were revealed to the Congregationalist in the believer's reading of the Bible and in the believer's conscience.

The Congregationalists took the freedom of Christians and their equality seriously. A church could only be a group of Christians united by a voluntary agreement. According to Robert Browne: "Christians are a companie or number of beleeuers, which by a willing couenaunt made with their God, are vnder the gouvernement of God and Christ and keepe his Lawes in one holie communion." [49] The church is gathered out of the mass of men by God's promises, his covenant, "Sec-

[49] Robert Browne, *Booke which showeth the Life and Manners of all True Christians* (p. 3), in Walker, p. 19.

ondlie by a couenant and condicion made on our behalfe,"
and these agreements are sealed by the sacrament of baptism.[50]

"We must offer and geue vp our selues to be of the church
and people of God." We must also offer up our children, and
others who are under age (provided that they are in our household and we have full power over them). "We must make profession, that we are his people, by submitting our selues to his
lawes and gouernement." [51]

Governors enter into their callings by assurance of their gifts
(for all, their knowledge and godliness, for some, age or birth);
by God's special charge (to further his kingdom by edifying
others, also by public or private revelation); and by agreement
of men. Browne goes on to ask,

> *what agreement must there be of men?*
> For Church gouvernours, there must be an agreement of the
> church.
> For ciuil Magistrates, there must be an agreement of the people
> or Common welth.
> For Housholders, there must be an agreement of the hous-
> houldes.[52]

For Browne, and for those (e.g., Henry Barrowe, John
Greenwood, John Robinson, John Smith) who thought similarly, societies, whether of Christians or of men, were necessarily gathered, formed by the agreements of men. (Browne
even distinguishes between the agreement that each Christian
makes as an individual to follow a pastor who is planting or
establishing a church, and the agreement, by an election, of an
established church to fill a vacant pastorate.)

Separate such a congregation from the Church of England,
it will establish itself as a church by making an agreement—a
church covenant. Separate such a group of men from an estab-

[50] *Ibid.*, Question 36 (p. 20), Walker, p. 18.
[51] *Ibid.*, Question 38 (p. 22), Walker, p. 20.
[52] *Ibid.*, Question 117 (p. 72), Walker, p. 25. The necessity of an agreement of
the household applies only to voluntary and not to natural relations.

lished society—they could not, after all, avoid the fact that there was an established government in England—send them, for example, from the Old World to the New, from old England to New England, and they will make the Mayflower Compact:

We, whose names are underwritten, the Loyal subjects of our dread Sovereign Lord King *James,* . . . Do by these Presents, solemnly and mutually in the Presence of God and one another, covenant and combine ourselves into a civil Body Politick.[53]

The theory that human societies were founded (at least in part) upon human agreements was not confined to the Brownists. Richard Hooker, that learned and judicious Anglican divine, referred to the possibility of such agreements when he argued that the law of nature and reason binds men "absolutely even as they are men, although they have never any settled fellowship, never any solemn agreement amongst themselves what to do or not to do." [54] But the law of nature and reason is not sufficient for men to live by, without some established law and society. Man has a natural tendency toward society because it is only in society that his needs are satisfied, that his defects are supplied. Man alone is not self-sufficient. This is the cause of political societies, and therefore governments and laws.

Two foundations there are which bear up public societies; the one, a natural inclination, whereby all men desire sociable life and fellowship; the other, an order expressly or secretly agreed upon touching the manner of their union in living together.[55]

---

[53] Poore, Part I, p. 931. See Osgood, p. 24:
"Transfer the idea of compact from ecclesiastical to political relations, and we have the underlying thought which is to be found in all the references made to government by the Puritan divines. The analogy between the gathering of a church and the formation of a corporation or state was a favorite one with them. In 1639 the clergy said: 'Every city is united by some covenant among themselves; the citizens are received into *jus civitatis,* or right of city privileges by some oath.' [See *Apologie* of the Churches of New England . . . touching the covenant (London, 1643)]."
[54] Hooker, *Of the laws of Ecclesiastical Polity,* I. x. 1, in *Works,* I, 184.
[55] *Ibid.*

Men are naturally sociable—indeed, they are all born into a natural society, that of the family. But in spite of this natural sociability, there was no natural peace and concord among men:

> If therefore when there was but as yet one only family in the world, no means of instruction, human or divine could prevent effusion of blood [Gen. iv. 8]; how could it be chosen but that where families were multiplied and increased upon earth, after separation each providing for itself, envy, strife, contention and violence must grow amongst them? For hath not Nature furnished man with wit and valour, as it were with armour, which may be used as well unto extreme evil as good? Yea, were they not used by the rest of the world unto evil; unto the contrary only by Seth, Enoch, and those few the rest in that line? [Gen. vi. 5; Gen. v.] We all make complaint of the iniquity of our times: not unjustly; for the days are evil. But compare them with those times wherein there were no civil societies, with those times wherein there was as yet no manner of public regiment established, with those times wherein there were not above eight persons righteous living upon the face of the earth [2 Pet. ii. 5]; and we have surely good cause to think that God hath blessed us exceedingly, and hath made us behold most happy days.
>
> [4.] To take away all such mutual grievances, injuries, and wrongs, there was no way but only by growing unto composition and agreement amongst themselves, by ordaining some kind of government public, and by yielding themselves subject thereunto; that unto whom they granted authority to rule and govern, by them the peace, tranquillity, and happy estate of the rest might be procured.[56]

Hooker believed that there were natural societies—individual families—in which the father is the ruler. He also was willing to admit that there is a natural right of the noble, wise, and virtuous to govern the naturally servile; "Nevertheless for manifestation of this their right, and men's more peaceable contentment on both sides, the assent of them who are to be governed seemeth necessary." To avoid the endless "envy, strife, contention and violence" of this state of nature, men

[56] *Ibid.*, I. x. 3–4, pp. 186–87.

(i.e., patriarchs, *patres familiarum*) agreed to some kind of government. Before this they had no obligation to obey anyone else; they might resist violence with violence; no man had a right to govern another without his consent because no man had the right to define his own authority. From this situation men were delivered either by their own consent to a public regiment, a result of "deliberate advice, consultation, and composition between men, judging it convenient and behoveful," or else by the immediate appointment of God.[57]

Voluntary agreement or consent could be the original source and the justification of society for Anglicans as well as for Separatists. This is not to say that their theories were identical. Congregationalism emphasized the immediate consent of the believer to the organization of church and state and to the governing authorities he was establishing in each. Anglicanism emphasized the implied consent of the Christian subject to his society and its historical constitution both civil and ecclesiastical. The point is that it was assumed by all that the consent of the ruled justified the exercise of government over him by the rulers. The language of natural equality, man's agreement, compact, covenant, and the establishing of authority to govern (by making and enforcing laws) was common to all, Presbyterian as well as Independent and Anglican.[58]

Sovereignty by Institution

Hobbes accepted the individualist assumptions and the legal terminology of the covenant argument: to be obliged to obey

[57] *Ibid.*, pp. 187–88.

[58] *Cf.* Samuel Rutherford, *Lex, Rex* (1644), Question II (quoted from Woodhouse, pp. 200–1):

"As domestic society is by nature's instinct, so is civil society natural *in radice,* in the root, and voluntary *in modo,* in the manner of coalescing. . . .

"We are to distinguish betwixt a power of government, and a power of government by magistracy. That we defend ourselves from violence by violence, is a consequent of unbroken and sinless nature; but that we defend ourselves by devolving our power over in the hands of one or more rulers, seemeth rather positively moral than natural, except that it is natural for the child to expect

an authority, one must have covenanted to obey. From them he drew an argument for absolute rather than limited government; the authority to which one owes obedience is, if correctly constructed and properly understood, an absolute sovereign. Hobbes argued that absolute power was based on universal consent. The principles of absolute sovereignty and of universal consent are both required to explain the existence of a society and its powers. Both requirements are satisfied by either of the methods that Hobbes offers of constructing societies: institution and acquisition.

Sovereignty is constructed by institution when a multitude of men unite themselves into a single body politic. This is done when a number of men, instead of having a number of wills, have a single will, i.e., when the will of one man or the will of one council (that is, a majority vote of that council) is taken for the will of each and every one of the multitude no matter what his actual individual will may be.[59]

This union is not a merely temporary agreement among themselves for a single action or a limited purpose, but something more. The concept of union and the method of achieving it and its implications were developed by Hobbes from the *Elements of Law* to *Leviathan*.

According to the earlier versions (the *Elements of Law, De Cive*),

The making of union consisteth in this, that every man by covenant oblige himself to some one and the same man, or to some one and the same council, by them all named and determined, to do those

help against violence, from his father. For which cause I judge . . . that princedom, empire, kingdom, or jurisdiction hath its rise from a positive and secondary law of nations, and not from the law of pure nature. The law saith, there is no law of nature agreeing to all living creatures for superiority; for by no reason in nature hath a boar dominion over a boar, a lion over a lion, a dragon over a dragon, a bull over a bull. And if all men be born equally free (as I hope to prove), there is no reason in nature why one man should be king and lord over another; therefore . . . I conceive all jurisdiction of man over man to be, as it were, artificial and positive, and that it inferreth some servitude whereof nature from the womb hath freed us, if you except that subjection of children to parents, and the wife to the husband."

[59] *Elements of Law* (I. xii. 8, II. i. 3), pp. 63, 109; *De Cive* (v. 6–7), *EW* II, 68.

actions, which the said man or council shall command them to do; and to do no action which he or they shall forbid, or command them not to do.[60]

In the case of a council, there is a stipulation that the command of the majority is to be held to be the command of the council. A *union* only exists when a number of men are obliged to some known and determined man or men. The obligation of the citizen arises from his covenant to subject his will to the command of the sovereign.[61] According to this account, each individual must covenant to allow the will of someone else to be taken for his will. The first step is then a concord—a unanimous agreement to erect a union by allowing either the will of a majority of them (a democracy), or the will of a majority of a named group (an aristocracy), or the will of a single man (monarchy), "to involve and be taken for the wills of every man." [62] But since monarchy and aristocracy both require an election of some individual or individuals out of the whole number, and such an election would have to be concluded by a majority vote before either an aristocracy or a monarchy could come into being, a democracy must first exist, since "where the votes of the major part involve the votes of the rest, there is actually a democracy." [63] This original democracy is made sovereign by the covenants of individual men, i.e., "every man with every man, for and in consideration of the benefit of his own peace and defence, covenanteth to stand to and obey, whatsoever the major part of their whole number, or the major part of such a number of them, as shall be pleased to assemble at a certain time and place, shall determine, and command." [64]

---

[60] *Elements of Law* (I. xix. 7), p. 103. *Cf. De Cive* (v. 6–9), *EW* II, 68–69, where Hobbes emphasizes the creation of a single will for a number of men.
[61] *Elements of Law* (I. xix. 7), p. 104; *De Cive* (v. 7), *EW* II, 68.
[62] *Elements of Law* (II. i. 3), p. 109.
[63] *Ibid.* (II. ii. 1), p. 118. Hobbes presumes that there will be no unanimous choice. *Cf. De Cive* (vii. 8, 11), *EW* II, 99, 100, where an original democracy is assumed, and *De Cive* (vii. 5), *EW* II, 96–97: "Those who met together with intention to erect a city, were almost in the very act of meeting, a democracy."
[64] *Elements of Law* (II. ii. 2), p. 119.

Hobbes defined the origin of political obligation as a sub-mission—subjecting one's own will to the will of another. (A society exists where a number of men are subject to a single will.) But since there is no designated sovereign to whom men may submit, Hobbes turns the original creation of a society into a paradox by describing their covenant of submission (a prom-ise to obey) as a covenant of each with each to create a union which each promises to obey, i.e., they oblige themselves to submit to an authority which only exists as the result of their submission. Hobbes does not make a double covenant out of this. He never says that the covenanters create a union by a covenant of each with each, to which union each individually obliges himself by a subsequent covenant. Apparently the sov-ereign is something like a third-party beneficiary of their con-tracts; each obliges himself to the sovereign by a donation, or conveyance of right, as well as obliging himself to his fellow citizens by covenant.

But though a government be constituted by the contracts of par-ticular men with particulars, yet its right depends not on that obliga-tion only; there is another tie also towards him who commands. For each citizen compacting with his fellow, says thus: *I convey my right on this party, upon condition that you pass yours to the same:* by which means, that right which every man had before to use his faculties to his own advantage, is now wholly translated on some certain man or council for the common benefit. Wherefore what by the mutual contracts each one hath made with the other, what by the donation of right which every man is bound to ratify to him that commands, the government is upheld by a double obligation from the citizens; first, that which is due to their fellow-citizens; next, that which they owe to their prince [*imperantem*]. Wherefore no subjects, how many soever they be, can with any right despoil him who bears the chief rule of his authority, even without his own consent.[65]

Each makes his submission to the body politic by his covenant, which is a covenant to obey, however much that covenant may seem to create only an obligation to submit.

[65] *De Cive* (vi. 20), *EW* II, 91–92; *LW* II, 234.

Hobbes gives substantially the same account of sovereignty by institution in *Leviathan,* but he has improved it in several ways. The theory of personation provides a general explanation of "systems"—organized groups, or "bodies politic." The unity of a system is the unity of its representative; the representative —a single man or a council—impersonates the whole group. The representative is severally authorized by each member of the group to act in his name. The state is a special case of this class of "systems"; the sovereign is a special case of an actor or representative, the case in which the authorization is general and unlimited—"owning all the actions the Representer doth." [66]

The covenants of each with each are restated as covenants of authorization. A common power is erected by the appointment of a Representative, authorized by each man to act for him in things concerning the common peace and safety. This unification into a single system is "made by Covenant of every man with every man, in such manner, as if every man should say to every man, *I Authorise and give up my Right of Governing my selfe, to this Man, or to this Assembly of men, on this condition, that thou give up thy Right to him, and Authorise all his Actions in like manner.*" [67]

This formula seems to be a conditional authorization. Each authorizes a determinate person provided that the others do the same. This eliminates the priority of any form of government; an original democratic assembly to choose the determinate persons to govern, is unnecessary when the government already has been determined by the covenants of each with each. The advantages of this form are that: (1) it stipulates the person to whom the author obliges himself at the same time as it creates the obligation; (2) it generalizes the covenant so that it is capable of creating any of the forms of government; (3) it

[66] *Leviathan* (16), p. 126.
[67] *Ibid.* (17), pp. 131–32. For another account of Hobbes's development emphasizing authorization even more strongly, see Pitkin, pp. 328–40, 902–18; see especially pp. 907–13.

establishes the society upon the unanimous agreement of those who join.

By the device of mutual covenants of authorization of a representative person, Hobbes achieves the difficult (some would say impossible) and paradoxical result of creating an absolute and unlimited sovereign on the basis of the consents of the subjects at the same time that the community is created. Because the creation of the community and the creation of the sovereign are accomplished by the same act, the community only exists by virtue of the existence of the sovereign, and the community can only act through its representative, the sovereign. Thus, the existence of a communal corporation independent of the sovereign is avoided. As a consequence, there is no person who can challenge the sovereign's authority.

Unfortunately this is not the only formulation of sovereignty by institution. At the beginning of Chapter XVIII, *Of the* RIGHTS *of Soveraignes by Institution* (i.e., on the next page), Hobbes gives another description of the act of instituting a commonwealth:

A *Common-wealth* is said to be *Instituted,* when a *Multitude* of men do Agree, and *Covenant, every one, with every one,* that to whatsoever *Man,* or *Assembly of Men,* shall be given by the major part, the *Right* to *Present* the Person of them all, (that is to say, to be their *Representative;*) every one, as well he that *Voted for it,* as he that *Voted against it,* shall *Authorise* all the Actions and Judgements, of that Man, or Assembly of men, in the same manner, as if they were his own, to the end to live peaceably amongst themselves, and be protected against other men.[68]

This formulation is derived from Hobbes's former contention that there had to be an original democracy. The agreement to appoint a representative by majority vote forms the society. But if this is the case, then the society must already be a democracy when it appoints the representative by majority vote. For if it had no representative at all, it would not be a society. If

[68] *Leviathan* (18), p. 133. In the first edition the two formulations occur on p. 87 and p. 88.

Hobbes supposed that this formulation was consistent with that of Chapter XVII, he went out of his way to avoid making it appear so. As it stands, it could be a special case, the implied appointment of a democracy, especially an original democracy.

Or alternatively, the formula could mean that a society can be formed by the agreement to appoint a representative. This has very great defects: (1) it creates a political society without the authorization of a determinate person; (2) a political obligation (unnecessarily, I think) is created in spite of the negative votes of a minority.

It seems to me that there is a third alternative explanation, more compelling than either of these. When Hobbes dropped the notion of an original democracy and reformulated the covenant to allow the original authorization of any form of government, he overlooked this inconsistent passage. This oversight may have occurred partly because the second formula seems to widen rather than restrict the original covenants since it avoids the necessity for a unanimous authorization. Hobbes's error was doubly unfortunate; the requirement of unanimity is tautological: those who do not authorize the representative do not become members of the society at the original authorization.

Sovereignty by Acquisition

In the state of nature it would be advantageous to form even a small society. A small group (perhaps as few as ten) would be secure against the attack of isolated individuals and it would be capable of enlarging itself by conquering others.[69] The formation of such a group should precipitate the formation of counter-groups of at least the same size. The danger to the unorgan-

[69] Hobbes is not precise about the minimum size of a society. It cannot be too small; two or three individuals are not enough. *De Cive* (v. 3), *EW* II, 65. But, *cf. Elements of Law* (II. iii. 2), p. 128, where Hobbes says that two men in a relation of master and servant make a small body politic. An extended family is sufficient. See *De Cive* (ix. 10, vi. 15), *EW* II, 121–22, 84; *Elements of Law* (II. iv. 10), p. 135.

ized and the possibility of discovering a way to reduce that danger have both been increased, as has the fear of those not in the society. The process of increase in the size of societies by either conquest or agreement would continue until the point was reached at which the increase in size of any one society no longer gave it such a clear superiority to the others that they could not defend themselves successfully. At that point, no group would be faced with the alternative of being conquered or instituting a larger society.

Until men live in societies so large, so well organized, and so well defended that each society must regard the outcome of a war against another society as uncertain, men are faced with the alternative: to fight or to surrender. Hobbes argues that both lead to the same result. To fight, men must organize a society for their defense—commonwealth by institution. To surrender is to submit to the conqueror—commonwealth by acquisition.

By conquest the victor gains power, physical control, over the vanquished. By the right of nature every man has a right to everything, so that the conquest is justified or at least justifiable. The conqueror may do with the conquered whatever he thinks necessary: he may turn him loose (perhaps irrationally but charitably); he may imprison him; he may kill him without violating the law of nature if this seems the only course consistent with his own safety. To kill for a reason, not from blood lust or cruelty, is justified by the right of nature in this situation.

A political relationship is not established by physical conquest, nor by the conqueror's grant of life to the conquered; it is created by the consent of the vanquished man, by his submission to the conqueror. He takes the political obligation upon himself by promising to obey. There is a contractual relationship between the victor and the vanquished, the lord or master and the servant, "In which contract, the good which the vanquished or inferior in strength doth receive, is the grant of his life, which by the right of war in the natural state of men he might have been deprived of; but the good which he promises, is his service and obedience." [70] In this contract, one party, the servant, makes a covenant to obey the other party, the lord, but the lord does not make any promises to the servant; he does not make a covenant to him. His part of the contract consists not in making a promise but in a performance—the granting of certain benefits. This performance consists in more than just a grant of life:

> Every one that is taken in the war, and hath his life spared him, is not supposed to have contracted with his lord; for every one is not trusted with so much of his natural liberty, as to be able, if he desired it, either to fly away, or quit his service, or contrive any mischief to his lord. . . . The obligation therefore of a *servant* to his *lord,* ariseth not from a simple grant of his life; but from hence rather, that he keeps him not bound or imprisoned. For all obligation derives from contract [*ex pacto,* i.e., from covenant]; but where there is not trust there can be no contract [*pactum*], as appears by chap. ii, art. 9; where a compact is defined to be the promise of him who is trusted. There is therefore a confidence and trust which accompanies the benefit of pardoned life, whereby the *lord* affords him his corporal liberty; so that if no obligation nor bonds of contract had happened, he might not only have made his escape, but also have killed his lord who was the preserver of his life.[71]

Hobbes distinguishes sovereignty by acquisition from sovereignty by institution only to assimilate them to each other. The result—a sovereign—is the same regardless of the motiva-

---

[70] *De Cive* (viii. 1), *EW* II, 109. *Cf. Elements of Law* (II. iii. 2), pp. 127–28: "For where every man (as it happeneth in this case) hath right to all things, there needs no more for the making of said right effectual, but a covenant from him that is overcome, not to resist him that overcometh. And thus cometh the victor to have a right of absolute dominion over the conquered."

[71] *De Cive* (viii. 2–3), *EW* II, 109–10; *LW* II, 250–51. In this passage, both "contract" and "compact" have been translated from the Latin *pactum,* i.e., covenant. The definition referred to is the definition of covenant; *De Cive* (ii. 9), *EW* II, 20: "where there is credit given, either to one or both, there the party trusted promiseth after-performance; and this kind of promise is called a *covenant* [*pactum*]." *Cf. Leviathan* (20), pp. 155–56; *Elements of Law* (II. iii. 3), p. 128.

tion of the subjects. All subjects in both cases are bound because they have consented; they have obliged themselves by covenant to each other or to the sovereign. Hobbes underscores the element of consent in sovereignty by acquisition:

It is not therefore the Victory, that giveth the right of Dominion over the Vanquished, but his own Covenant. Nor is he obliged because he is Conquered; that is to say, beaten, and taken, or put to flight; but because he cometh in and Submitteth to the Victor; Nor is the Victor obliged by an enemies rendring himselfe, (without promise of life,) to spare him for this his yeelding to discretion; which obliges not the Victor longer, than in his own discretion hee shall think fit.[72]

Although the subject is bound, the sovereign is free. The sovereign has made no promises to the subjects individually or collectively. The sovereign could not have covenanted with the subjects collectively because before the institution they were a multitude as yet "not one Person"; if the instituted sovereign had covenanted with each individual the covenants would be void after the institution—"What act soever can be pretended by any one of them for breach thereof, is the act both of himselfe, and of all the rest, because done in the Person, and by the Right of every one of them in particular." [73] Furthermore, there is no judge of the claim that the sovereign has broken his covenant (other than the parties to the dispute). Such a claim therefore involves a return to the state of nature. In the alternative case, the sovereign by conquest makes no covenant, although he accepts the covenants of others. Hobbes assimilates the position of the sovereign by acquisition to that of the sovereign by institution. Covenants made by the victor to the conquered are unnecessary under the circumstances, i.e., counter-factual, whereas those of the instituted sovereign are (where possible) void.[74]

[72] *Leviathan* (20), p. 156. [73] *Ibid.* (18), p. 134.
[74] It is interesting to note that Hobbes does not discuss the possibility that the victor might make covenants with some and not with others, in other words, that the terms of surrender might differ, some being allowed privileges that others were denied. Presumably this is excluded by the law of nature con-

Sovereignty by institution comes first for Hobbes, then, partly because it can be used as a model in which the sovereign makes no promises (because it does not exist as sovereign while promises are being made). Institution has, I think, a second function. A conqueror must be either a single individual or the leader of an organized group—an army. Since it is hard to argue that anyone would stay conquered in a state of nature, in which the conquered and the conqueror are both single presumably equal individuals, Hobbes has to provide a method by which organized groups capable of conquering others could come into existence. This method is institution: institution is the model method because it is rational; it does not need the historical occurrences of conquest or generation but only the rational element common to all three, i.e., consent. Because institution can be shown to be the same as conquest, Hobbes can argue that both sorts of sovereign are absolute and that in both cases the subject is bound by his own consent. Acquisition is thereby legitimized while institution is shown to be absolute.

Institution precedes acquisition because it provides an answer to the question: how did the leader of this conquering army have a right to rule his own army? The application to the conquest of England by William of Normandy is obvious.[75] Institution provided Hobbes with a possible answer to the question: "How did the leader of the conquering army have a right to command his followers?" other than the answer "by the right of conquest," an answer implying that men are not equal, that there are natural superiors and inferiors.

---

cerning equality. For the opinion that Hobbes attempts to argue that the sovereign is not a party to a covenant see Warrender, *The Political Philosophy of Hobbes,* pp. 125–40. Warrender confuses covenant and contract and therefore argues that Hobbes could not legitimately say that his sovereign by acquisition is not a party to a covenant. This is repeated by Pitkin, pp. 907, 914. The argument above admits that the sovereign by acquisition is necessarily a party to a contract but not that he covenants.

[75] Hobbes, like the Levellers and unlike those, e.g., Sir Edward Coke, who held that the English constitution as established had existed from time out of mind, casually affirms that William (the Conqueror) had conquered England. See *Leviathan* (24), p. 190; *Behemoth* (Dialogue 2), p. 71; and Pocock, pp. 148–70.

Hobbes was a man who valued peace so highly that he thought that the scientific description of war, its frightfulness, and of the causes of war would motivate men to seek to avoid it. It would have been paradoxical of him to have argued that society, and therefore peace, could only be brought about by conquest. Institution provides a means to avoid war and to avoid conquest. The fear of force, the fear of conquest, is a sufficient motive for the creation of society—but if this motive is insufficient or unsuccessful, then society will come about anyhow; men will be forced to submit to him who threatens them if they do not organize themselves against that threat. Because sovereignty by institution is the model, Hobbes can emphasize the consent of the conquered rather than the power of the conqueror. Institution and acquisition may each be regarded as a special case of the other. In submitting to the conqueror men authorize and institute as sovereign the threatening power; in instituting a sovereign men create a power sufficient to keep them in awe, a self-conquest.

There is another case of "natural dominion" recognized by Hobbes, paternal dominion. His contemporaries probably regarded the paternal dominion of the head of a family over his wife, his children and his servants as obvious and natural. Their knowledge of history, sacred and profane (especially Roman), supported their patriarchal practices. Filmer's statement of this position was more influential in the 1680s than it had been in the 1640s. Sir Robert Filmer, in spite of his "no small content" with Hobbes's conclusions "about the rights of exercising government, . . . cannot agree to his means of acquiring it." [76] Hobbes had put things backward by assuming that men sprang from the earth like mushrooms; deny this, and the state of nature with its right of nature is also denied:

I cannot understand how this right of nature can be conceived without imagining a company of men at the very first to have been all created together without any dependency one of another, or

[76] Filmer, p. 239.

as mushrooms (*fungorum more*) they all on a sudden were sprung out of the earth without any obligation one to another, as Mr. Hobbes's words are in his book *De Cive,* chapter 8, section 3: the scripture teacheth us otherwise, that all men came by succession, and generation from one man: we must not deny the truth of the history of the creation.[77]

All men are derived from a single source—the first man, created by God, Adam. Eve was made from Adam's flesh and subjected to him. Adam had dominion over his posterity by right of fatherhood and his posterity succeeded to this natural and inalienable right with which Adam was endowed by his Creator:

> For as Adam was lord of his children, so his children under him had a command over their own children, but still with subordination to the first parent who is lord paramount over his children's children to all generations, as being the grandfather of his people.
>
> I see not then, how the children of Adam, or of any man else, can be free from subjection to their parents. And this subordination of children is the fountain of all regal authority, by the ordination of God himself.[78]

All men are born into families, and consequently they are born into subordination to the heads of families. Since this has been true of every human being since Adam, it follows that, far from being born free, men are born into the bonds of obligation.[79]

Filmer's discontent with Hobbes's explanation of the way sovereignty is acquired was well founded, for Hobbes explicitly denies the cogency of Filmer's argument.

"Socrates *is a man, and therefore a living creature,* is right reasoning . . ." because the unstated minor premise, "a man is a living creature" is part of the definition of man:

> And this, *Sophronicus is Socrates' father, and therefore his lord,* is perhaps a true inference, but not evident; because the word

---

[77] *Ibid.,* p. 241.   [78] *Ibid.,* p. 57.
[79] *Cf.* Locke, *Second Treatise,* chap. vi, sec. 61; Laslett ed., p. 326. Men are "born free" according to Locke not in act but in potentiality (and in right). "Thus we are *born Free,* as we are born Rational; not that we have actually the exercise of either: Age that brings one, brings with it the other too."

lord is not in the definition of *a father:* wherefore it is necessary, to make it more evident, that the connexion of *father* and *lord* be somewhat unfolded. Those that have hitherto endeavoured to prove the dominion of a parent over his children, have brought no other argument than that of *generation;* as if it were of itself evident, that what is begotten by me is mine; just as if a man should think, that because there is a triangle, it appears presently, without any further discourse that its angles are equal to two right.[80]

On Hobbes's analysis, the right of the father is much less clear than that the sum of the angles of a triangle is two right angles. Generation gives the male parent no greater right than the female parent; for the generation of a child requires both of them. In which parent is dominion to lie? Not in both, for no one can have two masters. The usual position is that the child belongs to the father, because of the pre-eminence of the male sex. Although this is the ordinary situation in established societies—most societies are dominated by males—in the state of nature it is not the case that every man is superior to any woman. Furthermore, the evidence supports the contention that not all societies have been dominated by men; there have been societies controlled by women, viz., the Amazons, and there had been female rulers (e.g., Elizabeth of England) within Hobbes's memory. In fact, in a state of nature, a child is born into the power of its mother. Its life is hers to dispose of, for she may preserve it or expose it.[81] "Add also, that in the state of nature it cannot be known who is the *father,* but by the testimony of the *mother;* the child therefore is his whose the mother will have it, and therefore her's." [82]

If the mother abandons the child, she abandons her right to it as well. Whoever preserves the child, acquires the same dominion over it as the mother had. "Now the preserved oweth all to the preserver, whether in regard to his education as to a *mother,* or of his service as to a *lord.*" [83] If the mother is or be-

---

[80] *De Cive* (ix. 1), *EW* II, 114–15.
[81] *Elements of Law* (II. iv. 1–3, 5), pp. 131–33; *De Cive* (ix. 1–3), *EW* II, 114–17; *Leviathan* (20), pp. 153–55.
[82] *De Cive* (ix. 3), *EW* II, 116–17.   [83] *Ibid.* (ix. 4), *EW* II, 117.

comes a subject of another, then the child also is a subject of that other. The rights of parents, married or unmarried, in societies are determined by the laws within those societies. Where the laws permit, or in the state of nature, the dominion over the child may be specified by covenant. Men and women may make covenants of cohabitation or of copulation in which the rights to the offspring are specified. The Amazons covenanted that the father should have the males while they kept the females.[84] Marriage is a special case of a covenant of cohabitation, a "society for all things." One of the partners is subjected to the other by the marriage agreement. A society is established, therefore one must rule: either the man or the woman. Usually the husband rules "but because sometimes the government may belong to the wife only, sometimes also the dominion over the children shall be in her only; as in the case of a sovereign queen, there is no reason that her marriage should take from her the dominion over her children." [85]

Apparently the argument *Sophronicus is Socrates' father and therefore his lord* is a good deal less evident than *the sum of the angles of a triangle is 180°*. Unlike the latter, which is true for all triangles, the former is true if (a) the father is also the preserver of the child; (b) the father is so entitled by the agreement of the mother; (c) the father is also the master of the mother; or (d) the father is so entitled by the civil laws of a society.

Is the child to be regarded as the property of his preserver or master? The argument so far seems to have treated the child as a head of livestock rather than a human being. Does the child have any obligation to its parents, to its preservers? If it does, is this obligation based merely upon the fact that it is within the power of someone else? Since the child owes its life to its preserver, it ought to obey that preserver, no obligation

[84] *Elements of Law* (II. iv. 5), p. 133; *De Cive* (ix. 6), *EW* II, 118; *Leviathan* (20), p. 154.
[85] *Elements of Law* (II. iv. 7), pp. 133–34; *De Cive* (ix. 4–6), *EW* II, 117–18; *Leviathan* (20), pp. 154–55.

being owed to a non-preserving parent. "For it ought to obey him by whom it is preserved; because preservation of life being the end, for which one man becomes subject to another, every man is supposed to promise obedience, to him, in whose power it is to save, or destroy him." [86] In other words, the dominion is derived not from the generation of the child, "but from the Childs Consent, either expresse, or by other sufficient arguments declared." [87]

There are, Hobbes appears to be saying, two possible ways of deriving the obligation of children from their own consent. The child may expressly consent; this would be a consent in a form similar to the covenant by which a servant subjects himself to a lord. Alternatively, the child's consent may be declared by other sufficient arguments. The child may act in a way that implies that it has consented; by accepting the benefits offered by its preserver, the child sufficiently declares, by its own act, its consent. It obliges itself by accepting benefits—according to the laws of nature concerning gratitude.[88] Furthermore, there is a presumption that, where a child is within the power of another to preserve or destroy, and that other preserves the child rather than destroying it, that child has consented to obey. Hobbes even goes so far as to argue that there is a presumption of a promise to obey.[89]

The obligations of children are neither natural nor an ex-

---

[86] *Leviathan* (20), pp. 154-55.   [87] *Ibid.*, p. 153.

[88] See Warrender, *The Political Philosophy of Hobbes*, p. 136.

[89] *Elements of Law* (II. iv. 3), p. 132: "And though the child thus preserved, do in time acquire strength, whereby he might pretend equality with him or her that hath preserved him, yet shall that pretence be thought unreasonable, both because his strength was the gift of him, against whom he pretendeth; and also because it is to be presumed, that he which giveth sustenance to another, whereby to strengthen him, hath received a promise of obedience in consideration thereof."

De Cive (ix. 3), *EW* II, 116, is substantially similar: "If therefore she [the mother] breed him [the child], because the state of nature is the state of war, she is supposed to bring him up on this condition; that being grown to full age he become not her enemy; which is, that he obey her." Since every one acts for his own good, "it cannot be understood that any man hath on such terms afforded life to another, that he might both get strength by his years, and at once become an enemy."

ception to Hobbes's general position. These obligations are as artificial and as consensual as the obligations of citizens or of subjects. Children are obliged: (1) by their express consent (a covenant to obey); or (2) by acts amounting to consent (either by acts signifying a promise of obedience in return for sustenance, or by the acceptance of benefits which impose an obligation of gratitude). There is a presumption that the child has consented; this presumption is apparently to be regarded as an irrebuttable presumption of law: since the supposition that no one sustains or breeds his own enemy is a presumption of reason, all cases to the contrary must be regarded as cases of breach of obligation.[90]

Children stand in precisely the same relation to parents (provided that their parents are not members of a society) as servants stand to their lords, subjects to their rulers, the conquered to the conqueror, and citizens to the city. In the list of societies, various social relations between men and women must be included. Marriage, concubinage, and cohabitation are social arrangements involving agreements between the parties. Some forms of these agreements, especially those that are relatively more permanent, will involve either the setting up of a small society by institution or the subjection of one party to the other—a society by acquisition. The most natural of societies, the family, is composed of relationships based upon the same principle as the most artificial of instituted commonwealths; that principle is the consent of the parties. That the alternative to

[90] But Hobbes disliked irrebuttable presumptions; see *Leviathan* (26), pp. 214–15. The solution of an implied contract (either in law or in fact) merely raises the problem of consent in another form. *Cf. De Cive* (ix. 7–8), *EW* II, 119. A son is freed from bondage in the same manner as a subject or a servant (emancipation or manumission). The natural consequence of this freedom from the lord's power is the reduction of the honor paid to the father or former master (honor being the deference paid to those one thinks powerful). But the enfranchiser did not intend to make the enfranchised person his equal. "It must therefore be ever understood, that he who is freed from subjection, whether he be a *servant, son* or some *colony,* doth promise all those external signs at least, whereby superiors used to be honoured by their inferiors. From whence it follows, that the precept of *honouring our parents,* belongs to the law of nature, not only under the title of *gratitude,* but also of *agreement.*"

consenting to obey is present or future (probable) death does not invalidate the consent given. Such a consent is free although forced; terror of the alternative merely increases the rationality of consenting. For Hobbes the submission of the conquered, motivated by the fear of death, is equivalent to the submission of the child to be inferred from his acceptance of the means of life. (Is the choice more illusory in one case than in the other?) [91]

A family is a small society. The head of a family who has no earthly superior is a sovereign.

> By this it appears, that a great Family if it be not part of some Common-wealth, is of it self, as to the Rights of Soveraignty, a little Monarchy; whether that Family consist of a man and his children; or of a man and his servants; or of a man, and his children, and servants together: wherein the Father or Master is the Soveraign.[92]

This is true if the family is large enough to protect itself from aggression—large enough so that it cannot be subdued without the hazard of war.[93] No new relations are required to transform the family into a political society. Aristotle distinguished the political relationship from those of the family: husband-wife, parents-children, master-servants.[94] Hobbes does not distinguish these societies, provided only that the family be large enough to protect itself.

The state of nature is an imaginary political space in which societies may be formed. The concept of a state of nature, like the concept of space, is mainly negative; it is the description of the result achieved when the social world is imagined to be destroyed. The state of nature is what is not a society. The concept enables Hobbes to make a clear disjunction between the social and the non-social. The characteristics of the non-social

[91] *De Cive* (i. 14, ii. 16), *EW* II, 12–13, 23–24; *Leviathan* (14), p. 107; *Elements of Law* (I. xv. 13), p. 79.

[92] *Leviathan* (20), p. 157.

[93] *Ibid.*; *De Cive* (ix. 10), *EW* II, 121–22; *Elements of Law* (II. iv. 10), p. 135.

[94] *Politics* 1252 a–1255 b, pp. 1–18.

(the state of nature) are the negations of the characteristics of the social. In the state of nature there is no society, no security of person or property (except what each single person can provide), no redress against force except self-help, no guarantee that others will keep their agreements, no machinery, no arts, no sciences; nothing can exist that requires more than minimum human cooperation.

Hobbes regards all situations in which there is no known authorized sovereign, competent to make and enforce rules upon all persons (natural and artificial) in that situation, as actual or incipient states of nature. As long as there is no single (earthly) sovereign, i.e., as long as there are at least two independent societies, a state of nature must continue to exist. International relations are relations in a state of nature. A state of nature is only excluded where there is an effective sovereign; i.e., the state of nature is excluded by an organized society—at the level of family, tribe, city, or nation. Nevertheless, the residue of anarchy and insecurity exists wherever or whenever the effective control of the society begins to weaken. In areas remote from the power of the sovereign, bandits lurk. In the interstices of the society, psychological as well as physical, in the contempt of law-enforcing power as well as in the darkened back-alley, the state of nature is evident.

Nevertheless (again like space), the state of nature is not an absolute (moral) vacuum. Space in fact is supposed by Hobbes to be occupied by an ether, a very thin sort of body. The state of nature may contain very thin sorts of moral agreements. Contracts, even contracts of mutual covenants, can be made but they are precarious. The state of nature is a situation in which there is an unenforced and unenforceable moral code; far from excluding a morality, the natural condition describes that area in which morality does not exist, but can be constructed. Men are assumed to be possessed of speech, reason, and the desires which lead them to a society. They are not simply antisocial animals; although they have unsocial passions, they have not only the contrary passions but also the necessary tools (capable of being developed only within social situations) for constructing societies.

Just as space does not exclude the existence of physical bodies, so the state of nature does not exclude the existence of (political) bodies, but rather provides the framework in which they may be rationally analyzed.

6

SOVEREIGNTY AND GOVERNMENT

The Law is that which puts a difference betwixt good and evil, betwixt just and unjust; if you take away the Law, all things will fall into a confusion, every man will become a Law to himself, which in the depraved condition of humane nature, must needs produce many great enormities, Lust will become a Law, and Envy will become a Law, Covetousness and Ambition will become Laws; and what dictates, what decisions such laws will produce may easily be discerned * in the late Government of Ireland.

JOHN PYM IN HIS SUMMATION AGAINST THOMAS WENTWORTH, EARL OF STRAFFORD. (RUSHWORTH, VIII, 622)

The defining characteristic of every organized society is the existence of an authorized representative of that society. In an unorganized multitude each man speaks and acts for himself. The voice or action of the crowd is the voices or actions of those individuals who speak, shout, and act; even if a crowd should chant in unison, each man chants for himself. Even if a crowd acts together each man acts for himself and no man

* The part of this quotation ending at the asterisk was quoted by Charles I in answer to a petition of the Houses of Parliament to remove the magazine at Hull to London in April, 1642. (Edward, Earl of Clarendon, *History of the Rebellion*, II, 32.)

need avow the acts of his companions. But every organized society has a representative, a man or group of men (committee or assembly), that is authorized to act for the whole. In any such society, the actions of its representative—its government—are binding on every member.

What powers has such a government? What acts are binding on all the members of the society? What is the government authorized to do? What is it not authorized to do or perhaps even prohibited from doing? Are there any things that it is forbidden to omit? These questions may be asked for any organized society. To discover the answer for any subordinate organization, one would have to examine the charter of that organization in the light of the laws of the state to which it is subordinate. The problem for a sovereign state is somewhat more complicated, although some would say that it should only be necessary to examine the constitution and the law of the constitution of that state. Hobbes proposed to discover what should be the powers, the duties, and the limits of the powers of a correctly constructed sovereign state. He did not intend to describe the constitution and laws of England or France or any other state. He did not mean to inform his contemporaries about the powers exercised or claimed by states, or about the duties or limits they recognized. His inquiry was into the science of state construction and not into its practice. That men had always built their houses on sand could not invalidate a scientific theory of housebuilding that indicated that houses would be better built on firm ground.[1] Erroneous practice does not invalidate a true scientific theory; the science would be true if it correctly described the results of building houses on sand and on firmer ground. The science of politics indicates what powers are necessary to a state, and perhaps even what sorts of actions will make it strongest; it indicates the necessary limits of those powers and the duties of the sovereign.

Hobbes regarded the function of government as the preser-

---

[1] *Leviathan* (30), pp. 259–60.

vation of order or peace, the conditions necessary for the existence of human beings. He does not incline to Locke's view that
men are naturally peaceable, and therefore that government is
necessary only because of the activities of a few bestial ag-
gressors.[2] Hobbes's analysis of the state of nature inclines him
toward St. Augustine's opinion that peace is difficult to maintain among fallen men. It might even be argued that *Leviathan*
describes the political organization necessary for peace among
fallen men. This was not the only opinion that he could have
held, either logically or historically. He rejected the ancient
theory, held by both Plato and Aristotle, and revived in many
forms since, that society exists to promote the good life—the
life of virtue, or Christianity, or freedom, or morality, or culture, or worldly welfare. This kind of rationalist theory postulates an objective good, which it is the duty of the rulers to
know and to promote regardless of their own desires and the
desires of the members of the society. It has been the main
European political tradition, particularly in its Christian form.
(And if we now doubt the existence of objective goods of the
soul or the mind, we can still pursue happiness by attempting
to secure the more measurable goods of fortune.)

Hobbes also rejected the theory most opposed to this one,
i.e., the theory that government exists for the benefit of the
governors. He did not regard government as a swindle of the
foolish by the clever, or as a device for promoting the good
of the governors, or the governing class, at the expense of the
good of the governed. Hobbes could not accept a "power
struggle" theory of government (no matter whether the government is conceived of as participant, umpire, or merely as in-
dicator of who is winning), even though this conception of
politics would seem the most appropriate to his general approach. He develops a situation, the state of nature, in which
the actions of independent participants, whether individuals
or groups, are explained as a struggle for satisfactions and for

---

[2] Locke, *Second Treatise,* chap. ii, secs. 8–13; Laslett ed., pp. 290–94.

power. He does not take this to be a pattern for society, but for non-society. He rejects this model because he could not accept the presumption made by all power-struggle theories: that the struggle is limited, that it goes on in some sort of social framework in which the "rules of the game" *sunt servanda*, whether they are agreed on by the participants explicitly or implicitly, forced upon players by an umpire or the other players' reaction to their violation, or embodied in custom or in formal institutions. Since the laws of nature do not provide reliable limits to the conflicts of men in the state of nature, Hobbes could not accept a power-struggle theory. The main problem is to impose limits on the war of all against all. The limits are effectively imposed by a sovereign with a monopoly of the right to coerce and the power to use that right.

For Hobbes, then, the sovereign exists to maintain peace. What powers must the sovereign possess to do this? What must the sovereign do and what must it refrain from doing to establish and maintain peace, the prerequisite condition of civility?

The Limits of Sovereign Right

The sovereign is the exclusively authorized agent of the society. There can be but one sovereign at any time in any society. A man can be subject only to a single authorized sovereign at one time; no man can serve two masters. The authorization of a sovereign implies that there is no (still binding) previous authorization. Since the obligations incurred by an authorization are logically always the same, an existing obligation deprives one (as in the law of contracts) of the power to enter into the same obligation again.[3] The existence of such an obligation controls the extent of subsequent obligations; subjects may not undertake new obligations inconsistent with their subjection.

Subjects may not put off their obligations by their own ac-

---

[3] *Leviathan* (18), p. 133.

tions; they cannot withdraw their obligations to the sovereign. If a number of men have instituted a sovereign by mutual covenants, then any single objector prevents a mutual forgiving of all these obligations. Even their unanimous consent will not suffice to free the subjects from their obligations, for "they have also every man given the Soveraignty to him that beareth their Person; and therefore if they depose him, they take from him that which is his own, and so again it is injustice." [4] The subjects have obligations to the sovereign directly, not only indirectly through contractual relations among themselves. In sovereignty by acquisition, it is clear that each has bound himself by his own covenant to the sovereign. In sovereignty by institution, although there is no contractual relation between subject and sovereign, the subjects have given their authorization to the sovereign, and they may not take it back even if they should unanimously agree to do so. Although a promise to give is not binding (it transfers no right), a completed gift is an effective transfer of right. Since a change of government amounts to withdrawing authorization from one sovereign and conferring it on another, it follows that the subjects cannot change the form of government.

The sovereign has received the authorization of the subjects absolutely rather than conditionally. He can have agreed to no stipulation that is binding after he has become sovereign. He cannot have obliged himself to all collectively, because the collectivity did not exist before he was sovereign. Any stipulation to one or more individually ("I promise to maintain the following rights of John Doe . . .") would be both void and unenforceable. It would be void, because (after the society's establishment) the sovereign's acts are authorized by all. The sovereign, acting for the individual to whom he is obliged, may free himself from his obligations; the sovereign is in effect bound only to himself.[5] Such a stipulation would be unenforceable, because there is no judge instituted other than the

[4] *Ibid.*   [5] *De Cive* (vi. 14), *EW* II, 83–84.

parties involved. The result would be a return to the state of nature—a result contrary to the intention of the institutors: "It is therefore in vain to grant Soveraignty by way of precedent Covenant." [6] A sovereign by acquisition, although standing in a contractual relation with each subject, makes no promises in return for their submissions. The conqueror's part of the contract is not a covenant (a promise of future action) but a performance (allowing the vanquished man to live at liberty as an ordinary subject rather than in chains as a slave).[7] There are no conditions which the sovereign could break, therefore he cannot forfeit the sovereignty, "and consequently none of his Subjects, by any pretence of forfeiture, can be freed from his Subjection." [8]

Although the sovereign may not be deprived of his sovereignty by his subjects, he may divest himself of it and he may lose it. What the sovereign has he may convey. The sovereign may convey his sovereignty by appointing a replacement, by changing the form of government (e.g., a sovereign assembly may appoint a monarch), by submitting to or contracting with a foreign sovereign. The sovereign could divest himself of his sovereignty without appointing a successor.[9] This ungracious act, returning the society to the state of nature, is said by Hobbes to be contrary to the sovereign's obligation by the law of nature.[10] It is a violation of the law of nature forbidding ingratitude, it being ungrateful to allow this to happen to those who benefited him. It might also be contrary to the law of nature because it unnecessarily destroys a peace. Such a lapse

[6] *Leviathan* (18), pp. 134–35.

[7] *Ibid.* (20), pp. 155–56; *De Cive* (viii. 1–3), *EW* II, 108–10. Nevertheless, the fact is that many sovereigns have unfortunately made such agreements for the reason *"That a man to obtain a Kingdom, is sometimes content with lesse Power, than to the Peace, and defence of the Common-wealth is necessarily required."* In resisting these sovereigns' attempts to regain this necessary power, "such as will hold them [the sovereigns] to their promises, shall be maintained against them by forraign Common-wealths." *Leviathan* (29), pp. 247–48.

[8] *Leviathan* (18), p. 134.

[9] *Ibid.*, (19, 21), pp. 149–52, 170–71; *De Cive* (ix. 11–19), *EW* II, 122–25.

[10] *Ibid.* (19), p. 148. *De Cive* (vii. 16), *EW* II, 103; *Elements of* Law (II. ii. 9), p. 122.

into civil war would also be "contrary to the intention of them that did Institute the Common-wealth, for their perpetuall, and not temporary security." [11]

In order to insure the perpetuity of the institution, all sovereigns have the right to appoint their successors. Democracies and aristocracies are self-perpetuating: the democratic assembly can continue to exist as long as the population of the democracy continues to exist—"succession" is a result of reproduction; the aristocratic assembly may replenish its numbers by coopting new members, or by providing some other method of election. Assemblies perpetuate themselves by appointing a day for the next meeting; to adjourn *sine die* is to die. Monarchies must find more artificial ways of providing for a quasi-eternal existence. The power to appoint a successor is always in the hands of the present monarch who may designate his heir either expressly (by words or writing) or tacitly (by allowing a custom to stand, e.g., the custom of male succession or that of female succession). In the absence of another disposition, Hobbes asserts that there is a presumption in favor of (1) the continuance of monarchy, and (2) the succession of the nearest blood relative, preferably male.[12] Succession is a special case of the transfer of sovereignty which only arises where the sovereign is a natural person.

Although the sovereign may transfer sovereign power to another—by testament, sale, covenant, or gift—the sovereign may not grant away part of his sovereignty. Because the rights of sovereignty are inseparable, "it follows necessarily, that in whatsoever words any of them seem to be granted away, yet if the Soveraign Power it selfe be not in direct termes renounced, and the name of Soveraign no more given by the Grantees to him that Grants them, the Grant is voyd." [13] Either the sovereign grants away his sovereignty or he does not. If he does

[11] *Leviathan* (19), p. 149.
[12] *Ibid.*, pp. 150–51; *De Cive* (ix. 14–19), *EW* II, 123–25.
[13] *Leviathan* (18), p. 140. *Cf. De Cive* (vii. 17), *EW* II, 106; *Elements of Law* (II. ii. 13), pp. 125–26.

not, he must still be possessed of all the necessary rights and powers of sovereignty; therefore a grant of part of this power is "void," i.e., in this case logically impossible; either the whole is granted or none, either X is sovereign or X is not sovereign. Since the sovereign can grant away his sovereignty or even renounce it, it is to be presumed that no grant that does not grant away all sovereignty explicitly is meant as a grant of any part of sovereignty.[14]

The sovereign may divest himself of the obligations of specific subjects to obey. He does so in all cases in which he no longer protects the life of the subject. If a man be banished, if he be permitted to emigrate, if he be attacked, if he be commanded to kill or damage himself, if he be interrogated, or if he be commanded to kill someone else (except where a refusal would jeopardize the purpose of instituting a commonwealth), he is not obliged to obey.[15] If a subject is taken prisoner in a war, or if his "means of life" are within the power of the victor, he has the liberty to submit to that victor, thus becoming the subject of a new sovereign and no longer the subject of the old. If all of a sovereign's subjects were so conquered, all their obligations would be cancelled; the sovereign would lose his sovereignty, at least until the country were reconquered.[16] If so many of the subjects of a sovereign were conquered that the sovereign could no longer protect the rest, the result would be the same. It is essential to the maintenance of the state that the sovereign maintain the means of defending the state. If he allows his military power to decline because of ignorance, negligence, or stupidity, he is creating the necessary conditions for the destruction of his sovereignty.

The principle that the obligation incurred by a subject to his sovereign excludes a subsequent authorization of another sovereign must be modified by the provision that under some

[14] *Leviathan* (21), p. 169.

[15] *Ibid.*, pp. 167–71. *Cf. De Cive* (vi. 13), *EW* II, 82–83.

[16] Although the right of a monarchic sovereign cannot be extinguished, the obligation of the subjects may be. If the sovereign is an assembly, the extinction of the obligations to it destroys the assembly. *Leviathan* (21, 29), pp. 170, 257. *Cf. De Cive* (vii. 18), *EW* II, 106–8.

circumstances the subject is freed from his obligation. The obligation of the subject to the sovereign is defined by the covenant of the subject; it is defined not only by the words of the covenant but also by the intention of the covenant, i.e., by the purpose for which it was made. By his covenant of association or submission, the subject obliges himself to simple obedience, the greatest obedience that one man can perform toward another.[17] The subject's obligation of obedience is both the result and the logical correlative of the absolute power, the full authorization, that he has conferred upon the sovereign. The subject is obliged to obey the commands of the sovereign and his delegates, i.e., the public laws and orders of the society.[18] He is obliged to assist the sovereign, to "refuse him not the use of his wealth and strength against any others whatsoever; for he is supposed still to retain a right of defending himself against violence." [19] The subject transfers as much as he can transfer; he cannot transfer his actual "strength and power," he cannot transfer his right to preserve his life. He is not bound to be an Atilus Regulus, committing himself to torture and death for his country, nor is he bound to be a Lucius Junius Brutus, executing the death penalty upon his own sons, nor is he bound to show the courage of Horatius Cocles. He need not even face the enemy, for (unless the "Defence of the Commonwealth, requireth" everyone to bear arms) he may fulfill his obligation by providing a substitute soldier.[20]

The subject's authorization of the sovereign (*Leviathan*) or his transfer of the use of power and strength to him (*Elements of Law* and *De Cive*) obliges the subject to obey the sovereign,

[17] *De Cive* (vi. 13), *EW* II, 82; *Leviathan* (21), p. 166.
[18] *De Cive* (v. 7–8, 11), *EW* II, 68–69, 70; *Elements of Law* (II. i. 13), p. 113.
[19] *De Cive* (v. 7), *EW* II, 68. Cf. *Elements of Law* (I. xix. 7, II. i. 7–8), pp. 103–4, 111–12.
[20] *Leviathan* (21), pp. 167–68. Presumably the sovereign would determine, according to his assessment of the danger, when the subjects would be allowed to hire substitutes and when all would be required to serve. In the latter case, there is an obligation to serve: "And it is a Dictate of Naturall Reason, and consequently an evident Law of Nature, that no man ought to weaken that power, the protection whereof he hath himself demanded, or wittingly received against others." *Ibid.* (26), p. 210. Cf. *Leviathan* (Review and Conclusion), p. 548, where Hobbes adds to the Laws of Nature: "*That every man is bound by*

to assist the sovereign and his ministers, and not to "resist the Sword of the Common-wealth, in defence of another man, guilty or innocent." [21] He is free to resist force used against his person even if that force is force commanded by the sovereign. Hobbes says again and again that no one is bound to suffer bodily harm without defending himself.[22] The subject has authorized the actions of the sovereign (who may be doing no wrong); the subject may not accuse the sovereign of injustice in any case (even if he is innocent),[23] but if the sovereign comes against him with force he may resist, be he a criminal or a rebel, he may resist, even joining with others to do so.[24] The subject is obliged not to resist the will of the sovereign (*"obligat ad non resistendum* voluntati *illius* hominis *vel illius* concilii *cui se submiserit"*),[25] but he is free to defend himself against the force of the sovereign. The "right of resisting" with which the subject has parted [26] is:

(1) the right to deny the sovereign the use of his power when it is required; and

(2) the right to resist the sovereign by interfering in the sovereign's actions and interposing his (the subject's) strength on another subject's behalf against the sovereign (e.g., by defending another against the sovereign's punishment).

In the making of a Common-wealth, every man giveth away the right of defending another; but not of defending himselfe. Also he obligeth himselfe, to assist him that hath the Soveraignty, in the Punishing of another; but of himselfe not.[27]

Nature, as much as in him lieth, to protect in Warre, the Authority, by which he is himself protected in time of Peace." When the presence in arms of even the most timorous is required, the sovereign will assure it by offering them a choice between immediate punishment for refusing to serve and the remoter risks of service. Men will choose the lesser evil, in this case the more remote risk.

[21] *Leviathan* (21, 28), pp. 168, 238–39.

[22] *Ibid.* (21, 27, 28), pp. 167–68, 229–30, 238.   [23] *Ibid.* (21), pp. 163–64.

[24] *Ibid.*, p. 168.   [25] *De Cive* (v. 7), *EW* II, 68; *LW* II, 213–14.

[26] *De Cive* (v. 11), *EW* II, 70. References to the obligation not to resist should always be read as referring to the will of the sovereign or his force against another.

[27] *Leviathan* (28), pp. 238–39. *Cf. Elements of Law* (I. xix. 7, 10; II. i. 5, 14, 18), pp. 103–4, 110, 114, 116.

The subject does not confer on the sovereign a right to punish; the sovereign possesses that already in the right to everything of the state of nature. The subject's renunciation of his natural right and his obligation to the sovereign make the sovereign's right effective, strengthening his actual ability to punish.

Hobbes seems to suppose that the subject will not usually have to assist the sovereign; the sovereign's right and his possession of the means of rewarding service will induce some men to perform these tasks. Nevertheless the subject may be required to help.[28] The sovereign's right to use the power and wealth of the subjects, and the subjects' obligations to provide these, are what makes the sovereign able to provide the security that eliminates the state of nature. This is the power and strength "that by terror thereof, he [the sovereign] is inabled to forme the wills of them all, to Peace at home, and mutuall ayd against their enemies abroad." [29]

Sovereign Power: Force and Defense

The sovereign is created by the consents of the institutors.[30] The consent of each to obey, given in his authorization, is also

---

[28] *Leviathan* (28), p. 245: "REWARD, is either of *Gift,* or by *Contract.* When by Contract, it is called *Salary,* and *Wages;* which is benefit due for service performed, or promised. When of Gift, it is benefit proceeding from the *grace* of them that bestow it, to encourage, or enable men to do them service. And therefore when the Soveraign of a Common wealth appointeth a Salary to any publique Office, he that receiveth it, is bound in Justice to performe his office; otherwise, he is bound onely in honour, to acknowledgement, and an endeavour of requitall. For though men have no lawfull remedy, when they be commanded to quit their private businesse, to serve the publique, without Reward, or Salary; yet they are not bound thereto, by the Law of Nature, nor by the Institution of the Common-wealth, unlesse the service cannot otherwise be done; because it is supposed the Soveraign may make use of all their means, insomuch as the most common Souldier, may demand the wages of his warrefare, as a debt."

[29] *Ibid.* (17), p. 132. See Appendix 5.

[30] Sovereignty by institution is taken here as the paradigm. See above, p. 165, for some reasons. Institution exhibits an intention to create a society and a sovereign, as well as to avoid death. The motive for this is the fear of others inherent in the state of nature. Sovereignty by acquisition is less "rational";

his *Fiat civitas*. The institutors are motivated to create a society by the fear of death and the desire to avoid death and to have various satisfactions. Peace is the means to these ends, and the creation of a society the means to peace. If this intention is to be effected, the institutors must create the means to effect it. Not only must they oblige themselves but they must also create an agency with the right and the power to enforce their obligations. These are the conditions of "sufficient security," in which one cannot rightfully break an obligation; that is, the conditions under which obligations are valid—the conditions in which the excuses for failure to perform obligations are defined by the law and judged by the sovereign. Since the obligations are valid *in foro externo* only if the sovereign has the power to enforce them, the institutors are obliged to provide their force and wealth; obliged, that is, to enable the sovereign to maintain the conditions in which they will continue to be obliged. The function of the sovereign is to create and maintain these conditions. The means of doing so are the powers that the sovereign must have. The specification of these powers will also be a specification of the rights of the sovereign, and (because these rights need not be fully exercised) an exhibition of what may be the obligations of the subject.

Hobbes's argument was designed to demonstrate that the sovereign had the right to rule without limitation; the sovereign alone retains the right of nature to do anything required for his own preservation, the subjects having divested themselves of their natural rights and obliged themselves to the sovereign. To make his right effective, the sovereign must be able to force the unwilling to obey. The power of coercion is both part of the sovereign's right, and a necessary means to the effectiveness of that right.[31] The diminution of that power

---

the motive is again fear but this time fear of death at the hands of the victor. In submitting, the defeated need have no desire or intention to create a society. Their intention is to avoid death; there need be no other purpose.

[31] The sovereign alone retains the natural right to punish. See *Leviathan* (28), p. 239.

would mean that the subject, although intending to fulfill his obligations, might in many cases rightfully disobey the sovereign's commands. Where the power of the sovereign does not enforce, the writ of the sovereign does not run and the subject may discover that he is thrown back on his own resources.[32] The subject has no security; he is in a state of nature, or a social vacuum. Here he need not ensure his own destruction by acting as if his rights could be enforced.

This does not mean that the subject is always in a state of nature because he is the ultimate judge of his obligations. The subject does not claim to be the judge of good and evil in society; he only claims his unalienated right to preserve his life. The subject here recognizes his obligations; he is a "good subject" who makes no claims of right that are inconsistent with society or tend toward its dissolution. He does not claim the right to judge right and wrong by his own conscience rather than by the law; he does not claim that the sovereign power ought to be limited, divided, or less than absolute. He does not claim to be obliged to obey some other authority. He does not claim the right to resist or rebel.[33] Hobbes attempts to exclude the right of the private individual to judge between good and evil. He execrates the claim that the private moral conscience is superior to the laws. Can men holding such subversive opinions be distinguished from those who do not? Can men give up their private right to distinguish good and evil, or must they be continually thrown back into a state of nature? It is consistent to suppose that the good subject intends to obey the laws and tries to preserve the sovereign power. He attempts to fulfill his obligations. In this attempt, he is frustrated by his insecurity. He discovers that there is not sufficient force available to protect him and his rights against some other man, or perhaps the sovereign has not the power to recover his rights for him. In this case his private judgment is a judgment of

[32] *Ibid.* (21, 27), pp. 170, 224–25. When sovereign power ceases, crime also ceases.

[33] *Ibid.* (29), p. 249.

fact—the fact that there is no power sufficient to protect him. (A much more difficult problem arises if he refuses to obey the sovereign's command because he believes that the sovereign does not have the power to protect or aid him in its execution. If the subject refuses to obey, does he not contribute to the destruction of the society? Suppose that he is correct about the sovereign's impotence? In this case, if he has not contributed to the destruction of the society, the "good subject" is only rational in attempting to preserve his own life.)

The subject does not transgress against Hobbes's prohibitions when he decides that there is no *de facto* sovereign power. This is a private judgment, but not a claim that the sovereign's right ought to be limited or that the subject has a right to judge right and wrong where laws are enforced. The judgment is a judgment forced upon the subject by a situation; he perceives that he is endangered. If his perception is incorrect, he has no rightful plea to make against the sovereign's punishment. How can he claim a right to do what he did on the basis of a belief that the sovereign was powerless if brought before the sovereign's court? If his perception is correct he is justified by the law of nature; he is entitled to preserve himself. His right to preserve his life is not destroyed by the creation of a society; it is a right preserved even against the sovereign. In this sense a right of private judgment is retained but it is not judgment of good and evil. (The subject may intend peace, desire that there be a sovereign and that the laws be maintained, and yet be forced to decide that he is in a state of nature.)

Either there is a sovereign providing sufficient security, or there is not one. If there is one and the subject believes there is not, if he commits actions forbidden by law, he commits a crime punishable by law.[34] If there is no sovereign, and the subject has not contributed to this situation, he has done noth-

---

[34] *Ibid.* (27), p. 226. That he does not know that there is a sovereign is no excuse.

ing wrong and he can act to preserve himself. If there be a sovereign and the subject, erroneously believing that there is no sovereign, acts to preserve himself in a way that contributes to the dissolution of the sovereign power, the subject may have committed a crime—but that crime is no longer punishable. The subject has also committed a sin, breaking his obligations by the law of nature to the society. He has been imprudent and the result is to return him to the state of nature; this is a "natural punishment" of his error, for he has impaired his chances of attaining his ends and increased the likelihood of his own death.

The subject, then, is not only obliged to maintain the society by supporting the power of the sovereign to enforce peace, but also he has a "possible motive" to do so: the desire to avoid the consequences of a breakdown. The sovereign must be possessed of overwhelming force—as much of the combined total force, including the wealth, of the society as he thinks necessary to preserve peace. Peace is the necessary condition for the satisfaction of men's desires, the best means of self-preservation, the principle upon which the laws of nature concerning the life of men in society are founded, and the end toward which these laws are oriented.

What kind of peace does Hobbes propose be established? In what ways and in what areas should there be order? The purpose of the peace Hobbes advocates is the protection of the lives of the individuals composing the society. This involves two things: (1) internal peace, security of life within the society, and insofar as possible, the elimination of the use of force by one member against another; (2) preservation of the society and of its members against foreign invasion, armed attack from the outside.[35]

A society is a necessary means for the preservation of men's lives. The continuance of the society is the best way of ensuring their continued preservation. The destruction of a so-

[35] *Ibid.* (17, 25), pp. 132, 200.

ciety is likely to involve the premature death of many of its members, if not by invading armies, then as a result of the breakdown of internal peace—a return to the state of nature. This would be avoided only if the society surrendered itself completely or joined another without conquest, the sovereign of one becoming the sovereign of both by the submission of the other sovereign or, in an hereditary monarchy, by both crowns being inherited by the same man, as James VI of Scotland became James I of England in 1603.

Military force is necessary to prevent the destruction of a society by the military force of another society. Sovereigns face each other as gigantic individuals in a state of nature. They have desires and fears similar to the fears of individuals. They are "in the state and posture of Gladiators; having their weapons pointing, and their eyes fixed on one another." [36] Happily, men have not always been miserable as a result; societies are more self-sufficient than particular men.

The sovereign and the subjects depend for their safety upon the preservation of the society. Collectively they can defend themselves against external force. There is a sense in which the whole society may be regarded as a force organized by the sovereign for his own protection against attack by other men who may also be sovereigns wielding the aggregate power of a large number of men. Hobbes argues that the interests of sovereign and subject are not opposed. [37] Society was established for the benefit of all—i.e., for their peace and preservation.

And this benefit extendeth equally both to the sovereign, and to the subjects. For he or they that have the sovereign power, have but the defence of their persons, by the assistance of the particulars; and every particular man hath his defence by their union with the sovereign. [38]

---

[36] *Ibid.* (13), p. 98. *De Cive* (xiii. 7), *EW* II, 169.

[37] There is an obvious sense in which this is false. The subject's interests are harmed when he is put in direct danger of his life in defense of the state. The reply is that the subject has a prior obligation which he undertook because of the general advantages of the society. He cannot take the advantages and refuse the risks.

[38] *Elements of Law* (II. v. 1), pp. 137–38.

The sovereign needs this defense, for the sovereign is the head, i.e., not only the part which is responsible for the cares of the society, "but also [that] against which the stroke of an enemy most commonly is directed." [39]

"Military security" is perhaps too narrow a label for the set of powers required for the preservation of a society against external force: (1) the power to organize for war—raising, arming, and paying the military personnel, and appointing the officers (who should be able and popular, but loyal); [40] (2) the supreme command—judging where and when the forces are to be employed, i.e., political and military strategy. (The war power is the sovereign's, "And therefore whosoever is made Generall of an Army, he that hath the Soveraign Power is alwayes Generallissimo." [41]); (3) the power to make war and peace, i.e., the conduct of foreign policy (insofar as it is not included above).

The rules for the conduct of one sovereign toward another are laid down in the Law of Nations; this is precisely the same as the Law of Nature. There are no absolutely valid rules, either moral or prudential, for conducting foreign policy: "every Soveraign hath the same Right, in procuring the safety of his People, that any particular man can have, in procuring the safety of his own Body." [42] Peace, or at least truce, provided that others will maintain it, even in an insecure and hostile state of nature, is desirable. But since it is not enforced by men, but only by God, whose laws apply to the consciences of princes, there can be no security against a resort to force. Hobbes seems to envision a relatively stable state of suspicion

---

[39] *Ibid.* (II. v. 2), p. 139. *Cf. De Cive* (x. 2), *EW* II, 128; *LW* II, 266: "both he that commands, and he who is commanded, to the end that he may defend his life makes use at once of all his fellow-citizens [*utitur simul omnium concivium*]." (I have corrected the translation to conform to the Latin.) *N.B.* in *De Cive* and *Leviathan* the sovereign is always the soul, and never the head, of the commonwealth.

[40] *Leviathan* (30), pp. 272–73.

[41] *Ibid.* (18), p. 138. *Cf. De Cive* (vi. 7–8), *EW* II, 76–77; *Elements of Law* (II. i. 8–9), pp. 111–12.

[42] *Leviathan* (30), p. 273.

with occasional use of force rather than an all-out continuous struggle. Hobbes, unlike Harrington, does not propose that the state be constituted for the purpose of expansion by military conquest. The desire for continuous expansion is a disease of the state, a bulimia; it frequently results in incurable wounds from the enemy; or "the *Wens,* of ununited conquests, which are many times a burthen, and with lesse danger lost, than kept." [43]

If the sovereign is to secure the society against disturbance from without he must have the power to decide foreign policy, as well as the military power, one of the means of action in foreign affairs. In order to perform the first of these functions effectively some subordinate powers are necessary: (1) the powers to negotiate and to appoint public ministers to foreign states; (2) the power to take counsel—to receive advice from the expert and the experienced, from those who have knowledge of a science or experience in affairs. If counsel is to be informed, then the sovereign must also have (3) the power to collect information abroad, e.g., by sending private agents.[44]

Some powers within the society are implicit in the external powers of the sovereign. The sovereign must have the means to carry on these activities. Subordinate officials, civil and military, must be appointed and rewarded for their services with money, or honors, or both; the materials of war or defense must be provided. To Hobbes, who discarded the demand that the king should live of his own, this meant that the government must have the power to tax. The military power is as necessary to internal peace as it is to external security, for it is the means necessary for guaranteeing internal order.

Sovereign Power: Justice

Defense against external violence and maintenance of internal order are inseparable. The continued existence of the

[43] *Leviathan* (29), p. 257. *Cf. Elements of Law* (II. ix. 9), p. 184.
[44] *Leviathan* (23, 25), pp. 187–88, 199–200; *De Cive* (xiii. 7-8), *EW* II, 169–70.

society requires that the society protect itself, politically and militarily, from external threats. The organization and provision of the means (men, money, supplies) of protection require that the society (i.e., its government) decide policy, raise and dispense funds, and appoint, empower, supervise, and dismiss officials. These powers are equally necessary for the maintenance of an internal order. The armed forces guarantee, and perhaps create, the sovereign's power to keep an internal peace; the power that protects all collectively protects each individually—each from the other. The sword of war and the sword of justice are in the same hands; "and consequently those two swords are but one." [45]

The "sword of justice" guarantees the enforcement of a peace within the society. Peace is a harmony imposed upon the conflicts and collisions of constantly moving, desiring individuals. Since desire cannot be eliminated, conflict cannot be completely eliminated. It is not simply desire and conflict that make the state of nature terrible, but these in a situation in which quiet enjoyment is unlikely and every clash of desire can lead to a life-and-death struggle. The elimination by force of a competitor is the only sure, though completely unsafe, way of settling a disagreement. The resort to force, and consequently fear, are maximized.

The internal peace of the society is the limitation and minimization of conflicts and of the use of force in settling them— the maximization of quiet enjoyment. One part of avoiding clashes between individuals is the limitation of their rights. In the state of nature, right is unlimited except by conscience; in society, rights are defined by law. The establishment of general rules of property prescribes a protected area of safety to the individual in the enjoyment of his own. His enjoyment is protected by the power of the society, and the same power hedges him off from the violation of the legal rights of others

[45] *Elements of Law* (II. i. 8), pp. 111–12; *Leviathan* (18), p. 139; *De Cive* (vi. 7), *EW* II, 76.

because he can now know precisely what their rights are. The law, as a set of rules defining property rights: (1) establishes an area of safety for these rights; (2) allows each individual to know precisely what his rights are; (3) warns the intentional transgressor that society will punish or rectify his transgression; and (4) provides the knowledge of what is a transgression to the innocent who might have come into conflict with others by accident or inadvertence.

It is the sovereign, the representative of the society, that lays down the rules for distinguishing what belongs to one subject from what belongs to another, "the Rules, whereby every man may know, what Goods he may enjoy, and what Actions he may doe, without being molested by any of his fellow Subjects." [46] The sovereign is legislator of all the rules of the society: those prohibiting behavior as criminal as well as those defining property rights.

Law, according to Hobbes, is command—a direction issued by a sovereign to those already obliged to obey.[47] All laws for the members of a society derive their validity from having been commanded by the sovereign. Customs are laws because they are silently approved by the sovereign.[48] The laws of nature are truly laws only in a commonwealth, being then commanded by the commonwealth. The commonwealth makes the laws of nature into civil laws by specifying, for example, what constitutes a contract and a breach of contract, and what conduct is so unsociable, uncivil, or disturbing to the social peace that it is a punishable offense (a crime), or a legally actionable offense (a wrong).[49]

---

[46] *Leviathan* (18), p. 137.

[47] *Ibid.* (26), p. 203; *De Cive* (vi. 9, xiv. 1), *EW* II, 77, 182–83; *Elements of Law* (II. x. 1–3), pp. 184–86. This raises the problem of the sense in which the "laws" of nature are laws properly speaking. They are "laws" only to those who are obliged to obey a sovereign who has commanded them, i.e., either to those obliged to obey a civil sovereign or to those obliged to obey God.

[48] *Leviathan* (26), pp. 204–6; *De Cive* (xiv. 15), *EW* II, 195; *Elements of Law* (II. x. 10), p. 190.

[49] *Leviathan* (26), pp. 205–6; *De Cive* (xiv. 15), *EW* II, 189–91; *Elements of Law* (II. x. 5), pp. 186–87. The laws of nature and the civil laws are mutually inclusive. The civil law contains the natural law by making it into specific rules

The sovereign is the ultimate legislator for the society; all laws are applied by his authority. Laws and binding interpretations of laws are not valid without that authority. The laws of nature, insofar as they are left unwritten by the civil law, and the civil law itself, must be interpreted. Law is interpreted by officials having their authority from the sovereign. Their interpretations of the civil laws are to be made according to the meaning of the law, i.e., the intention of the legislator. In interpreting the law of nature, applying it to the case before him, "the Judge doth no more but consider, whither the demand of the party be consonant to naturall reason, and Equity." [50] The interpretation of the laws of nature differs from the interpretation of the civil laws in but one respect: an interpretation, even if approved by the sovereign, cannot change a law of nature, "the Eternall Law of God," or create a precedent binding in future cases:

For though a wrong Sentence given by authority of the Soveraign, if he know and allow it, in such Lawes as are mutable, be a constitution of a new Law, in cases, in which every little circumstance is the same; yet in Lawes immutable, such as are the Lawes of Nature, they are no Lawes to the same, or other Judges, in the like cases for ever after.[51]

The sovereign is the ultimate interpreter of the law. It is by his authority that all laws are interpreted. Inferior judges' interpretations are valid unless invalidated by the sovereign or by his authority. The binding interpretations of law are given by his authority and not by the authority derived from

---

—defining its terms. Conversely, the law of nature commands the performance of the covenants of society. "Whence it follows, that no civil law whatsoever, which tends not to a reproach of the Deity, (in respect of whom cities themselves have no right of their own, and cannot be said to make laws), can possibly be against the law of nature." *De Cive* (xiv. 10), *EW* II, 190–91. *Cf.* St. Thomas Aquinas, *Summa Theologica* I–II, Question 95, Article 2.

[50] *Leviathan* (26), pp. 207–13. It may seem niggardly of Hobbes not to provide criteria for deciding specific cases according to "Equity" or the laws of nature, but since the laws of nature are themselves such criteria, and since they have been spelled out, there are no further instructions to be given about how to be fair in practice.

[51] *Ibid.*, p. 213.

a professional education, precedent, famous commentaries, or even natural reason.

The validity of all law in the state is conferred by the authority of the sovereign. The authenticity of any particular rule of law may be verified by examining the evidence of its authorization by the sovereign in the public registers and records. The authority of any official or judge may be verified by examining the evidence of his authorization by the sovereign—his sealed commission.[52]

The sovereign's legislative power is not limited by the existing laws and customs. He may abrogate legal rules by making new laws; no one but the sovereign has the power to do this. Since customary law is valid by virtue of his tacit approval, he has the power to judge which customs are reasonable and to be retained and which are unreasonable and to be abolished.[53] The sovereign has the power to eliminate inconsistencies in the law, and to resolve conflicts of law or of interpretation. "To him therefore there can not be any knot in the Law, insoluble; either by finding out the ends, to undoe it by; or else by making what ends he will, (as *Alexander* did with his sword in the Gordian knot,) by the Legislative power; which no other Interpreter can doe." [54]

The sovereign, therefore, is not subject to the civil law. Since he can make new laws and repeal old ones, he is bound to the old laws only by his own will to continue them. He is bound, then, to himself and therefore not bound at all. The sovereign is not bound by the laws; *princeps legisbus solutus est.*[55] True, the sovereign is bound by natural law, which it is not in his power to change. But he is bound to that law only as a man in the state of nature is bound, viz., *in foro interno,* to his own interpretation. He is responsible only to God and not to the members of the society; they cannot punish him for any pretended breaches of the laws of nature.[56]

[52] *Ibid.,* pp. 210–11.   [53] *Ibid.,* pp. 204–5.   [54] *Ibid.,* p. 212.
[55] *Digest* i. 3. 31. See *Leviathan* (26), p. 204.
[56] *Leviathan* (28, 29, 30), pp. 241, 250, 258.

The sovereign's legislative power is not restricted to any set of human activities, nor is it forbidden to be exercised on some subjects. No human activity is *ultra vires* of the sovereign power. The sovereign is legislator of the rules of property and of transfer of property; [57] he is legislator of the limitations on the powers of subordinate bodies politic; [58] he is the source of the laws of honor, and the distributor of honors; [59] the sovereign has the power to tax,[60] the power to encourage and promote industry,[61] the power to establish an obligatory public religion whether Christian or not, and to determine which opinions and doctrines may be publicly taught and which may not.[62] Furthermore, there are no fundamental or constitutional laws which are beyond the legal power of the sovereign to alter. Fundamental laws are laws necessary to the existence of the commonwealth—the basic rules for the constitution of a social order and the particular rules by which this particular social order is constituted. The sovereign has the power to change the constitution by changing the form of sovereignty and the power to dissolve the society by intention and by neglect.[63] There are, then, no laws beyond the sovereign's legislative capacity.

The sovereign is not bound by the laws in regard to the property of the subject. Civil laws guarantee the subject his rights against other subjects but not against the sovereign. The doctrine that the subject has a propriety in his goods that excludes the sovereign is a doctrine tending toward the dissolution of the commonwealth. The laws of property are the sovereign's laws; the introduction of property (private right exclusive of other men) is an effect of the commonwealth, i.e., the sovereign representative and the civil laws.[64] Changes in the civil laws (which the sovereign may make) necessarily would result

---

[57] *Ibid.* (18, 24), pp. 137, 189–93.   [58] *Ibid.* (22), pp. 172–73.
[59] *Ibid.* (18), p. 139.   [60] *Ibid.* (18, 30), pp. 138, 258.
[61] *Ibid.* (30), p. 267.   [62] *Ibid.* (18, 42), pp. 136–37, 421–23.
[63] *Ibid.* (26), p. 222.
[64] *Ibid.* (24, 29), pp. 189–93, 250–51; *De Cive* (vi. 15, xii. 7), *EW* II, 84–85, 157–58.

in the changing of the rights of individuals under those laws.[65] If the sovereign is legislator, capable of changing laws, private rights are not secure against public invasion. If the sovereign could not deprive private individuals of their rights then laws would be contracts; each person would have to give his consent to a change in his rights.[66] Such a condition exists only in the state of nature. In a society, there exists a sovereign representative empowered to act for the preservation of each and all, and therefore empowered to change the law without injury to anyone. The power of the sovereign to act for the public good extends beyond his power to change the rules of property to a power to assert an overriding public right when the assertion of this right is necessary. The sovereign is, of course, the judge of the necessity, just as he is the judge of the necessity to make or change a legal rule.

The overriding right of the sovereign will not always be exercised. Normally, the subject will have his goods and liberties within the limits of the law. In those areas in which the sovereign has not legislated, the subject will have complete liberty. Otherwise he will be subject to the enacted taxes and services. If the subject claims a debt against the sovereign (acting here as representative of a corporation that can make valid contracts), if he has a legal dispute with the sovereign about property, about the taxes or services demanded from him according to law, or about a legal penalty or punishment, the subject may institute a legal action against the sovereign in the usual courts just as if the sovereign were a subject.

For seeing the Soveraign demandeth by force of a former Law, and not by vertue of his Power; he declareth thereby, that he requireth no more, than shall appear to be due by that Law. The sute therefore is not contrary to the will of the Soveraign; and consequently the Subject hath the Liberty to demand the hearing of his Cause; and sentence, according to that Law.[67]

[65] For example, the value of the local coinage may be changed by the sovereign. See *Leviathan* (24), p. 194.
[66] *De Cive* (xiv. 2), *EW* II, 184–85.
[67] *Leviathan* (21), p. 169. *N.B.* that it is the case in most states that the state may not be sued without its permission.

Nevertheless, the sovereign is not limited in his actions to what he may demand by law; the sovereign possesses a reserve of power—prerogative power—to act without law. If the sovereign acts in virtue of his power, for example confiscating the subject's goods, the subject has no legal remedy.

Hobbes did not accept the constitutionalist saw: To the king belongs government, to the subject belongs property. Neither fundamental law, nor constitutional law, nor natural law guarantees the property rights of the subject against the sovereign. The logic of his argument for absolute sovereignty drove Hobbes to deny the existence of absolute property rights in the subject. He could do so because the society was not founded upon the right of the individual to property, but upon the right and the desire of the individual to preserve his life. All other rights were superfluous, and therefore not immune from the sovereign's invasion.

Hobbes did not achieve his radical position in regard to property rights easily. He had originally thought that men could enter society retaining the rights they had previously acquired by contract in the state of nature.[68] Even in *Leviathan* there is a trace of the absolute right of subjects to property; after land has been distributed by the sovereign, he may not redistribute it:

For seeing the Soveraign, that is to say, the Common-wealth (whose Person he representeth,) is understood to do nothing but in order to the common Peace and Security, this Distribution of lands, is to be understood as done in order to the same: And consequently, whatever Distribution he shall make in prejudice thereof, is con-

[68] An early version of the *Elements of Law* in the Hardwick papers (denoted by Tönnies "H," now A_2B) has the following passage struck out at Part I, Chap. xvii, Sect. 2, p. 89n: "Of the law of nature also it is: that entering into peace every man be allowed those rights which he hath acquired by the covenants of others." A later version, B. M. Harl. mss, 4235 (Tönnies' "A"), had: "Another, that men entering in peace, retain what they have acquired." These reservations based on formal parity of right were replaced by the provision that each man allow others to retain any right he claims himself. The actual reservation of right (for not all liberties must be divested), at *Elements of Law*, I. xvii. 2, is a reservation of the rights to things necessary for life: one's own body, its defense, fire, water, air, and "place to live in." Cf. *Leviathan* (21), p. 167.

trary to the will of every subject, that committeth his Peace, and safety to his discretion, and conscience; and therefore by the will of every one of them, is to be reputed voyd.[69]

This passage no longer contradicts the absolute right of the sovereign in the Latin version of *Leviathan;* there it has disappeared completely.[70]

Although there are no legal limitations on the sovereign, there are limits to what the sovereign can do by law. Laws are commands, the orders of the commonwealth through its representative to all subjects or some group of subjects. Civil laws are rules by which the subjects are to regulate their actions— doing what the laws enjoin and avoiding what the laws forbid. The laws are supposed to be means by which the sovereign can influence the actions of the subject; civil laws are "Artificiall Chains" which men have "fastned at one end, to the lips of that Man, or Assembly, to whom they have given the Soveraigne Power; and at the other end to their own Ears. These Bonds in their own nature but weak, may neverthelesse be made to hold, by the danger, though not by the difficulty of breaking them." [71] The chains of law are chains of words addressed to the subject.

The purpose of giving a law is to influence the conduct of the subject. His conduct can be influenced if the existence of the law and the penalties of disobeying it enter into his deliberation. In other words, laws are means by which the sovereign can influence or control the subject insofar as they are causes of his will—items taken into account when he sums up the consequences of any action.

The nature and purpose of law limit what can be done by law. Laws do not speak to those who are not obliged to obey, nor to those who are incapable of understanding them, nor to

---

[69] *Leviathan* (24), p. 191. But the passage goes on to forbid the subject to make war on the sovereign, or accuse him of injustice, or even to speak evil of him. The passage may have been directed against the sequestering of the lands of "disaffected persons" and "delinquents."

[70] *LW* III, 186–87. See Appendix 6.   [71] *Leviathan* (21), pp. 162–63.

those who have no means of taking notice of them. A law must be published to those whom it is to affect. Those having incomplete or undeveloped minds incapable of deliberation (e.g., children, fools, the insane, the injured, animals) are excused because of their impediments.[72]

To inflict harm on persons who cannot have conformed their conduct to the rule (1) because they are incapable of obeying any rule,[73] or (2) because the rule was not announced to them (and they had no opportunity to take notice of it),[74] or (3) because there was no rule when they acted,[75] or (4) despite the fact that they have acted in obedience to the rule (i.e., they are innocent),[76] or (5) without a trial prior to the infliction of harm,[77] is not to punish such persons for their crimes against the law. The harm inflicted in such cases is not an act of punishment—an evil inflicted on a lawbreaker to dispose his will or the will of others to obedience—but an act of hostility.[78]

Nevertheless, the sovereign may commit acts of hostility against subjects without their having any remedy. Here too, *princeps legibus solutus est;* the sovereign can act outside the law. Jeptha's sacrificing his daughter and David's killing Uriah were acts of hostility although neither act "injured" the harmed person.[79] Moreover, not all acts of hostility are injuries to God: a dangerous psychopath could be imprisoned (an act of hostility) for the safety of others. An innocent or ignorant or incapable person might be forced to obey what was not a law to him, e.g., a traffic rule, a black-out in war-time, avoidance of a restricted area under the Emergency Powers (Defence) Act. The force used would be a kind of act of hostility, but clearly, no crime or sin would have been committed. These are

---

[72] *Ibid.* (26), p. 208. Since some of these sorts of creatures are capable of obeying direct orders they are excused because they cannot take notice of commands in general terms—rules given for unspecified future application rather than particular immediate commands. See Warrender, *The Political Philosophy of Hobbes,* pp. 21–24, 80–87, 254–56.

[73] *Leviathan* (26, 27), pp. 208, 231.   [74] *Ibid.,* pp. 208, 225.

[75] *Ibid.* (27, 28), pp. 226, 240–41.   [76] *Ibid.* (26, 28), pp. 213–14, 244.

[77] *Ibid.* (28), p. 239.   [78] *Ibid.,* pp. 238–40.   [79] *Ibid.* (21), pp. 163–64.

cases in which the sovereign acts by virtue of his power rather than by the ordinary course of law.

The sovereign, then, is the legislator for the commonwealth. He makes civil laws and translates natural law into civil law. He is ultimate controller of the interpretation of the law. There are no limits of subject to his power to legislate. He is bound neither by past law, nor by his own legislation, nor by any other man's interpretation of natural or civil law. The sovereign is not bound to act by law; he may act by virtue of his prerogative power. Although the sovereign need not act by law, law will usually be the best means of action available to him —it conforms others' actions to the rules by the threat of physical coercion or punishment rather than by the use of force.

The second function of the sovereign in preserving the internal order of the society is the administration of government. The sovereign is the executor of the rules and the decisions of the society, i.e., his own rules and decisions.

The sovereign is the executor of the law in its application to individuals. One of the inconveniences of the state of nature is the lack of a way to settle conflicts over goods without resorting to force. The corresponding benefit in civil society is the existence of a judge with the power "of hearing and deciding all Controversies, which may arise concerning Law, either Civill, or Naturall, or concerning Fact." [80] The subject is not free to use or ignore the judge as he pleases, for if he were to attempt to vindicate his rights by force, he would violate the peace of the society and break its laws. Although the parties might be free to settle their differences by a private agreement (provided it was not illegal), either party could appeal to the sovereign or to his appointed delegate for protection of his rights. The subject is only free forcibly to vindicate his rights if he is permitted to do so by law or if he is assaulted and fears that he will be killed. Since the law cannot arrive in time to protect him, he may protect himself.[81]

[80] *Ibid.* (18), p. 138. *Cf.* Locke, *Second Treatise*, chap. ix, sec. 125; Laslett ed., p. 369.
[81] *Leviathan* (27), p. 230.

In bringing their controversy before the sovereign's courts, the subjects bring it before judges agreeable to both parties. A litigant may even bring suit against a judge he accuses of having been partial. Both parties have already accepted the sovereign as judge, but they have not accepted his delegate.[82] The complainant, in bringing his case to court, accepts that court. The defendant may take exception to the judges whom he suspects of being interested; those judges to whom he makes no exception he accepts. The defendant may appeal to another judge, in which case he has chosen that judge. As a final recourse, there is the possibility of appealing to the sovereign.[83]

Hobbes regards the impartiality of the judge as important. He approves of the English system under which both lords and commoners received justice from their equals in rank—the House of Lords and the local jury respectively. In both sorts of cases, the party is judged by judges of his own choice.[84] The judge ought to give his judgment according to the facts established by witnesses. His judgment ought to be equitable, according to the law of nature or the civil law equitably interpreted. The interpretation of the law may be presented to the judges (i.e., the jury), as it is in England, by an official appointed by the sovereign for that purpose.[85]

The administration of justice is not completed by the decision of the particular case by the officials appointed by the sovereign. It is also necessary that the decision be executed by other officers appointed by the sovereign.[86]

It is the sovereign's function to make sure that the society keeps going, that those tasks are performed which must be performed if the society is to go on. The sovereign is the

[82] I do not believe that Hobbes is inconsistent here. If the subject expects the sovereign to be hostile he has no recourse. Presumably the sovereign wishes to appoint a judge as a means of keeping peace between the parties. If either party suspects the judge of personal hostility or interest (the judge being a natural as well as an official person), it is against the sovereign's purpose to appoint him in that case.

[83] *Leviathan* (23), pp. 186–87.

[84] *Ibid.* See also *De Cive* (xiii. 17), *EW* II, 180–81; *Elements of Law* (II. i. 11; II. ix. 6), pp. 112, 182.

[85] *Leviathan* (26), pp. 216–17.   [86] *Ibid.* (23), p. 187.

legislator of the rules of the society and the administrator of those rules. The sovereign appoints officials, delegates to them their powers, and supervises their activities; the appointed officials do the actual executing of the sovereign's rules and decisions.[87] The sovereign may appoint officials to do anything that the sovereign could do, anything necessary for the peace, security, and prosperity of the commonwealth. (The maxim *Delegata potestas non potest delegari* does not apply.) The sovereign may appoint a governor (for the whole state or for any part of it) that the subject is bound to obey as long as the governor acts within his powers and in the sovereign's name. Officials may be appointed to care for the economic activities of the country, to collect taxes and other public revenue, to dispense funds, to account for the public money. Military and diplomatic officers may be appointed; the former to command the forces of the commonwealth, the latter to represent its person to other states. Judicial officials may be provided by the sovereign; other officials may be authorized to carry out the judgments of the sovereign's courts. Still other public officials apprehend and imprison criminals, publish the laws, or preserve the peace. Since one of the most effective ways to preserve the peace is to dispose men to act rightly—and men who calculate correctly (i.e., understand their duties and do not hold doctrines subversive to the commonwealth) are more likely to act rightly—the sovereign will appoint teachers to explain to the citizens their obligations, and preachers to encourage obedience.[88]

To perform the sovereign's functions (to make foreign and domestic policy, to legislate, to judge, to appoint subordinate officials, to command the forces of the society, to authorize doctrines), and especially to perform them in such a way as to strengthen the state (and the sovereign's position in it), requires intelligent calculation. Information must be gathered, experiences reported, consequences calculated. The sovereign, if he

[87] *Ibid.* (18), p. 138.   [88] *Ibid.* (23), pp. 184–88.

is to act most effectively, will seek out the best information and the best advice available. The best counsellors are disinterested, precise, informed, and expert, either because of their experience or their science.[89] Counselling is giving advice aimed at the benefit of the person advised. No one has a right to be another's counsellor, or to demand that his advice be taken. Such a demand implies that a command is being given that the other is obliged to obey. Conversely, since the request for advice authorizes the counsellor to give his opinion, he cannot be equitably punished for that opinion.[90] The sovereign is free to take advice from a number of counsellors, and should consult them separately rather than as a group.

Hobbes believed monarchy superior to conciliar governments because a monarch was more likely to be well counselled. Sovereign assemblies consult among themselves, and in these consultations the opinions of the members are presented in lengthy, persuasive orations.[91]

A man that doth his businesse by the help of many and prudent Counsellours, with every one consulting apart in his proper element, does it best, as he that useth able Seconds at Tennis play, placed in their proper stations. He does next best, that useth his own Judgement only; as he that has no Second at all. But he that is carried up and down to his businesse in a framed Counsell, which cannot move but by the plurality of consenting opinions, the execution whereof is commonly (out of envy, or interest) retarded by the part dissenting, does it worst of all, and like one that is carried to the ball, though by good Players, yet in a Wheelebarrough, or other frame, heavy of it self, and retarded also by the inconcurrent judgements, and endeavours of them that drive it.[92]

In Hobbes's commonwealth there is provision for the discussion of policy. This discussion takes place during the sovereign's deliberation; if the sovereign is a single natural person, deliberation occurs within the sovereign's mind, or with such

[89] *Ibid.* (25), pp. 198–201. [90] *Ibid.*, p. 196.
[91] *Ibid.* (19, 25), pp. 144, 200–2. *Cf. De Cive* (x. 9–12), *EW* II, 136–39; *Elements of Law* (II. v. 4), pp. 141–42.
[92] *Leviathan* (25), p. 202.

advisers as he chooses; if the sovereign is a group of men, they deliberate among themselves, or with such advisers as the assembly chooses. But there is no place for an organized opposition. Such a group would be an unlawful league in a monarchy, an unlawful conspiracy in a sovereign assembly—in short, a faction.[93] To consult several advisers may be wise as long as the decision rests with a single person. Many eyes see more than one, but "because many eyes see the same thing in divers lines, and are apt to look asquint towards their private benefit; they that desire not to misse their marke, though they look about with two eyes, yet they never ayme but with one." [94]

Governmental Policy

The sovereign's function is to preserve the society, to establish an internal order or peace, and to defend that peace against external violence. Society exists so that men may live. Hobbes emphasizes the precariousness of human life and the difficulty of keeping men's desires in check. In this emphasis he follows Augustine (probably because of Calvin) rather than Plato and Aristotle; society exists to maintain life rather than to attempt to attain the good life.[95] The state does not aim at the achievement of beauty, nobility, virtue, holiness, or wisdom. The common good, whether conceived as moral or economic, is not the primary aim of society but a means to the preservation of life. The sovereign provides an impartial justice neither because he is obliged to do so,[96] nor because individual men

[93] *Ibid.* (22), pp. 181–82. Assemblies are particularly subject to factional differences which develop into a civil war. See *ibid.* (19), p. 145. No large popular commonwealth has ever maintained itself (save those unified by a foreign enemy) without a single outstanding man, a cabal, or the mutual fear of equal factions. Small republics may be more united, but "there is no humane wisdome can uphold them, longer then the Jealousy lasteth of their potent Neighbours." *Ibid.* (25), p. 202. (*N.B.* this passage does not occur in the Latin version of *Leviathan, LW* III, 196.)

[94] *Leviathan* (25), p. 202.

[95] Compare, *Politics* 1252 b, p. 5: "while it [the *polis*] grows for the sake of mere life, it *exists* for the sake of a good life."

[96] The sovereign is obliged to do this by the laws of nature, but the obligation is not enforced by other men.

have a right to demand it of him, but because law equitably administered by impartial judges is the most effective means of preventing and resolving conflicts among the members of the society. Public teaching of religion, even the Christian religion, is a means not to salvation but to peace. Public care for the economy—the welfare of the members of the society— although it benefits the individuals, is primarily intended to strengthen and secure the society.

ECONOMIC POLICY

The sovereign's end is the safety of the people; the sovereign is obliged to God to promote this end by the law of nature. "But by Safety here, is not meant a bare Preservation, but also all other Contentments of life, which every man by lawfull industry, without danger, or hurt to the Common-wealth, shall acquire to himselfe." The sovereign is not limited to a negative promotion of the safety of the people. He is not restricted to his usual function of protecting individuals from injuries on their complaint; he (like God) is to exercise "a generall Providence, contained in publique Instruction, both of Doctrine, and Example," and to make and execute good laws.[97]

Good laws are laws that are needed for the good of the people, i.e., laws ought not to be superfluous, their purposes should be clear, and clearly stated.[98] But is there not a distinction between laws for the good of the sovereign and laws for the good of the members of the society? Since the sovereign is supported by the society, is it not to his benefit to take more than the minimum from the subjects so that he may live in luxury, and support the relatives, favorites, and friends of the monarch or the sovereign assembly?[99] The sovereign's private and personal good is only apparently in conflict with the public

---

[97] *Leviathan* (30), p. 258. *Cf. De Cive* (xiii. 6, 14), *EW* II, 169, 176–78; *Elements of Law* (II. ix. 4), pp. 180–81.

[98] *Leviathan* (30), pp. 268–69.

[99] This is usually an objection to monarchy, but Hobbes turns it against republics. *Ibid.* (19), pp. 144–45; *De Cive* (x. 6), *EW* II, 131–32; *Elements of Law* (II. v. 5), p. 142.

good. The strength and wealth of the sovereign are derived from, and dependent upon, the strength and wealth of the members. Conversely, a society is weak if the sovereign cannot command its wealth and power.

The good of the sovereign and the good of the members are inseparable.[100] To view the sovereign's good and the subjects' good as separable is to court disaster. Such a view encourages the opinion that the sovereign is demanding the subjects' goods unnecessarily, or that the subjects have absolute ownership in their properties and can refuse to pay taxes. To circumvent this limitation the sovereign strains to find money, often by petty legal devices enacted as "trapps for Mony." [101] The opposition of the subjects' good to that of the sovereign weakens the state if the sovereign does nothing, complicates and corrupts the laws if the sovereign attempts to get around the resistance, or leads to a direct clash between sovereign and subjects, which must result either in the victory of the sovereign over the rebels, or the destruction of the commonwealth. All unnecessarily, for

the greatest pressure of Soveraign Governours, proceedeth not from any delight, or profit, they can expect in the dammage, or weakening of their Subjects, in whose vigor, consisteth their own strength and glory; but in the restiveness of themselves, that unwillingly contributing to their own defence, make it necessary for their Governours to draw from them what they can in time of Peace, that they may have means on any emergent occasion, or sudden need, to resist, or take advantage on their Enemiés.[102]

Truly, "Common-wealths can endure no Diet." [103]

The sovereign's promotion of the economic well-being of the community begins with the distribution of property and the enactment of the laws defining property rights and the

[100] *Leviathan* (19, 30), pp. 144, 268; *De Cive* (x. 2), *EW* II, 127–29; *Elements of Law* (II. v. 1), pp. 137–38. Of course, it may be necessary to curb excessively powerful, popular, or rich subjects. See *Leviathan* (30), p. 270.
[101] *Leviathan* (29, 30), pp. 255–56, 268.   [102] *Ibid.* (18), p. 141.
[103] *Ibid.* (24), p. 191.

rules of exchange.[104] But the sovereign's functions in the economy are not exhausted by the establishment of private property, the means for securing and maintaining property, and legal methods of transferring it, not even if the guarantees and conveniences for property are extended to include a currency system (a system which the sovereign can only partially control because the value of precious metals is determined in an international market).[105]

The sovereign, in addition to providing the legal framework for property, has functions in the economy of the state which may be inconsistent with a private-property–free-market system. God has placed the means of plenty before men. Plenty can be purchased from nature by labor, which is itself a thing of value, capable of being bought and sold. Some nations, poor in resources, have even lived from the sale of their labor in manufacturing and trading.[106] And it is the sovereign that regulates this foreign trade. The sovereign may (and Hobbes expects that he will) assign, approve, and disapprove, both the places to which men may trade and the goods in which they may trade. The sovereign may forbid trade with the enemy in strategic materials and prevent the importation of harmful things.[107] Clearly the sovereign has the power to incorporate groups of merchants for trade to particular places; this involves the right to create a kind of double monopoly: the sole buying at home and selling abroad of goods traded to that area; and the sole

[104] *Ibid.* pp. 189–93. Hobbes seems to think that property, especially property in land, will be owned by individuals. However, there is no theoretical reason why this should be the case. Artificial persons may hold property: e.g., the sovereign (p. 191) or a (public or private) subordinate corporation that can, by its representative, have whatever powers are granted by the sovereign's charter or by the laws, including the powers to make contracts, incur debts, participate in a common venture. A family is such a corporation, albeit private, authorized by the ordinary laws of the commonwealth, rather than public, authorized by charter. (See *ibid.* [22], pp. 173–79 *passim*.) There is no reason why any of these organizations could not be the subject of legal rights, and in the seventeenth century, as well as in this century, they were.

[105] *Ibid.* (24), pp. 193–94.

[106] *Ibid.*, p. 189. *De Cive* (xiii. 14), *EW* II, 176–78.

[107] *Leviathan* (24), p. 192.

buying abroad and selling at home of the goods of that area traded to the home market. Hobbes turns out to be something less than a mercantilist, and also something less than a free trader; he recommends that the company retain monopoly practices abroad (a single seller or purchaser has a bargaining advantage), but that each individual trade for himself at home (presumably lowering the prices at which the imported goods are sold but raising the prices of goods produced within the society).[108]

The sovereign has a labor policy as well as a trade policy. Those who are able to work are to be forced to work. The sovereign ought to encourage navigation, agriculture, fishing, and manufacture so that there can be no "excuse of not finding employment." If the population increases still more, some are to be sent to more sparsely inhabited areas. "And when all the world is overcharged with Inhabitants, then the last remedy of all is Warre; which provideth for every man, by Victory, or Death."[109]

The taxation policy suggested by Hobbes favors mercantilist thrift over luxurious consumption—on the principle of equality.

To Equall Justice, appertaineth also the Equall imposition of Taxes; the Equality whereof dependeth not on the Equality of riches, but on the Equality of the debt, that every man oweth to the Common-wealth for his defence. It is not enough, for a man to labour for the maintenance of his life; but also to fight, (if need be,) for the securing of his labour. They must either do as the Jewes did after their return from captivity, in re-edifying the Temple, build with one hand, and hold the Sword in the other; or else they must hire others to fight for them. For the Impositions, that are layd on the People by the Soveraign Power, are nothing else but the Wages, due to them that hold the publique Sword, to

---

[108] *Ibid.* (22), pp. 177–78.

[109] *Ibid.* (30), p. 267. *N.B.* that the colonists are not to exterminate the native inhabitants of the new territory but merely to make them develop intensive cultivation instead of grazing or gathering. See also *ibid.* (24), p. 190. *Cf. Elements of Law* (II. ix. 3), pp. 179–80, where the sovereign's duty includes the obligation to promote the increase of population, especially by suitable marriage laws.

defend private men in the exercise of severall Trades, and Callings. Seeing then the benefit that every one receiveth thereby, is the enjoyment of life, which is equally dear to poor, and rich; the debt which a poor man oweth them that defend his life, is the same which a rich man oweth for the defence of his; saving that the rich, who have the service of the poor, may be debtors not onely for their own persons, but for many more. Which considered, the Equality of Imposition, consisteth rather in the Equality of that which is consumed, than of the riches of the persons that consume the same. For what reason is there, that he which laboureth much, and sparing the fruits of his labour, consumeth little, should be more charged, then he that living idlely, getteth little, and spendeth all he gets; seeing the one hath no more protection from the Commonwealth, then the other? But when the Impositions, are layd upon those things which men consume, every man payeth Equally for what he useth: Nor is the Common-wealth defrauded, by the luxurious waste of private men.[110]

Finally, those who by "accident unevitable" are unable to work, are to be supported by the state. They should not be exposed to the hazard of private charity, but have their necessities provided by public charity.[111]

The good laws that Hobbes hopes the sovereign will make are laws that aim at the inseparable good of sovereign and subject. Good laws are simple, easily understood because clearly expressed in a few words, and set out with the reasons for their enactment.[112] The avoidance of ambiguity in the commands of the commonwealth is as useful for correct action as the avoidance of ambiguity in reasoning is necessary to correct conclusions.

[110] *Leviathan* (30), pp. 266–67. *Cf. De Cive* (xiii. 10–11), *EW* II, 173–74, where Hobbes, following the same line of reasoning, considers, and rejects, taxing gains equally: "But if we consider, where monies are raised according to wealth, there they who have made equal gain, have not equal possessions, because that one preserves what he hath got by frugality, another wastes it by luxury, and therefore equally rejoicing in the benefit of peace, they do not equally sustain the burthens of the commonweal: and on the other side, where the goods themselves are taxed, there every man, while he spends his private goods, in the very act of consuming them he undiscernably pays part due to the commonweal, according to, not what he hath, but what by the benefit of the realm he hath had." See also *Elements of Law* (II. ix. 5), pp. 181–82.
[111] *Leviathan* (30), p. 267.   [112] *Ibid.,* p. 268. *Cf.* Plato, *Laws,* 722 ff.

Despite the legal competence of the sovereign to do whatever is deemed necessary for the society, and despite the sovereign's power to promote prosperity, Hobbes does not expect the sovereign to regulate everything. On the contrary, laws may be superfluous, unnecessary, and therefore not good. Hobbes expects that the sovereign will leave the subject free to buy and sell, and to contract with others, to choose his own manner of life (abode, diet, trade) and to educate his children as he thinks fit.[113] Laws are not intended to prescribe all the subjects' actions, but rather to limit their choices, "to direct and keep them in such a motion, as not to hurt themselves by their own impetuous desires, rashnesse, or indiscretion; as Hedges are set, not to stop Travellers, but to keep them in the way." [114]

SOCIAL POLICY

In the state of nature, men are naturally equal; it is a law of nature that they acknowledge their equality. Some aspects of man's equality continue to exist in society, others are abrogated.

Society introduces differences of condition among men. It is only in society that the variations in power and in ability develop to the extent of being inequalities in condition. It is in society that proficiency in the arts and sciences develops; such proficiency depends on the existence of arts and sciences, and these exist only in society. In addition to the natural distinctions among men, society artificially introduces distinctions in power, honor, rank, and property. In a commonwealth, the sovereign power is the fountain of honor. The sovereign sets the public value of a man by employing him in public office, giving him power, or by giving him a "title of honor." (These titles were themselves originally titles of public office and command.) [115] Property, another social inequality, is derived from

[113] *Leviathan* (21), pp. 163, 168–69.
[114] *Ibid.* (30), p. 168. *Cf. De Cive* (xiii. 15), *EW* II, 178–79; *Elements of Law* (II. ix. 4), pp. 180–81.
[115] *Leviathan* (10), pp. 68, 69–70, 73–74.

the distribution of the sovereign, and supported by the sovereign's laws.[116] The sovereign power may even transfer the property of one man to another without a crime by the first, without pretence of public benefit, and without injury.[117] Man's natural equality is superseded by social inequality based on the sovereign's distribution of political office, political power, honor, and property (one form of reward within the sovereign's gift). Political power is the cause of social inequality rather than its result.[118]

Men are, or are to be accounted, equal, mainly because most of them refuse to be regarded as inferior. Very few men will object to being honored as superior; in fact men tend to demand this because they overvalue themselves and undervalue others. In order to prevent the consequent quarrels, "It is necessary that there be Lawes of Honour, and a publique rate of the worth of such men as have deserved, or are able to deserve well of the Common-wealth; and that there be force in the hands of some or other, to put those Lawes in execution." [119] The sovereign establishes orders of rank and dignity, confers them on individuals, and legislates the protocols of respect.

Despite the inequality consequent upon society, the equality of men is not entirely destroyed. The inequalities are conventional, not natural; they may be taken away by the sovereign. These inequalities of rank and power disappear in the presence of the sovereign; before him all subjects are to be regarded as equal in power and in honor. "And though they shine some more, some lesse, when they are out of his sight; yet in his presence, they shine no more than the Starres in presence of the Sun." [120] The equality of subjects before the sovereign is especially important in the dispensation of justice. There are vainglorious men who believe themselves to be naturally superior to others, immune from the ordinary laws and punish-

[116] Ibid. (18, 24, 29), pp. 137, 189–91, 250–51.
[117] *Elements of Law* (II. v. 2), p. 140.   [118] *Cf.* Dahrendorf, pp. 104–5.
[119] *Leviathan* (18), p. 139.   [120] *Ibid.*, p. 141.

ments.[121] Yet "the safety of the People" requires that justice be done to the rich and powerful as well as the poor and impotent. The sovereign is bound by the law of nature to punish the great when they injure the mean; equity requires the equal administration of justice to all degrees of men.[122] The privileges of the nobility in Europe (e.g., to sit in the Council of State by inheritance), privileges derived from their ancestors, absolute lords, who insisted on such privileges when they confederated to conquer others, are inconsistent with sovereign power. The nobility's privileges are kept by the sovereign's permission, "but contending for them as their Right, they must needs by degrees let them go, and have at last no further honour, then adhæreth naturally to their abilities." [123] The natural equality of men persists in society in equality before the sovereign, and before the law, and in the tendency for natural abilities and disabilities to produce their natural consequences on the power, honor, and rank of their possessors.

RELIGIOUS AND EDUCATIONAL POLICY

For the sake of peace, the sovereign must have the right to control the expression of opinion. Men's actions follow from their opinions; men who believe it legitimate to kill tyrants will assassinate their rulers; men who believe it justifiable to rebel will rebel; men who believe that priests control greater powers of punishment and reward than kings will obey priests rather than kings.[124] It is not possible for the sovereign to control the internal thoughts and beliefs of the subjects (thought is free), nor is it desirable that he should inquire into men's thoughts. (It is even against the law of nature for him to do so.) [125] The sovereign cannot oblige men to believe, but he

[121] *Ibid.* (27), pp. 228–29.
[122] *Ibid.* (30), pp. 265–66, 269; *Elements of Law* (II. ix. 6), p. 182.
[123] *Leviathan* (30), p. 272. Hobbes, although not a Leveller, is egalitarian, yet this position on natural nobility as opposed to nobility of blood was a Renaissance commonplace.
[124] *Ibid.* (18, 30, 38, 46), pp. 136–37, 258–65, 345, 526–27.
[125] *Ibid.* (37, 40, 46), pp. 345, 364, 534.

can order them to obey. He can also permit the teaching and publication of some opinions and forbid the teaching and publication of other opinions. The public teaching of doctrine conducive to peace may indeed cause men to believe it; especially so, since truth is never really repugnant to peace. New truth may expose an incipient war; it never really starts one.[126] For, according to Hobbes, truth is exhibited in his own moral philosophy. The truth about men's obligations and the powers of the sovereign leads as certainly to peace and obedience as the laws of nature are the necessary means to peace. The happy consistency of truth and peace in moral philosophy is matched by the tendency of true religion to peace. Natural sciences, especially mathematics, do not affect most men's interests, and therefore disputes in these sciences do not usually endanger the peace of the state. But religion, like politics, may be dangerous to the state. Religion is naturally based on man's curiosity, the desire to know causes. Curiosity compounded with ignorance produces fear of imaginary powers, and therefore worship. Curiosity combined with knowledge produces reverence for God, and therefore worship. The worship of God has been cultivated in two ways: by human invention, and by God's commandment. Both these sorts of religion are conducive to peace.[127] In order to understand why this is so, we must examine the two different ways that God has commanded men: naturally and prophetically.

God's natural kingdom over men is not simply God's natural power over them. To call God's irresistible power over all things a kingdom "is but a metaphoricall use of the word." [128] Although God's right to rule is derived from his irresistible power, it is exercised over subjects who have submitted by recognizing that power. God is the first, unlimited cause. Men who acknowledge

---

[126] *Ibid.* (18), p. 137. Nevertheless, Hobbes does excuse the novelty of his doctrine by arguing not only that it is true and conducive to peace but also that it is not disturbing a settled situation. See *ibid.* (Review and Conclusion), p. 555.

[127] *Ibid.* (12), pp. 82–85.　　　[128] *Ibid.* (31), p. 274.

God's existence and his power, viz., theists, are God's subjects. They believe that God governs the world, i.e., that there is a causal order. God has given them a sufficiently clear promulgation of his commands, his rewards, and his punishments. through the dictates of natural reason. Theists acknowledge that the laws of nature (knowledge of the causes of peace) are commanded by God, and they acknowledge that the effects of obedience and disobedience are the natural rewards and punishments provided by God as sanctions for these laws.[129]

To acknowledge the power of God is almost to worship him. To worship is to exhibit external signs of honor; "Honour consisteth in the inward thought, and opinion of the Power, and the Goodnesse of another: and therefore to Honour God, is to think as Highly of his Power and Goodnesse, as is possible." [130] God's goodness is not as evident to reason as is his power; still, since God's power is acknowledged as irresistible by the theist, he has accepted God as ultimate sovereign and consequently he has no right to judge God, or God's actions, evil.[131] External worship may use either natural or conventional signs of honor. So that men do not offend each other, the sovereign may prescribe the conventions of the public worship of God. Public worship is appropriate because it exhibits to the eyes of others that honor of God which men should have; and, since a commonwealth is a single person, its subjects ought to be commanded to exhibit a uniform public worship of God.[132] Otherwise, the commonwealth could not be said to be of any religion at all. Men are free to think as they please about the "civil religion," provided that they obey the commands of the sovereign as they are obliged to. In private they may worship as they please.[133]

[129] See above, pp. 107–28.   [130] *Leviathan* (31), p. 277.

[131] Although the confirmation of revealed religion is inadmissible here, it should be noted that Hobbes mentions God's justification of Job's afflictions by his power. (Job 38:4) *Leviathan* (31), pp. 276–77.

[132] *Ibid.*, pp. 277–83; *De Cive* (xv. 15–18), *EW* II, 216–25. Nevertheless, the Romans tolerated any religion that was not subversive. Hobbes does not condemn them for it. See *Leviathan* (12), p. 90.

[133] *Leviathan* (31), p. 279.

By natural reason we can know that God is, and that he is the cause of the world. We can honor him by using words that express our ignorance of his nature and our reverence for his power and goodness. According to natural reason, God's attributes are negative (infinite, eternal, incomprehensible), or superlative (most high, most good), or indefinite (good, holy, just, etc.). To attempt to determine God's nature any further is frivolous; it dishonors him to do so.[134]

Religion was cultivated by the founders and legislators of states among the Gentiles to promote peace and obedience. They inculcated the belief that their religious precepts were supernaturally revealed; they taught that the gods were displeased by what the laws forbade; they prescribed appropriate ceremonies; and, although the contrary opinion was allowed, they promoted the belief in rewards and punishments after this life. In short, they reinforced the authority of the state and the laws by pretended supernatural revelation, pretended prophecy, and pretended miracles.[135]

It is now necessary to examine the effect that a true revealed religion has on the rights of sovereigns and the duties of subjects. There have been only two such religions; first Judaism, later Christianity.

The tenets of a revealed religion are not discoverable by natural reason, but reason and experience are not renounced in understanding revelation. Revelation does not contradict sense, experience, and reason. In things beyond our understanding, men may be obliged to submit not their minds but their wills, i.e., where obedience is due.[136]

God speaks to men in two ways: (1) directly; (2) through the mediation of another man.

(1) Direct revelation, or sense supernatural. God has spoken to some men directly. Christians believe this, for they are told

---

· [134] *Ibid.*, pp. 279–82. See Appendix 7.
   [135] *Leviathan* (12), pp. 85, 89–90. *Cf.* Machiavelli, *Discourses*, I. 11–15; Walker trans., I, 240–51.
   [136] *Leviathan* (32), p. 287.

in the Bible that God spoke to Moses, to the prophets, and to Job. Most men do not have this experience, and so they are unable to understand exactly how God speaks to a man directly. God has directly commanded particular men to do various things (e.g., he commanded Jonah to preach), but no general commands have been promulgated by direct revelation to an entire community (e.g., God revealed the Ten Commandments to Moses directly, but to the Hebrews indirectly through Moses). It follows that there is no Kingdom of God which he rules by direct revelation.[137]

The claim to have received a direct revelation from God is vulnerable to skeptical attack. To say that God spoke through the Scriptures is not a claim to have had an immediate revelation. If a man says that God spoke in a dream, it "is no more then to say he dreamed that God spake to him." Visions, dreams, voices, and enthusiasms are more likely to be illusory experiences of revelation due to natural causes, than true revelations. "So that though God Almighty can speak to a man, by Dreams, Visions, Voice, and Inspiration; yet he obliges no man to beleeve that he has so done to him that pretends it; who (being a man) may erre, and (which is more) may lie." [138]

(2) Mediate revelation. The consideration of direct revelation has led to the problem of mediated revelation: through which man has God revealed his will? Or how can true prophets be distinguished from false ones?

There is no infallible natural mark of having received divine revelation. Qualities by which men naturally test holiness are: especial wisdom; sincerity; love of others; supernatural signs—miracles or extraordinary felicity. Men naturally tend to lose faith or disbelieve in the supernatural revelation of those who exhibit the contrary qualities: ignorance, e.g., enjoining belief in logical contradictions; insincerity—acting as if they do not believe what they tell others to believe; self-

---

[137] *Ibid.* (31, 32), pp. 275, 287.   [138] *Ibid.* (32), pp. 287–88.

interest, e.g., requiring beliefs tending to enhance the power and wealth of the preacher; no supernatural signs.[139]

The Holy Scriptures establish two characteristics, which taken together are the marks of a true prophet: teaching the established religion and not any other; doing miracles.[140]

The Scriptures repeatedly warn against prophets who do miracles and teach doctrine that varies from the doctrine of the Scriptures.[141] But teaching the true doctrine without miracles is not sufficient to verify the claim to revelation.

Hobbes's critique of the marks of revelation is intended to establish a skeptical attitude to all claims of direct communication with God. Most prophets are self-anointed frauds; and even true prophets have been deceived by false ones.[142] Miracles, supposedly supernatural signs of divine revelation, are also suspect. A miracle is a wonder worked by God for the purpose of securing the belief of the elect (i.e., those God has chosen for salvation) in God's messenger or prophet. If an event has not this purpose, it is no miracle although it may exhibit God's power. To qualify as miraculous, an event must be both rare and not explicable by natural causes. If an event is ordinary, it is not a miracle. Any event, no matter how unusual, which can be explained by science is no miracle. Events may be miraculous to the superstitious and ignorant which appear perfectly natural—indeed inevitable in the course of nature—to the scientific, e.g., an eclipse.[143] Not only is the scope of the miraculous increased by ignorance, but it may also be expanded by trickery and enchantment; and enchantment is not causing effects by words,

but Imposture, and delusion, wrought by ordinary means; and so far from supernaturall, as the Impostors need not the study so much as of naturall causes, but the ordinary ignorance, stupidity,

---

[139] *Ibid.* (12), pp. 90–92.   [140] *Ibid.* (32), p. 288.
[141] *Ibid.*, pp. 288–89. Hobbes cites Deut. 13:1–5, Matt. 24:24, and Gal. 1:8.
[142] *Leviathan* (32, 36), pp. 287–89, 326–37.
[143] *Ibid.* (37), pp. 338–41. *Cf.* Plato, *Timaeus*, 40 c–d.

and superstition of mankind, to doe them; . . . So that all the Miracle consisteth in this, that the Enchanter has deceived a man; which is no Miracle, but a very easie matter to doe.[144]

A little knowledge or skill beyond the ordinary enables the trickster to impress his fellow men by sleight-of-hand, or ventriloquism. A crafty fortune teller needs only a bit of unexpected information. The possibilities of fraud by a man if he has assistants are immense.[145]

Men are not obliged to believe that any reported revelation is authentic. Men may believe that a revelation is authentic; they may be obliged—by the lawful government—to acknowledge the authenticity of a revelation even if they do not believe it. The force of miracles as proof of a revelation is limited: (1) the revelation may not be contrary to the already revealed word of God; (2) very miracles are unusual, unexplainable, and unlikely.

To know the obligations of Christians to their governments and to God requires an examination of the Holy Scriptures and a historical account of the Kingdom of God. Miracles having ceased, Christians need not accept any doctrine inconsistent with the Scriptures. Since Christ's time, the Scriptures, wisely and carefully interpreted, have been the source of human knowledge of God's commands.[146] What books of Scripture are to be acknowledged as canonical? What is their authority? No one can know that the Scriptures are God's Word except those to whom God revealed it supernaturally. Why then do we believe they are God's word? To this question there is no single answer, for men may believe this for various reasons. Correctly stated the question is: Why are we obliged, or by what authority are the Scriptures made law?

(1) Insofar as they are identical to the laws of nature, the Scriptures are God's law published to all men with natural reason.

[144] *Leviathan* (37), p. 342.   [145] *Ibid.*, p. 343.   [146] *Ibid.* (32), p. 290.

(2) The Scriptures oblige those to whom God has revealed supernaturally that he commands them.

(3) The Scriptures oblige those who are commanded to obey them by the sovereign, who already is empowered to make law. (A "church" with power to oblige obedience is a commonwealth.) [147]

Otherwise the individual Christian and the individual man is free to believe as he chooses. In a state without a legally established church, religious associations would be "subordinate systems" (public or private, legal or illegal).

If there were a single universal Christian church (a commonwealth composed of all Christians), a kingdom of God in this world, ruled by God or his representative, then, unless this church was identical to a single universal Christian State, there could be a conflict of authority between church and state, and conflicts in the duties of Christian subjects. God has had three sets of representatives on earth: (1) Moses and his successors; (2) Christ when he lived on earth; (3) the Apostles and their successors.[148] The "Kingdom of God" is not a mere metaphor for eternal felicity, but God's monarchy over a particular group of human beings, Israel. This is not a Kingdom by virtue of God's natural power, but a Kingdom in which God's sovereignty was acquired over the subjects by their own consent: "constituted by the Votes of the People of Israel in peculiar manner; wherein they chose God for their King by Covenant made with him, upon Gods promising them the possession of the land of Canaan." [149]

From the beginning God exercised sovereignty over some men directly, e.g., Adam and the survivors of the Flood. Later, God and Abraham contracted—Abraham obliging himself and his posterity to be God's subjects, subjects to God's positive law as well as to the moral law, to which Abraham was already

[147] *Ibid.* (33), pp. 300–2.   [148] *Ibid.* (33, 39), pp. 299, 362–63.
[149] *Ibid.* (35), p. 314. (See also pp. 317, 319.)

obliged. Isaac, Jacob, and Moses renewed this covenant with God.[150] The Israelites were obliged to obey Moses as God's lieutenant, although he was not the legitimate heir of Abraham, Isaac, and Jacob, and whether or not they continued to believe that God spoke directly to him, because they promised to obey him. They submitted to him as Civil Sovereign and God's representative. After his reign the Kingdom descended (according to its constitution) to Aaron and his successors as High Priest, all of whom had sovereign power in religious as well as civil matters.[151]

God's previous sovereignty was cast off (with his consent) by the Israelites when they chose to have a human monarch as sovereign. Saul and his successors had sovereign power, including sovereign power in religion; the priest's office became ministerial.[152] Despite the propensities of the Jews to revolt for civil or religious reasons, and to follow prophets rather than their rightful governors, the right of civil and religious sovereignty was always in the same hands as long as their commonwealth lasted, i.e., until the Captivity. Under the Old Covenant the sovereign represented God's person.[153]

Jesus Christ, the Messiah, was first of all a savior and redeemer. In his sacrifice he took upon himself (by God's mercy and ordination) the sins of mankind. Second, he undertook the office of a pastor, a counsellor, a teacher, and a prophet, to convert those elected by God to salvation. This work is continued by his ministers. Third, at his coming again he will begin the glorious reign as King over the elect; to this promised Kingdom, the elect submit themselves in baptism. Christ's first coming was not as a King but to renew God's covenant with the faithful by baptism, and to preach to them that he was the prophesied Messiah to persuade men to prepare themselves for his Kingdom when he should come to take possession of it. Christ preached no rebellion against the legitimate civil au-

---

[150] *Ibid.* (35, 40), pp. 315–16, 363–65.   [151] *Ibid.* (40), pp. 365–69.
[152] *Ibid.*, pp. 370–71.   [153] *Ibid.*, pp. 372–74.

thority, but submitted to it; he broke no laws.[154] But when he comes again, he will exercise power as God's Vicegerent; he will be, as Moses was, God's representative.[155]

Christ, God's son, left to the Apostles and their successors (the third representative of God) the power to preach, to advise, and to persuade; but he left them no power to coerce men to obedience, no power to punish men for not believing or contradicting, no power to rule over them. Christ left to all sovereigns the authority they had before his coming; in fact he bade men obey them in all things.[156]

Christians are obliged to obey a non-Christian sovereign in all that he commands, even if he should command actions or words denying Christianity. It is not within the sovereign's power to command belief or disbelief, for this is a gift of God. Christians have the liberty to conceal their belief allowed by Elisha to Naaman the Syrian. Suppose there were a secret Mohametan subject in a Christian commonwealth, commanded by his sovereign to attend a Christian church on pain of death; would that Mohametan be obliged to suffer death rather than obey? If there is such an obligation (on Moslems, Christians, or anyone else), then men may claim the privilege of disobeying their sovereigns in the maintenance of their religions, true or false. If not, then a privilege is claimed by Christians which they deny to others contrary to the Golden Rule and the law of nature. In such cases, the external acts are compelled, and are therefore the acts of the sovereign commanding them.[157]

Have all Christian martyrs vainly cast away their lives, then? To be a martyr means to be a witness of Christ's resurrection. Only someone who saw Christ on earth could bear witness to his rising from the dead, e.g., one of Christ's original disciples. Other men can be only hearsay witnesses at a second remove from the event. It is not required of a Christian that he die for every point of doctrine that he or another draws out of the

[154] *Ibid.* (41), pp. 374–79.   [155] *Ibid.*, pp. 379–81.
[156] *Ibid.* (42), pp. 381–87.
[157] *Ibid.* (42, 43, 45), pp. 387–88, 441–42, 460, 470, 509.

Scriptures. Nevertheless Hobbes does allow a limited class of men to suffer death for their faith: men sent to preach the fundamental article of Christianity (that Christ is the Messiah), not having taken this calling upon themselves but having been sent to convert non-Christians.[158] Christian pastors, lawfully called to teach and direct others, and others who have a public reputation for knowledge, ought not to worship idolatrously unless they make their fear and unwilling obedience to the sovereign's command as evident as their worship. Such men have a greater obligation because of their position. As for the private and unlearned Christian in the power of an idolatrous state "if commanded on pain of death to worship before an Idoll, he detesteth the Idoll in his heart, hee doth well; though if he had the fortitude to suffer death, rather than worship it, he should doe better." [159] Unlike a Christian pastor, but like the Moslem, he has no obligation to die for his faith.

Moreover, if we examine Christianity before there were Christian sovereigns, we discover that no one was obliged to believe in any particular interpretation of the Scriptures. For the Apostles and their successors could only persuade others of their opinions; no interpretation of the Scripture was law.[160] The assemblies of Apostles and elders did not destroy the liberty of individuals to read and interpret the Scriptures, although they did agree on an interpretation they would teach. The offices of bishop, elder, and deacon were filled by men elected by plurality of votes in their local assembly of Christians, rather than by men appointed by a superior ecclesiastic.[161]

Before there were Christian civil sovereigns, no one was obliged to be a Christian or to profess Christianity. To refuse Christianity was not a sin, although men who did not accept it died in their sins. Nor was it unjust to disobey or disregard the precepts of Christ, or of the Apostles, or of any other pastors

[158] *Ibid.* (42), pp. 388–90.   [159] Ibid. (45), p. 512.
[160] *Ibid.* (42), pp. 399–402, 406–8.   [161] *Ibid.*, pp. 408–17.

of the church.[162] Their precepts were not laws but counsels.

When a sovereign becomes Christian, he submits himself to God (but to no man) and accepts the fundamental tenet of Christianity: Jesus is the Messiah. He makes the New Testament a law for himself, and he may make it a law to his subjects, just as the old heathen religion was legally binding on them. A Christian sovereign has as much power as a heathen to judge what doctrines are fit for peace and who shall preach them.

Since the Christian sovereign represents the Christians in his society, he acts as a representative of the church in authorizing doctrine and in choosing pastors subordinate to himself, the supreme pastor.[163] It follows that the sovereign is (*jure divino*) the supreme authority over religious doctrine and religious personnel. The sovereign stands in the same position as authenticator of prophets, miracles, and doctrine, as did Moses. The clergy—of whatever denomination—exercise a delegated authority, an authority *jure civili* and not *jure divino*.[164] Christian sovereigns have the authority to preach, baptize, administer the sacraments, and ordain; of course, this authority, like the authority to sit in legal judgment, is usually exercised by the sovereign through his appointees rather than in person.[165]

Hobbes denies that there is any danger to the salvation of a Christian subject in his supreme Erastianism. He also denies that (in the absence of any special revelation) there is any conflict between the obligations a Christian owes to his Christian sovereign and to God. There are two things necessary to salvation: faith and obedience. The faith necessary to salvation is summed up in one necessary article: that *Jesus is the Christ*. This one article includes the existence of God the Father, the Sonship of Jesus the Messiah, etc.[166] Under a Christian sovereign there can be no problem of obedience, for the sovereign as

---

[162] *Ibid.*, pp. 406–10.   [163] *Ibid.*, pp. 408, 409, 421–23.
[164] *Ibid.*, pp. 422–23.   [165] *Ibid.*, pp. 424, 427–28.
[166] *Ibid.* (43), pp. 458, 462. Hobbes offers five arguments to prove this at pp. 462–68.

Christian allows the belief in the one article (and its concomitants) necessary to salvation. It doesn't really matter if some false doctrines or absurd ceremonies are taught as well. The belief in Christ is the foundation, and the rest is superstructure; it does not affect salvation and the subject is not responsible for it.[167] On this account the pope is not Antichrist, but a Christian sovereign (over the papal states), who has attempted to usurp power over other Christians not under his civil authority by promoting certain doctrines and ceremonies.[168]

The obedience required for salvation by God, who accepts the will (or serious intention or endeavor) to obey for the deed, is obedience to the laws men are already obliged to obey: the laws of nature and the laws of the sovereign.[169] It turns out that, in the absence of special revelation, there is no conflict between God's laws and the civil laws of a Christian state, or even of any state that does not forbid the profession of Christianity. Furthermore, all special private revelations are suspect; they can oblige only the individual who believes himself to have had a command from God and no one else. In fact, God's revealed religion is so consistent with Hobbes's doctrine of sovereignty that the Ten Commandments are an exposition of it: the first table contains the law of sovereignty; the second, the duties of men to each other.[170]

In the period between 1638 and 1650, religious conflict became so important an obstacle to civil peace that Hobbes thought it necessary to devote half of *Leviathan* to the discussion of religion. Religion could not be ignored because to control the church was to control the main influence on the formation of public opinion. Hobbes argued that there could be no peace unless the sovereign was rightfully the head of the church and the supreme authority over religious doctrine and ceremony. The sovereign also had the right to control what

---

[167] *Ibid.*, pp. 468–70.　　[169] *Ibid.* (42, 44, 47), pp. 432–33, 474–77, 537–41.
[168] *Ibid.* (43), pp. 457–59.　　[170] *Ibid.* (42), pp. 402–4.

could be taught publicly in universities and published in print.

Although he regarded the establishment of the right of the sovereign as necessary, Hobbes found the situation in England, while there was no established doctrine, congenial. The progressive destruction of the powers of the bishop of Rome, the English episcopate, and the local congregations, had left the English in the same condition of independency as the primitive Christians. If this could be preserved "without contention, and without measuring the Doctrine of Christ, by our affection to the Person of his Minister," it would perhaps be the best condition, because there ought to be no power over the consciences of men but that of God's word, and "because it is unreasonable in them, who teach there is such danger in every little Errour, to require of a man endued with Reason of his own, to follow the Reason of any other man, or of the most voices of many other men; Which is little better, then to venture his Salvation at crosse and pile." [171]

Hobbes must have regarded toleration as a remote possibility, conceivable only if men do not fight over religion, and if the sovereign holds as wide a view of Christianity as Hobbes did and thinks it best to allow liberty. Religion is as much subject to the sovereign's rightful regulation as any other area of human conduct. This is true on natural and rational principles; it is only contradicted in a few minor cases on the nonrational revealed principles of Christianity.

[171] *Ibid.* (47), p. 543.

7

CONCLUSION:
THE EXPLANATION OF
POLITICAL PHENOMENA

Thomas Hobbes was one of those extraordinary little upstarts whom the chaotic motions of the Renaissance tossed into an eminence which they hardly deserved and have never lost.

T. S. ELIOT, "JOHN BRAMHALL," p. 312

Hobbes attempted to create a philosophic system which embraced the science of natural bodies and extended the methods of that science to human actions and political bodies. He believed that he had succeeded. Natural philosophy might be young (being the product of Copernicus, Galileo, Kepler, Gassendi, and Mersenne), and the science of man's body still younger (having originated with Harvey), but youngest of all was civil philosophy—no older than *De Cive*.[1] Apparently, Hobbes was never in any doubt about the scientific character of his political philosophy; he published *De Cive* in 1642 under the title, *Elementorum Philosophiae, Sectio Tertia, De Cive*. In 1646, concluding *A Minute or first Draught of the Optiques*, he claimed to be the inventor of two new sciences:

[1] *De Corpore* (Ep. Ded.), *EW* I, viii–ix.

How doe I feare that ye attentive reader will find that which I have delivered concerning ye *Optiques* fitt to bee cast outt as rubbish among the rest. [That is, with the old worthless opinions.] If hee doe, hee will recede from ye authoritie of experience, which confirmeth all I have said. Butt if it bee found true doctrine, (though yett it wanteth polishing), I shall deserve the reputation of having beene ye first to lay the grounds of two sciences; this of *Optiques,* ye most curious, and yt other of *Natural Justice,* which I have done in my booke DE CIVE, ye most profitable of all other.[2]

Should Hobbes's claim that he had produced a science of natural justice or of politics be taken seriously? Or should his triumphant assertions be dismissed as nothing more than blatant self-praise? To put the question more precisely, did Hobbes have any reasonable or legitimate ground for his claim that his political theory was scientific?

On Hobbes's own terms, a political science or philosophy has to be similar to natural science. Hobbes's natural science and his political science both begin with the imaginary annihilation, by analysis, of the phenomena to be explained. A conceptual apparatus is then elaborated by definition and deduction.[3] In political science, human nature, the state of nature, natural right, the laws of nature, the construction of a society, and the powers of the sovereign must all be elaborated. Finally, the conceptual tools must be used to explain the phenomena. Natural science is used to give explanations of the observed phenomena of nature.[4] If Hobbes's political theory is scientific, it too must explain the observed phenomena—the experiences of men in society.

Hobbes applies his political science to at least three sorts of phenomena: (1) law; (2) religion; (3) history.

(1) Law. On Hobbes's account, the law of a state is the command of the sovereign to the subjects.

CIVILL LAW, *Is to every Subject, those Rules, which the Commonwealth hath Commanded him, by Word, Writing, or other suffi-*

---

[2] *EW* VII, 470–71.
[3] For an analysis of Hobbes's natural science, see above, pp. 1–14, 38–47.
[4] See above, pp. 35–38.

cient Sign of the Will, to make use of, for the Distinction of Right, and Wrong; that is to say, of what is contrary, and what is not contrary to the Rule.[5]

Hobbes's definition makes the sovereign the absolute source of law in the state. There are, within the state, no laws that are not the sovereign's laws. Conversely, that which is not authorized by the sovereign is no law. It follows that the decisions of judges, the opinions of learned lawyers (or *responsa prudentium*), the orders of subordinate assemblies, and interpretations of natural or divine law, are only law if they are authorized as law by the sovereign. Hobbes dissolves the authority of custom into the authority of the sovereign, the authorizer of custom. To Sir Edward Coke's conception of legal reason as a "mystery" or craft to be practiced by lawyers, Hobbes opposes his own view, that legal reason is the natural reason of the sovereign or the sovereign's appointees. The scientific position thus explains away the superficial difficulties and, at the same time, debunks and destroys the doctrines of those common lawyers who, like Coke, assert the superiority of the law to the sovereign.[6] According to the common-law position, the law provided a barrier against the acts of any official power, supposedly sovereign or not. The common law protected the rights and privileges of Englishmen, especially the rights and privileges of the more substantial Englishmen. Strafford was guilty, not merely of acting arbitrarily and oppressively, but of so acting against persons of quality. John Pym, speaking against Strafford, expressed what most of his colleagues thought about law:

The Law is the safeguard, the custody of all private interest, your Honors, your Lives, your Liberties and Estates, are all in the keeping of the Law; without this, every man has a like right to any

[5] *Leviathan* (26), p. 203. *Cf. De Cive* (xiv. 1–2), *EW* II, 182–85; *Elements of Law* (II. x. 8), pp. 188–89. See above, pp. 192–206.

[6] See *A Dialogue between a Philosopher and a Student of the Common Laws of England*, *EW* VI, 3–15; *Leviathan* (26), p. 207. Hobbes takes the same general position in all four of his discussions of law: *Elements of Law* (II. x), pp. 184–90; *De Cive* (xiv), *EW* II, 182–202; *Leviathan* (26), pp. 203–23; *A Dialogue of the Common Laws*, *EW* VI, 3–160. See also Campbell, pp. 20–45.

thing, and this is the condition into which the *Irish* were brought by the Earl of Strafford: And the reason which he gave for it hath more mischief in it than the thing it self, *they were a conquered people*.[7]

Hobbes's political science provides an explanation of law that exhibits the authority of all law, no matter how customary or judge-made it seems, as derived from the authority of the sovereign. By reducing the phenomena to an intelligible pattern, the explanation clarifies the legal structure of the state; it shows that all lawmaking and law-enforcing agencies derive their powers and jurisdictions from the sovereign, thus clarifying the relations among the laws, orders, and decisions of these agencies. Politically, this amounts to an attack on the common-law position, and on the supporters of Parliament, for at the beginning of the Civil War almost everyone admitted that the King, or at most the King in Parliament, was sovereign.[8] It was not until 1649 that the office of king was declared abolished, and England became a republic.[9]

(2) Religion. Hobbes's political science explains the phenomena of religion as thoroughly as it explains the phenomena of law. The psychological foundations of false religion and of true religion are discovered.[10] The place of religion in the state is described. The sovereign, whether Christian or not, is authorized to regulate the expression of opinion and the public worship of God. All socially established religion has its force *jure civili* and not *jure divino*. No claim to direct revelation, no pretended miracle, need be acknowledged by any person unless the sovereign commands that it be acknowledged. What men believe in the privacy of their minds is their own affair,

[7] Rushworth, VIII, 662. See Hill, *The Century of Revolution, 1603–1714*, pp. 60–68; Ogilvie, pp. 1–8, 134–68; Pocock, pp. 30–55.

[8] As far as I know, the first to hold that Parliament was sovereign without the king was Henry Parker. See Salmon, pp. 81–88; Hill, *The Century of Revolution*, p. 175. Even William Prynne, it appears, was something of a "royalist"; see Lamont, pp. 85–118.

[9] See Gardiner, *Constitutional Documents of the Puritan Revolution*, pp. 291–97.

[10] *Leviathan* (12), pp. 81–94.

provided that they obey the laws. Since this conception of re-ligion is entirely compatible with the Scriptures, correctly in-terpreted, it follows that the various claims to divine authoriza-tion by the warring factions of Christians are all without foundation. Christianity requires only a simple belief in Christ and obedience to the sovereign; the other doctrines are im-posed on believers to enhance the power of one or another ambitious group of clerics.[11]

The explanation of religion, like the explanation of law, is a polemic, both philosophical and political, against views inconsistent with Hobbes's "scientific" Erastianism.[12] As re-ligion became a more and more important source of the dis-turbance of the social peace after 1640, Hobbes devoted more and more space to his polemic against various kinds of fanati-cism.[13]

(3) History. Hobbes also attempts to explain the phenomena of history. The explanation of history is a more difficult and a more important test of Hobbes's political philosophy than are the explanations of law and religion. Both law and religion can be explained by dissolving the claims of alternative ex-planations which are not consistent with Hobbes's science. The explanations that Hobbes offers involve the reduction of the phenomena into Hobbesian categories. Thus, the phenomena are organized into an elaborate pattern that is both intelligible and illuminating. Hobbes is satisfied if many phenomena are thereby consistently and simply explained. If another theory explained more phenomena more simply, it would presumably be a better and more acceptable theory.

But these criteria are not sufficient, for they do not provide criteria for falsifying theories by testing them against the facts. The absence of criteria of falsification is a weakness of Gali-lean, as well as Hobbesian, science. Theories explain, or "save," the phenomena. But, because there are no specific criteria for

[11] See above, pp. 214–27.   [12] See Dewey, pp. 88–115.

[13] Since it would be tedious to rehearse all of Hobbes's discussions of religion, I shall mention only the extended discussions in his major works: *Elements of Law* (I. xi, xviii; II. vi–vii), pp. 53–59, 95–99, 144–67; *De Cive* (iv, xv–xviii), *EW* II, 50–62, 203–319; *Leviathan* (12, 32–47), pp. 81–94, 286–546.

proving a theory false, the explanations tend to fit the phenomena to the theory.[14] Law is always the command of the sovereign because law is defined as the command of the sovereign. If the judges appear to make law, if they seem to be independent law-creators, then the appearances must be deceiving. It is only the sovereign's tacit consent to the rules so made, a consent exhibited in the sovereign's inaction, that makes those rules laws. So, no matter who has formulated and announced the rules, the rules are laws only because they are authorized by the sovereign. Hobbes's explanation is protected, by definition, against being proved wrong. No amount of evidence about the provenance of various legal rules can overthrow his position. The same is true of the explanation of religion. Established religions are religions obligatory by the laws of the state; tolerated religions are religions that citizens are permitted by law to profess; forbidden religions are prohibited by law. True revelation and true prophecy are distinguishable from fantasy and false prophecy only by doctrine (for the private believer), or by authority of the state. In other words, there is no independent evidence of the truth in this area; religion is law and not philosophy.

History provides a more challenging test of Hobbes's science. The phenomena of history, like the phenomena of nature, occur in sequence in time. A causal explanation of the sequences of events is precisely what we would like to have. And a causal explanation is what Hobbes ought, on his own principles, to give us.

Knowledge of historical occurrences is a kind of knowledge of fact. Such knowledge is not, by itself, scientific, but merely prudential. It is knowledge of events, but not scientific knowledge of causes and effects. Some people think that all knowledge is experiential, knowledge of the sequence of events.

But this is an error; for these signs are but conjectural; and according as they have often or seldom failed, so their assurance is more or less; but never full and evident; for though a man hath

[14] See above, pp. 38–47.

always seen the day and night to follow one another hitherto; yet can he not thence conclude they shall do so, or that they have done so eternally. Experience concludeth nothing universally. If the signs hit twenty times for once missing, a man may lay a wager of twenty to one of the event; but may not conclude it for a truth.[15]

Observation and experience provide immediate knowledge of phenomena and conjectural prudence; science alone provides causal knowledge.[16]

Hobbes uses his scientific, or philosophical, position to explain the events in several ways. First, philosophy provides a critical standpoint from which to evaluate and correct the reports of the events. Historians and witnesses, like miracle-mongers, are not always to be believed. Marcus Brutus is said to have seen Caesar's ghost before Philippi; "but considering the circumstances, one may easily judge [the fearful apparition] to have been but a short Dream." [17]

To adopt a critical attitude toward the acceptance of historical evidence is not to offer a philosophic or scientific explanation of history; but Hobbes does more than adopt a critical attitude: he occasionally explains historical sequences of events by showing that they exhibit a synthetical or analytical development. The early Christians revered and obeyed the Apostles. Later, the presbyters agreed on certain doctrines among themselves, and imposed those doctrines on other Christians by refusing to keep company with them if they would not accept the doctrines. Second, the presbyters of the more important cities were able to increase their authority over the other presbyters, thus becoming bishops. Third, the bishops of Rome, the imperial city, took upon themselves (partly by the Emperor's authority, and after the decline of imperial power by the privileges of St. Peter) authority over the other bishops, "Which was the third and last knot [on Christian liberty], and the whole *Synthesis* and *Construction* of the Pontificall Power." [18]

<hr>

[15] *Elements of Law* (I. iv. 10), p. 16.   [16] See above, pp. 1–14 *passim*.
[17] *Leviathan* (2), p. 16. Cf. *ibid*. (7, 46), pp. 52, 535–36.
[18] *Leviathan* (47), p. 543.

The reversal of this process, its resolution back to the independency of the primitive Christians, is what had occurred in England since Elizabeth's time. Papal authority was dissolved by Queen Elizabeth; the Presbyterians in Parliament destroyed episcopacy, and then lost their power in turn.[19]

Although this form of explanation has a few attractions, e.g., the superficial assimilation to analytic-synthetic method, it has great weaknesses. It does not specify the causes of the developments. To get an adequate explanation of the causes of the historical phenomena, the causes of the authority of the Apostles and of the subsequent successes of presbyters, bishops, and popes must be added, as must the causes of the resolution of these powers. Perhaps the more particular causes of the developments could be specified, but if they were the explanation might lose its attractive similarity to the analytic-synthetic model.

The main sort of historical explanation that Hobbes offers for events, and especially for the events of the Civil War, is also causal. In the *Elements of Law,* and in his subsequent writings, Hobbes attempted to identify the causes of the War. He recognized, perhaps before anybody else did, that the Civil War was imminent, and that sovereign power was disputed.[20] In *Behemoth,* his most elaborate explanation of the War, he describes the events that took place as a series of struggles over sovereign power, a series that began with the implicit challenge of the King's rights by Parliament (at least, that is, by some members who intended to set up a parliamentary oligarchy).[21] Hobbes's account of Parliament's accusations against the King and of its actions shows that it aimed at gaining control over one element of sovereignty after another: militia, taxation, justice, legislation, religion, and counsel.[22] The King having been defeated and imprisoned, sovereign power was "contended for, as in a game at cards, without fighting, all

[19] *Ibid.*   [20] *Elements of Law* (II. viii. 3), pp. 169–70.
[21] *Behemoth* (Dialogues 1, 2), pp. 27–28, 74–75.
[22] *Ibid.* (Dialogue 2), pp. 80–85, 97–98, 101–2.

the years 1647 and 1648, between the Parliament and Oliver Cromwell, lieutenant-general to Sir Thomas Fairfax." [23] Hobbes proceeds to describe the conflict between Cromwell, supported by the Army and the sectarian fanatics, and Parliament supported by the City of London. Parliament is defeated and purged. The King is killed. The Rump of the House of Commons, an oligarchy calling itself Parliament and claiming the powers claimed by Parliament, then becomes the apparent possessor of sovereignty.[24] But it was Cromwell who really possessed effective power, power which he used to get himself a title to sovereignty granted by another Parliament.[25] So eventually, what we see is a "circular motion of the sovereign power."

For (leaving out the power of the Council of Officers, which was but temporary, and no otherwise owned by them but in trust) it moved from King Charles I. to the Long Parliament; from thence to the Rump; from the Rump to Oliver Cromwell; and then back again from Richard Cromwell to the Rump; thence to the Long Parliament; and thence to King Charles II., where long may it remain.[26]

But why did this motion occur? The explanation is all too simple. It was caused by the seditious machinations of men who were motivated by ambition for power and office, men who believed or pretended to believe false and dangerous doctrines about politics and religion, and who organized themselves into factions, hampered the King's government, seduced the common people, and made the Civil War. Hobbes's explanation, then, emphasizes three elements: (1) the motivations of individuals and groups, both leaders and led; (2) the ideologies, the political, legal, and religious doctrines, put forward as pretenses to various rights and powers; (3) the organization of the leaders and the manipulation of the populace.

Unlike Plato and Aristotle, Hobbes does not think that every society is really composed of two conflicting economic

[23] *Ibid.* (Dialogue 3), p. 135.   [24] *Ibid.* (Dialogue 3, 4), pp. 154–56, 161.
[25] *Ibid.* (Dialogue 4), pp. 179–83.   [26] *Ibid.*, p. 204.

groups, the rich and the poor. Although he admits that men may be discontented, and consequently seditious, because they fear actual distress or imprisonment, and that men actually have rebelled because of oppressive taxation, he denies that these motives are relevant to the origin of the Civil War. It was not a rising of the poor, the downtrodden, or the over-taxed; "mark the oppression; a Parliament-man of 500*l.* a year, land-taxed at 20*s.!*" [27] The motive for the discontent in England was ambition—the desire for power in church and state of certain Presbyterian ministers and Parliament-men.[28]

Revolution or resistance based on actual necessity needs little or no ideological justification; even Hobbes's own philosophy allows resistance for the purpose of preserving one's own life. But a revolution that is motivated by a desire for power needs a firm ideological basis —a justification of resistance in the name of the rights of those resisting. To our not very great surprise, the rights pretended by the King's opponents turn out to be based on doctrines that are contradicted by Hobbes's political doctrines.[29] The incorrect, i.e., un-Hobbesian, opinions asserted are all false doctrines about the powers of the sovereign and the rights of the subject: (a) there is some authority, either each man's private conscience or some church, greater than the sovereign's in religion; [30] (b) there is no absolute sovereign, either because the sovereign is subject to the laws or because there is some kind of mixed constitution; [31] (c) the subject has an absolute right to property, i.e., a right to property against the sovereign; [32] (d) there is more liberty in a republic than in a

---

[27] *Ibid.* (Dialogue 1), p. 37.
[28] *Elements of Law* (II. viii. 2–3), pp. 169–70; *Behemoth* (Dialogue 1), p. 23.
[29] See Appendix 8.
[30] *Elements of Law* (II. viii. 4–5), pp. 170–71; *De Cive* (xii. 1–2, 6), *EW* II, 149–52, 156–57; *Leviathan* (29), pp. 249–50, 253–54; *Behemoth* (Dialogue 1), pp. 2–3, 21–23, 25.
[31] *Elements of Law* (II. viii. 6–7), pp. 172–73; *De Cive* (xii. 4–5), *EW* II, 153–56; *Leviathan* (29), pp. 250, 254–55; *Behemoth* (Dialogues 1, 2, 3), pp. 26–28, 33, 36–37, 76–77, 97–98, 112.
[32] *Elements of Law* (II. viii. 8), p. 174; *De Cive* (xii. 7), *EW* II, 157–58; *Leviathan* (29), pp. 250–51; *Behemoth* (Dialogue 1), pp. 3–4, 36–38.

monarchy, and tyrants may be killed, i.e., the doctrines of classi-cal republicanism.[33]

In short, Parliament-men and Presbyterian preachers held false opinions about politics and religion; they propagated those opinions in the press and from the pulpit; they attacked the King's government; and thus deceiving themselves and others, they brought down the government and plunged the country into Civil War.[34] From those troubles, the country could have been extricated by a sovereign—by the Rump (if it had had enough honesty and intelligence to govern well), or by Oliver Cromwell, or even by his son, Richard.[35] But no one knew the principles of political science, although they had been clearly demonstrated.

The craftiest knaves of all the Rump were no wiser than the rest whom they cozened. For the most of them did believe that the same things which they imposed upon the generality, were just and reasonable; and especially the great haranguers, and such as pre-tended to learning. For who can be a good subject to monarchy, whose principles are taken from the enemies of monarchy, such as were Cicero, Seneca, Cato, and other politicians of Rome, and Aristotle of Athens, who seldom speak of kings but as of wolves and other ravenous beasts? You may perhaps think a man has need of nothing else to know the duty he owes to his governor, and what right he has to order him, but a good natural wit; but it is other-wise. For it is a science, and built on sure and clear principles, and to be learned by deep and careful study, or from masters that have deeply studied it. And who was there in the Parliament or in the nation, that could find out those evident principles, and derive from them the necessary rules of justice, and the necessary con-nexion of justice and peace? [36]

The people had only one day a week on which they heard instruction. They were instructed badly—irreverently by the controversial preachers, irrelevantly by the elegant preachers, and seditiously by the Presbyterians and Independents and

[33] *Elements of Law* (II. viii. 9–10), pp. 174–75; *De Cive* (xii. 3), *EW* II, 152–53; *Leviathan* (29), pp. 252–53; *Behemoth* (Dialogue 1), pp. 3, 23.
[34] *Behemoth* (Dialogue 1), pp. 24–28.
[35] *Ibid.* (Dialogue 4), pp. 156, 180–81, 192–93.   [36] *Ibid.*, pp. 158–59.

fanatics. Neither the preachers nor those whom they duped lacked intelligence, "but the knowledge of the causes and grounds upon which one person has a right to govern, and the rest an obligation to obey; which grounds are necessary to be taught the people, who without them cannot live long in peace among themselves." [37]

Hobbes's view of the Civil War as primarily an ideological conflict is by no means patently ridiculous. No attempt to demonstrate that the Civil War was really a class war has succeeded.[38] S. R. Gardiner agrees with Hobbes in describing the conflict between King and Parliament as a dispute over sovereignty.[39] The importance to the revolution of Puritanism, and of the alliance between the Puritans and the Parliament-men, is well known. Even Hobbes's violent diatribes against the universities for imbuing future preachers and members of Parliament with the false doctrines of classical republicanism have some basis in fact. The universities were turning out men trained in classical literature (perhaps too many for the available livings in the church) ; it was becoming more and more common for the sons of the nobility and the gentry, men who might sit in Parliament, to get some university education.[40]

Hobbes's explanations are occasionally quite perceptive. He may have been correct in his belief that there would have been no Civil War "but for that unlucky business, of imposing upon the Scots who were all Presbyterians, our book of Common-prayer." [41] Unnecessary doctrinal quarrels did help to disturb the state; Laud, "standing upon punctilios," was partly at fault.[42] Hobbes points out that the destruction of a society does not

[37] *Ibid.*, p. 160. See also (Dialogue 1) , pp. 37–40.
[38] For a discussion of the problem, see Hexter, "Storm Over the Gentry," in his *Reappraisals in History*, pp. 117–62. For other recent work, see Laslett; Aylmer, *The King's Servants;* Simpson, *The Wealth of the Gentry, 1540–1640.*
[39] Gardiner, *History of England*, VI, 119 ff.; X, 184.
[40] See Curtis, "The Alienated Intellectuals of Early Stuart England," pp. 25–43; Curtis, *Oxford and Cambridge in Transition, 1558–1642;* Hexter, "The Education of the Aristocracy in the Renaissance," in *Reappraisals in History,* pp. 45–70.
[41] *Behemoth* (Dialogue 1) , p. 28.   [42] *Ibid.* (Dialogue 2) , pp. 62, 73.

automatically construct a new society. It was far easier for the Parliament to defeat the King than it was for it to maintain control of the situation.[43] The result was a continuous struggle for sovereignty.[44] Such a struggle is not a decline into a war of all against all, but it does have some of the uncertainty and insecurity of the state of nature. Perhaps men learn something from their experience in such a situation, but ultimately it is only the science of just and unjust—Hobbes's political philosophy—applied in practice that can prevent the recurrence of civil wars and other partial returns to the state of nature.[45]

In spite of its considerable virtues, Hobbes's explanation of the Civil War is not satisfactory. Why were seditious doctrines in politics and religion allowed to arise? Hobbes's explanation makes the doctrines and the revolution the result of a subversive conspiracy. This will not do. Any sovereign who allowed such a situation to develop could not have been exercising his power properly. A sovereign, acting correctly, would have acted in such a way that the causes of the revolution would not have existed. Hobbes never suggests that King Charles was responsible for the Civil War. He does suggest that Laud was not a good choice for his position, and that some of the King's officials, even during the fighting, were infected with the doctrines of the opposition; they (and among them Hobbes probably would include Clarendon) thought that England was a mixed monarchy, a *mixarchy*.[46] The King, then, should have appointed other counsellors, but he still should never have gotten into a situation of this sort. Hobbes was a royalist; he intended to blame the other side for all the troubles. But, on his own principles, he must blame the King, and the King's government too. Hobbes recognized that his philosophy was not always favorable to the royal cause. It does, after all, justify the right of the conqueror (e.g., Parliament, Oliver Cromwell),

[43] *Ibid.* (Dialogue 3), pp. 109, 155.   [44] *Ibid.* (Dialogue 4), pp. 195–96.
[45] *Ibid.* (Dialogues 1, 2), pp. 39–40, 70; *Leviathan* (18, Review and Conclusion), pp. 139–40, 556.
[46] *Behemoth* (Dialogue 3), p. 125.

and allow the conquered subject to acquire an obligation to the usurper. He should have given a better account of the causes of the War. And, if necessary, he should have apologized again to the King, as he had in 1662, when he asked Charles II not "to think the worse of me, if snatching up all the weapons to fight against your enemies, I lighted upon one that had a double edge." [47]

Suppose, however, that there never has been a full sovereign in England. The pope and other clergymen have always maintained a claim of right; the nobility and gentry have often claimed their liberties. Hobbes's newly discovered science has never been applied in practice. This does save the King (and perhaps some of his enemies as well) from blame, provided that he acted to the best of his knowledge and ability to vindicate his sovereign right as he understood it. But this supposition and its consequences will not save Hobbes's theory. For although it is an illuminating and perceptive account, Hobbes's explanation seems to simplify the phenomena too much. Can the problems of England in the seventeenth century be entirely explained by blaming them upon the malicious activities of a small group of wrongheaded men? The explanation of the phenomena is accomplished too easily if all that is required is an exhibition of the lack of a Hobbesian sovereign. The Civil War becomes an obvious case of the situation that always existed, viz., the absence of a sovereign. If there had been a sovereign, it would have applied the necessary means to cause peace. Where there is an outbreak of war, the cause is the failure to apply Hobbes's doctrine—the failure to have a sovereign. The phenomena of history, like the phenomena of law and religion, are explained by reducing them to the categories of Hobbes's theory.

Finally, even if there is a sovereign, Hobbes's theory provides no assurance that it will act as a sovereign should act. There is no way to make certain that the sovereign will be rational and

[47] *Seven Philosophical Problems* (Ep. Ded.), *EW* VII, 6.

not unnecessarily oppressive. (Short of the millennium, there is no way to assure this.) In Hobbes's defense, it must be said that he lived before the modern sovereign state existed; every twentieth-century state, no matter how democratic or libertarian, probably exercises more control over its citizens' lives and thoughts than even the most absolute seventeenth-century state did. Against the possibility of real oppression, Hobbes's subject has only his pious hopes and his ultimate right to defend himself.

I think that I have shown that Hobbes attempted to create a scientific or philosophic system on the assumptions and methods of Galilean science. He attempted to show that a science of natural bodies, a science of man, and a science of political bodies could all be elaborated systematically. The elaboration of the conceptual apparatus of the political science is Hobbes's political theory; it is, on any account, a brilliant piece of work. Hobbes's political science, however, exhibits the weakness of Galilean science in an especially noticeable way. This weakness is the absence of criteria for falsifying the theory by an empirical test. The theory is allowed to explain the phenomena, but it is not permitted to be tested by them.

Hobbes's success outweighs his failings. Upon the methods and assumptions of Galilean natural science, he proposed a new understanding of political society. Desirous individuals, naturally dissociated, would associate themselves through force and consent in a state ruled by a sovereign. And after Hobbes had invented his Leviathan—his theory of the modern state— it could no more be ignored than the reality it anticipated and described.

APPENDIXES

Appendix 1

According to Strauss, "On the Basis of Hobbes's Political Philosophy," in *What Is Political Philosophy?*, p. 178*n*4., "Hobbes seems to have thought that this view [that what is not body is nothing] supports sufficiently his contention that only the pleasures and pains of the body are genuine, whereas the pleasures and pains of the mind are vain or fantastical; *cf. De Cive*, I, 2 [*EW* II, 5] and *Leviathan*, ch. 27 [pp. 229–30] with *Leviathan*, ch. 6 [p. 42]. Or, in other words, he seems to have thought that his corporealism legitimates the polarity of reasonable fear and unreasonable glory."

This interpretation misrepresents Hobbes's position, for he did not think that "corporealism" implied the unreality or irrationality of imaginary pleasures (or imaginary pains). The pleasures and pains of imagination (desire, aversion, hope, fear, joy, grief) are no less real, and no less motion in a body, than is that pleasure or pain that "seemeth to affect the corporeal organ of sense." (*Elements of Law* [I. vii. 9], p. 31.) Imagination is decaying sense; the pleasures and pains of the imagination are merely weakened forms of the pleasures and pains of sensation. Imagination differs from sense because the object is absent. (*Elements of Law* [I. vii. 4], p. 29; *Leviathan* [6], p. 42.)

Hobbes distinguishes between pleasures and pains of sense, which arise from something present and apparently are felt in a particular part of the body, and pleasures and pains of imagination or mind, which are not so localized. The latter are really no less bodily motion in brain or heart than the former. See *Leviathan* (11), p. 76, for a peculiar example:

"Desire of Fame after death does the same. [Like desire for praise, it disposes men to laudable actions.] And though after death, there be no sense of the praise given us on Earth, as being joyes, that are either swallowed up in the unspeakable joyes of Heaven, or extinguished in the extreme torments of Hell: yet is not such Fame vain; because men have a present delight therein, from the foresight of it, and of the benefit that may redound thereby to their posterity: which though they now see not, yet they imagine; and any thing that is pleasure in the sense, the same also is pleasure in the imagination."

Appendix 2

Some commentators who have described Hobbes's pattern of aristocratic behavior are Leo Strauss, Dorothea Krook, and Michael Oakeshott.

Strauss, in *The Political Philosophy of Hobbes*, chapters iv and vii, pp. 44–58, 108–28, argues that Hobbes's model of virtuous conduct went through a process of development from an aristocratic model based on pride and magnanimity to a bourgeois model in which fear and reason have become the source of moral conduct. (Strauss's attempt to establish Hobbes's intellectual development, the basis and genesis of his thought, should be compared to Werner Jaeger's attempt to do the same for Aristotle.) Raymond Polin has shown that Hobbes's references to honor and courage, to aristocratic or heroic virtue are infrequent; these references occur in Hobbes's last writings as well as in earlier ones. To give three widely scattered examples: (1) The Letter Dedicatory to Hobbes's translation of Thucydides' *History* (1629), *EW* VIII, iii–v. (See Macdonald and Hargreaves, #1, p. 1.) (2) *Answer to the Preface before Gondibert* (dated January 10, 1650), *EW* IV, 443–44. (See Macdonald and Hargreaves, #38, pp. 24–25.) (3) Preface to Homer's *Iliads and Odysses* (first published in the edition of 1675), *EW* X, iv. (See Macdonald and Hargreaves, #77, p. 59.) According to Polin, Hobbes never held a moral theory based on honor. Honor and courage are virtues appropriate to war, and therefore to a state of nature. Furthermore, the most persuasive passages cited by Strauss come from the dedication of the translation of Thucydides to the Earl of Devonshire, Hobbes's patron; others were written for other literary occasions. (For a full statement, see Polin, pp. 159–64).

Dorothea Krook (*Three Traditions of Moral Thought*, pp. 127–31) has also discovered a second sort of man in Hobbes's writings, primarily in *Leviathan*. Most men are driven by fear, but inconsistently Hobbes allows that there are some rare generous natures. Hobbes's Gallant Man is similar to Aristotle's Magnanimous Man; neither of them hates evil or injustice as such, but both are too proud to commit it. Miss Krook holds that the Gallant Man is inconsistent with Hobbes's system because his morality is grounded, not on fear, but on the Satanic sin of pride.

Michael Oakeshott, in "The Moral Life in the Writings of Thomas Hobbes," in *Rationalism in Politics, and Other Essays*, pp. 248–300, has argued that aristocratic virtue has a place in Hobbes's philosophy. (Professor Oakeshott kindly allowed me to read this essay before its publication.) My account of the man of pride is indebted to Oakeshott, pp. 288–94.

Appendix 3

Hobbes formulated the laws of nature three times, in the *Elements of Law*, in *De Cive*, and in *Leviathan*. In my discussion I have followed the formulation of the *Leviathan*, the final version. In all three versions, the substance of the rules remains the same, the changes being mainly verbal.

The differences between *De Cive* and *Leviathan* (apart from slight differences in wording) are minor. In both versions, the first law of nature is accounted first and fundamental, and from it the other laws are to be derived. In *De Cive*, those other laws are called "special" laws (in the margin), or precepts, and they are numbered separately so that *Leviathan*'s law of nature #2 is *De Cive*'s law #1, and so forth. The order of the laws in these two versions is precisely the same. *De Cive* formulates two rules which *Leviathan* does not: #19 (there is to be no contract between the judge and the parties) and #20 (on drunkenness). *Leviathan* omits the former, subsuming it under the general rule that the judge deal equitably (equally) with the parties. *Leviathan* (15), p. 120, mentions "other things tending to the destruction of particular men; as Drunkenness, and all other parts of Intemperance; which may therefore also be reckoned amongst those things which the Law of Nature hath forbidden." But here, unlike *De Cive,* none of these is formulated as a specific rule.

The *Elements of Law* contains a less explicit formulation than the later versions. The laws of nature (again apart from minor differences of wording) are fewer in number and some of them are more general in scope: there are only fifteen laws, for the three rules on the division of property of *Leviathan* are but two rules in the *Elements of Law* (the forms of lot being a corollary), and the rules on arbitration are a single rule in the *Elements of Law.* In both cases the same points are mentioned in the discussion. The order of the laws in the *Elements of Law* differs slightly from that of the later versions; in particular, the rule about safe-conduct for mediators of peace comes ninth in the *Elements,* fifteenth in *Leviathan.* The *Elements of Law* formulates the first and fundamental law of nature as a definition rather than as a rule. "There can therefore be no other law of nature than reason, nor no other precepts of NATURAL LAW, than those which declare unto us the ways of peace, where the same may be obtained, and of defence where it may not." (I. xv. 1, p. 75.)

The *Elements of Law,* although like *De Cive* and unlike *Leviathan* it has the rule against the judge contracting with the parties, does not contain a rule about witnesses. (*Leviathan* (15), p. 120; *De Cive* [iii. 23], *EW* II, 43.) The only part of the discussion of the laws of nature in the *Elements of Law* that anticipates the later versions in referring to laws that apply to the preservation of the single individual, occurs in a discussion of virtue and vice; "the habit of doing according to these and other laws of nature that tend to our preservation, is that we call VIRTUE; and the habit of doing the contrary, VICE. As for example, justice is that habit by which we stand to covenants, injustice the contrary vice; . . . temperance the habit by which we abstain from all things that tend to our destruction, intemperance the contrary vice." (I. xvii. 14, p. 94.)

The *Elements of Law* contains two rules that are eliminated in the later versions of the laws of nature: "*That men allow commerce and traffic indifferently to one another*" (I. xvi. 12, p. 87); "*That no man obtrude or press his advice or counsel to any man that declareth himself unwilling to hear the same*" (I. xvii. 8, p. 91). The rule requiring free commercial intercourse may have been dropped because it can be regarded as a special case of the preceding rule, which forbids showing hatred or contempt for another; for, to deny a man commerce is to show hatred of him and to declare war on him. But Hobbes may have dropped this rule for another reason, for he tends to deny more and more forcefully the possibility of property rights, and therefore commercial intercourse, in the state of nature. By the time he produced the final version of the *Elements of Law,* Hobbes had already deleted from an earlier version (at I. xvii. 3, p. 89*n.*) a rule that allowed men to bring into society property rights acquired in the state of nature. The second rule, quoted above, is apparently directed against officious busybodies and Dutch uncles, but its political application in 1640 is obvious. The Parliament-men, the Puritans, the common lawyers, and the King's other political opponents have no right to give the King advice; they should wait until their advice is requested.

Appendix 4

For Hobbes's explanation of the passage quoted above p. 112, see *An Answer to Bishop Bramhall, EW* IV, 294–95: "In the seventh paragraph of chapter xv. of my book *De Cive,* he found the words in Latin, which he here citeth. And to the same sense I have said in my *Leviathan,* that the right of nature whereby God reigneth over men, is to be derived not from his creating them, as if he required obedience, as of gratitude; but from his irresistible power. This he says is absurd and dishonourable. Whereas first all power is honourable, and the greatest power is most honourable. Is it not a more noble tenure for a king to hold his kingdom, and the right to punish those that transgress his laws, from his power, than from the gratitude or gift of the transgressor. There is nothing therefore here of dishonour to God Almighty. But see the subtilty of his disputing. He saw he could not catch *Leviathan* in this place, he looks for him in my book *De Cive,* which is Latin, to try what he could fish out of that: and says I make our obedience to God, depend upon our weakness; as if these words signified the *dependence,* and not the *necessity* of our submission, or that *incumbere* and *dependere* were all one."

Hobbes interprets that passage as I do: men, realizing their relation to God, realize that they cannot avoid subjection, thus making an intellectual submission. Unlike F. C. Hood (pp. 51–53), I can find in this passage neither a suggestion that the doctrine of *De Cive* differs from that of *Leviathan,* nor support for the view that "The obligation to obey God does not depend in any way upon man." But Hobbes holds that atheists are not obligated while those who acknowledge God's power are. See above, pp. 110–12.

For another view of man's relation to God, see Warrender, *The Political Philosophy of Hobbes,* pp. 278–98. My opinion is that salvation is relevant only in a prophetic kingdom where there is a prophetic, rather than a natural, obligation to God.

For a rather different critique of the "Taylor-Warrender thesis" of the laws of nature as categorical moral rules legislated by God, see Watkins, *Hobbes's System of Ideas,* pp. 85–99.

Appendix 5

John Plamenatz has argued that the power of the sovereign by institution is illusory. The sovereign's power to terrify the subjects into obedience and the performance of their covenants is based on the subjects' keeping their covenants. But these covenants are invalid without the power to enforce them. Hobbes's argument is circular. See "Mr. Warrender's Hobbes," pp. 295–308.

But as Plamenatz has since pointed out in *Man and Society,* I, 132–38, each man does have an interest in making sure that other men keep their covenants, i.e., an interest in enforcing the covenants of others.

The power of the sovereign does depend upon the obedience of some men to his commands (as what power beyond a single man's strength does not?), but Hobbes does argue that the sovereign has a right to that obedience from subjects who are bound to assist him and from officers who may be paid to do so. It is treason, a violation of natural law, not to obey; and, Hobbes refuses to distinguish between active and passive obedience. See *De Cive* (xiv. 20–23), *EW* II, 199–202.

Sovereignty by institution requires a greater rationality than sovereignty by acquisition because it requires the intention of the institutors to create a society. But if men are rational enough to make covenants to institute a society, some men ought to be rational enough to fulfill their obligations. Furthermore, Hobbes does argue that it is to men's self-interest to have a society, and that their covenanted obligation is precisely what Plamenatz argues that it is their interest to do, i.e., assist the sovereign against others

Michael Oakeshott has also argued that it is not unreasonable for a man to be a first performer of this covenant, for unlike other covenants it is only necessary that some rather than all perform their obligations at any particular time. It is to be expected that some will perform, not only because the gains are much greater than the losses, but also because there may be a few generous natures too proud to break their word. See "The Moral Life in the Writings of Thomas Hobbes," in Oakeshott, *Rationalism in Politics*, pp. 294–300.

Appendix 6

Leviathan was first published in Latin in Hobbes's *Opera Philosophica, Quae Latinè scripsit, Omnia* (1668). Henry Stubbe was busily translating *Leviathan* into Latin in 1656. Of a collection of twenty-three "Letters to Thomas Hobbes, 1664–1675," British Museum, Additional MSS, 32553, sixteen are from Stubbe. (There is also one from Stubbe to Crooke, Hobbes's publisher.) The first of these is dated July 8, 1656, and the last, May 6, 1657. The letters report the doings of Hobbes's enemies at Oxford (especially Dr. Wallis), the support of various people at Oxford for Hobbes, and other gossip. Stubbe also reports his progress in translating *Leviathan* in several letters. In the first letter (fol. 5), he writes that he hasn't had time to transcribe all that he has translated; on January 30, 1656/7 (fol. 25), he reports that he is working four hours a day on the translation. In the possession of the Duke of Devonshire at Chatsworth, there is a box of letters to Hobbes (uncatalogued when I saw them). In one letter, Stubbe mentions that he is leaving out redundant words in the translation. Two of these letters are reproduced in Francis Thompson, pp. 99–106. See also Lubienski, pp. 253–74.

Although this documentary evidence does not categorically demonstrate that no Latin draft of *Leviathan* existed before 1656, or that the Latin *Leviathan* published in 1668 was (at least partly) the work of Stubbe, it does support both hypotheses. Hood, pp. 42, 54–56, who suggests the priority of a Latin version of *Leviathan*, has overlooked these letters in supposing that (except for the conclusion of the Latin version, and its Appendix) there is nothing beyond textual comparison to rely on but subjective impression.

Appendix 7

To attempt to analyze Hobbes's conception of God any further is to become involved in paradox, e.g., God is an infinite corporeal spirit, i.e., God is a body. (See *An Answer to Bishop Bramhall, EW* IV, 302–14 *passim*. [*N.B.*, although written in 1668, this *Answer* was not published until 1682.]) The universe is the aggregate of all bodies. (*Leviathan* [34, 46], pp. 302, 524.) Therefore God (being a body) is either part of the universe or the whole of the universe. But Hobbes denies both of these alternatives: (1) God is not the whole world, for if he is then the world has no cause; therefore there is no God; and (2) God is not part of the world. For if he is part of the world, he is limited and not infinite. (*Leviathan* [31], pp. 279–81.) If God is not a body, then he does not exist, for that which is not a body is no thing and no where. (*Leviathan* [34, 46], pp. 302, 312, 524.)

Does Hobbes mean us to conclude that there is no God? Has he covertly presented us with an argument of which the conclusion is that God does not exist? I think not. Hobbes's theological unorthodoxy is derived from his natural philosophy. The universe is an aggregate of bodies (all substances), and its phenomena are to be explained as caused by motion, i.e., second causes. God has no place within a determined universal order of second causes. He can only exist as a first cause—the cause of causes. All that be said of such a cause is that it is; the nature of the first cause is incomprehensible (as Hobbes repeatedly asserts). If this sort of negative theology is atheistic, then there have been many supposedly orthodox Christian theologians who were atheists.

Nevertheless, Hobbes has often been accused of atheism, not only in the seventeenth century by Alexander Ross, Bishop Bramhall, and Henry More (among many others), but also in this century by Leo Strauss and Raymond Polin. See Bowle; Mintz, especially pp. 39–62; Strauss, *The Political Philosophy of Hobbes*, especially pp. 71–78; Polin, pp. xv–xvi.

It has been argued above that Hobbes was not (strictly speaking) an atheist, for he does argue for the existence of a first cause. Although it is possible that Hobbes's argument is not to be taken seriously, there is no evidence and no reason why it should not be accepted as his position. Had Hobbes wished to avoid the accusation of atheism (i.e., to disguise his "atheism" successfully), he would have adopted an innocuous position on God's nature, e.g., that he was incorporeal. That he did not do so supports the contention that he held the position stated in his published works.

Hobbes could have been a theist without being a Christian. The argument that he was a theist has the same defects as the argument for his atheism. Hobbes professed to be a Christian (of a somewhat peculiar sort, it is true). He conformed to the Church of England. Clearly he did not like some of the doctrines current in the Church of England, the Roman Catholic Church, or the Reformed Churches. The faith required of Christians is simple; but it is to the benefit of the clergy (of whatever denomination) to complicate Christianity by confounding it with vain philosophy and the relics of heathen superstition while, at the same time, they pretend to great holiness and inspiration, the better thereby to increase their power over men's minds, hearts, and pockets—the Kingdom of Darkness. See *Leviathan* (43–47), pp. 457–546 *passim; De Cive* (xviii), *EW* II, 298–319; *Elements of Law* (II. vi. 1–9), pp. 144–55.

Hobbes denied that he was an atheist and defended his assertion that God must be corporeal rather than incorporeal in several minor works: *An Historical Narration Concerning Heresy, EW* IV, 385–408; *Considerations upon the Reputation, Loyalty, Manners and Religion of Thomas Hobbes, EW* IV, 409–40 (see 425–35).

Finally, Hobbes died a conforming Anglican. There is no evidence that he was anything other than what he professed to be, i.e., a slightly heterodox Erastian; there is no reason to believe that he held any secret disguised position.

For the argument that Hobbes was a good orthodox Christian, see Hood, pp. 4–5 and *passim*. A position closer to that adopted here has been put forward by K. C. Brown, who argues that Hobbes was a deist; see pp. 336–44.

Appendix 8

Hobbes's later position on historical explanation is distinguished from his position in what he wrote on Thucydides (1628) by his concern for sovereignty and by his discovery of the cause of civil war in the ignorance, or denial, of political-scientific truth. To be sure, he exhibits some characteristic opinions in the prefaces to his translation of Thucydides' *History,* e.g., fear is an important element in deliberation (*EW* VIII, xvi); monarchy is the most preferred form of government (*EW* VIII, xvi–xvii); Thucydides is defended against Dionysius Halicarnassus' criticism that he did not give a sufficient account of the causes of the war (*EW* VIII, xxi, xxiv–xxviii); history is to give instruction, to make men able to bear themselves prudently in the future, and Thucydides' *History* (of all merely human history) instructs men best (*EW* VIII, vii).

But although Hobbes's sentiments in the earlier work are typical, the general, philosophical element, so strong later on, is missing. Hobbes always preferred monarchy, but he recognized that this was merely a preference—an opinion—all sovereigns have the same rights. Hobbes always thought prudence a good thing, but he came to regard science as a better one. Significantly, the writer of a Thucydidean history of the Great Rebellion, exhibiting the moral for men in the deeds and words of the actors, was not Hobbes, but Clarendon. Hobbes wrote *Behemoth,* a set of dialogues, which attempts, while tracing the events, to exhibit the consequences of not following the correct, Hobbesian, science of politics.

For other discussions of Hobbes's view of history, see Strauss, *The Political Philosophy of Hobbes,* pp. 79–108; Schlatter, pp. 350–62.

BIBLIOGRAPHY

Works and Correspondence of Thomas Hobbes

MANUSCRIPTS

1. Manuscripts and papers of Thomas Hobbes in the collection of the Duke of Devonshire at Chatsworth.
2. Manuscripts in the British Museum:
The Elements of Law, Natural and Politic. Egerton MSS, 2005, Harleian MSS, 1325, 4235, 4236, 6858.
A Minute, or first Draught of the Optiques. Harleian MSS, 3360.
Leviathan, or The Matter, Forme, & Power of a Common-wealth Ecclesiasticall and Civill. Egerton MSS, 1910.
Letters to Thomas Hobbes, 1656–1675. Additional MSS, 32553.

PUBLISHED WORKS

1. Works edited by Sir William Molesworth:
The English Works of Thomas Hobbes of Malmesbury. Now first collected and edited by Sir William Molesworth, Bart. 11 vols. London, John Bohn, 1839–1845.
Thomae Hobbes Malmesburiensis—Opera Philosophica quae Latine scripsit Omnia. In unum corpus nunc primum collecta studio et labore Gulielmi Molesworth. 5 vols. Londini, apud Joannem Bohn, 1839–1845.
2. Other editions:
Behemoth; or, The Long Parliament. Edited for the first time from the original MS. by Ferdinand Tönnies. London, Simpkin, Marshall, and Co., 1889.

The Elements of Law, Natural and Politic. Edited with a preface
and critical notes by Ferdinand Tönnies. London, Simpkin,
Marshall, and Co., 1889.
The Elements of Law, Natural and Politic. Edited with a preface
and critical notes by Ferdinand Tönnies. Cambridge, Cambridge
University Press, 1928.
Hobbes's Leviathan. Reprinted from the edition of 1651, with an
essay by the late W. G. Pogson Smith. Oxford, Clarendon Press,
1952. A complete modern reprint from the "Head" edition.
*Leviathan, or The Matter, Forme, & Power of a Common-wealth
Ecclesiasticall and Civill.* London, printed for Andrew Crooke
at the Green Dragon in St. Paul's Church-yard, 1651. The "Head"
edition.
*Leviathan, or The Matter, Forme, & Power of a Common-wealth
Ecclesiasticall and Civill.* London, printed for Andrew Ckooke
(*sic*), at the Green Dragon in St. Paul's Church-yard, 1651. The
"Bear" edition.
Opera Philosophica, Quae Latinè scripsit, Omnia. 2 vols. Amstelo-
dami, Apud Ioannem Blaev, 1668.

Other Works

Aaron, R. I. "A Possible Early Draft of *De Corpore*," *Mind*, LIV
(1945), 342–56.
Aristotle. *The Politics of Aristotle.* Translated with an introduc-
tion, notes, and appendixes by Ernest Barker. Oxford, Clarendon
Press, 1948.
Aubrey, John. *'Brief Lives,' chiefly of Contemporaries, set down
by John Aubrey, between the Years 1669 & 1696.* Edited from the
Author's MSS by Andrew Clark. 2 vols. Oxford, Clarendon Press,
1898.
Augustine. *The City of God.* Translated by Marcus Dods. New
York, Modern Library, 1950.
Aylmer, G. E. *The King's Servants: The Civil Service of Charles I,
1625–1642.* London, Routledge & Kegan Paul, 1961.
—— *A Short History of Seventeenth-Century England: The Strug-
gle for the Constitution, 1603–1689.* New York, New American
Library, Mentor, 1963.
Barker, Ernest, ed. *From Alexander to Constantine: Passages and
Documents Illustrating the History of Social and Political Ideas,*

336 B.C.–A.D. *337*. Translated with introductions, notes, and essays. Oxford, Clarendon Press, 1956.

Bodin, Jean. *Method for the Easy Comprehension of History*. Translated by Beatrice Reynolds. New York, Columbia University Press, 1945.

—— *Six Books of the Commonwealth*. Abridged and translated by M. J. Tooley. Oxford, Basil Blackwell, 1955.

Bowle, John. *Hobbes and His Critics: A Study in Seventeenth Century Constitutionalism*. London, Jonathan Cape, 1951.

Brandt, Frithiof. *Thomas Hobbes' Mechanical Conception of Nature*. Copenhagen, Levin & Munksgaard, 1928.

Brown, J. M. "A Note on Professor Oakeshott's Introduction to the *Leviathan*," *Political Studies*, I (1953), 53–64.

—— "Hobbes: A Rejoinder," *Political Studies*, II (1954), 168–72.

Brown, K. C. "Hobbes's Grounds for Belief in a Deity," *Philosophy*, XXXVII (1962), 336–44.

Brown, S. M. "Hobbes: The Taylor Thesis," *Philosophical Review* LVIII (1959), 303–23.

Burrell, S. "The Covenant Idea as a Revolutionary Symbol: Scotland, 1597–1637," *Church History*, XXVII (1958), 338–50.

Burtt, E. A. *The Metaphysical Foundations of Modern Science: A Historical and Critical Study*. Rev. ed. Garden City, N.Y., Doubleday, Anchor, 1954.

Campbell, Enid. "Thomas Hobbes and the Common Law," *Tasmanian Law Review*, I (1958), 20–45.

Carlyle, R. W. and A. J. Carlyle. *A History of Mediæval Political Theory in the West*. 6 vols. Edinburgh, William Blackwood, 1950.

Clarendon, Edward, Earl of. *The History of the Rebellion and Civil Wars in England begun in the Year 1641*. Edited by W. Dunn Macray. 6 vols. Oxford, Clarendon Press, 1888.

Clark, G. N. *The Later Stuarts, 1660–1714*. (*Oxford History of England,* Vol. X.) 2d ed. Oxford, Clarendon Press, 1955.

Colie, Rosalie L. *Light and Enlightenment: A Study of the Cambridge Platonists and the Dutch Arminians*. Cambridge, Cambridge University Press, 1957.

—— "Spinoza in England, 1665–1730," *Proceedings of the American Philosophical Society*, CVII (1963), 183–219.

Cowley, Abraham. *The Works of Mr. Abraham Cowley*. London, printed by J. M. for Henry Herringman at the Sign of the Blew Anchor in the Lower Walk of the New Exchange, 1668.

Crombie, A. C. *Medieval and Early Modern Science.* 2 vols. Garden City, N.Y., Doubleday, Anchor, 1959.

Curtis, Mark H. "The Alienated Intellectuals of Early Stuart England," *Past and Present,* XXIII (November 1962), 25–43.

—— *Oxford and Cambridge in Transition, 1558–1642.* Oxford, Clarendon Press, 1959.

Dahrendorf, Ralf. "On the Origin of Social Inequality," in P. Laslett and W. G. Runciman, *Philosophy, Politics and Society.* (Second Series) Oxford, Basil Blackwell, 1962.

Davies, Godfrey. *The Early Stuarts, 1603–1660.* (*Oxford History of England,* Vol. IX.) Oxford, Clarendon Press, 1952.

De Jouvenel, Bertrand. *The Pure Theory of Politics.* Cambridge, Cambridge University Press, 1963.

Descartes, René. *Philosophical Works of Descartes.* Rendered into English by E. S. Haldane and G. R. T. Ross. 2 vols. New York, Dover, 1955.

Dewey, John. "The Motivation of Hobbes's Political Philosophy," *Studies in the History of Ideas,* I (1918), 88–115.

Dijksterhuis, E. J. *The Mechanization of the World Picture.* Translated by C. Dikshoorn. Oxford, Clarendon Press, 1961.

Eliot, T. S. *Selected Essays.* New edition. New York, Harcourt, Brace, 1950.

Engel, S. Morris. "Analogy and Equivocation in Hobbes," *Philosophy,* XXXVII (1962), 326–35.

—— "Hobbes's Table of Absurdity," *Philosophical Review,* LXX (1961), 533–43.

Filmer, Sir Robert. *Patriarcha, and Other Political Works.* Edited from the original sources and with an introduction by Peter Laslett. Oxford, Basil Blackwell, 1949.

Fink, Zera S. *The Classical Republicans, An Essay in the Recovery of a Pattern of Thought in Seventeenth Century England.* Evanston, Northwestern University Press, 1945.

Firth, Sir Charles Harding. *The Last Years of the Protectorate, 1656–1658.* 2 vols. London, Longmans, Green, 1909.

Frank, Joseph. *The Levellers: A History of the Writings of Three Seventeenth-Century Social Democrats: John Lilburne, Richard Overton, William Walwyn.* Cambridge, Mass., Harvard University Press, 1955.

Franklin, Julian H. *Jean Bodin and the Sixteenth-Century Revolution in Law and History.* New York and London, Columbia University Press, 1963.

Fussner, F. Smith. *The Historical Revolution: English Historical Writing and Thought, 1580–1640.* New York, Columbia University Press, 1962.

Gardiner, S. R. *History of England from the Accession of James I to the Outbreak of the Civil War, 1603–1642.* 10 vols. London, Longmans, Green, 1883–1884.

—— *History of the Commonwealth and Protectorate, 1649–1660.* 3 vols. London, Longmans, Green, 1903.

—— *History of the Great Civil War, 1642–1649.* 4 vols. London, Longmans, Green, 1893.

Gardiner, S. R., ed. *Constitutional Documents of the Puritan Revolution, 1628–1660.* Oxford, Clarendon Press, 1889.

Gierke, Otto. *Natural Law and the Theory of Society, 1500–1800.* Translated with an introduction by Ernest Barker. Boston, Beacon Press, 1957.

—— *Political Theories of the Middle Age.* Translated with an introduction by F. W. Maitland. Cambridge, Cambridge University Press, 1938.

Gilbert, Neal W. *Renaissance Concepts of Method.* New York, Columbia University Press, 1960.

Gooch, C. P. *English Democratic Ideas in the Seventeenth Century.* Second edition with supplementary notes and appendixes by H. J. Laski. Cambridge, Cambridge University Press, 1954.

Gough, J. W. *The Social Contract: A Critical Study of Its Development.* Oxford, Clarendon Press, 1936.

Greenleaf, W. H. *Order, Empiricism and Politics: Two Traditions of English Political Thought, 1500–1700.* London, Published for the University of Hull by the Oxford University Press, 1964.

Hall, A. R. *The Scientific Revolution, 1500–1800: The Formation of the Modern Scientific Attitude.* Boston, Beacon Press, 1957.

Haller, William. *Liberty and Reformation in the Puritan Revolution.* New York, Columbia University Press, 1955.

—— *The Rise of Puritanism; or, the Way to the New Jerusalem as set forth in Pulpit and Press from Thomas Cartwright to John Lilburne and John Milton, 1570–1643.* New York, Columbia University Press, 1938.

Hamilton, Bernice. *Political Thought in Sixteenth-Century Spain: A Study of the Political Ideas of Vitoria, De Soto, Suárez, and Molina.* Oxford, Clarendon Press, 1963.

Harrington, James. *Oceana.* Edited with notes by S. B. Liljegren. (*Publications of the New Society of Letters at Lund,* Vol. IV.)

Heidelberg, Carl Winters Universitätsbuchhandlung, 1924.

Havelock, E. A. *The Liberal Temper in Greek Politics*. London, Jonathan Cape, 1957.

Hexter, J. H. *Reappraisals in History: New Views on History and Society in Early Modern Europe*. New York, Harper Torchbooks, 1963.

—— *The Reign of King Pym*. (*Harvard Historical Studies*, Vol. XLVIII.) Cambridge, Mass., Harvard University Press, 1941.

Hill, Christopher. *The Century of Revolution, 1603–1714*. (*A History of England*, Vol. V.) Edinburgh, Thomas Nelson, 1961.

—— *Puritanism and Revolution: Studies in Interpretation of the English Revolution of the 17th Century*. London, Secker & Warburg, 1958.

Hood, F. C. *The Divine Politics of Thomas Hobbes: an Interpretation of Leviathan*. Oxford, Clarendon Press, 1964.

Hooker, Richard. *Works*. 2 vols. Oxford, Oxford University Press, 1850.

Horace. *The Works of Horace in English Verse*. By Mr. Duncombe, Sen., J. Duncombe, M. A. and other Hands. Vol. III. 2d ed. London, printed for B. White, in Fleet-street; T. Becket and P. A. De Hondt, in the Strand; and W. Nicoll, in St. Paul's Churchyard, 1767.

James, D. G. *The Life of Reason: Hobbes, Locke, Bolingbroke*. London, Longmans, Green, 1949.

Kantorowicz, Ernst H. *The King's Two Bodies: A Study in Mediaeval Political Theology*. Princeton, Princeton University Press, 1957.

Krook, Dorothea. "Mr. Brown's Note Annotated," *Political Studies*, I (1953), 216–27.

—— "Thomas Hobbes's Doctrine of Meaning and Truth," *Philosophy*, XXI (1956), 3–22.

—— *Three Traditions of Moral Thought*. Cambridge, Cambridge University Press, 1959.

Kuhn, Thomas S. *The Copernican Revolution*. New York, Random House, 1959.

Laird, John. *Hobbes*. London, E. Benn, 1934.

Lamont, William D. *Marginal Prynne, 1600–1669*. London, Routledge & Kegan Paul, 1963.

Lamprecht, Sterling P., ed. *De Cive or The Citizen* by Thomas Hobbes. Edited with an introduction. New York, Appleton-Century-Crofts, 1949.

—— "Hobbes and Hobbism," *American Political Science Review,* XXXIV (1940), 31–53.

Laski, Harold J. *A Defence of Liberty Against Tyrants: A translation of the Vindiciae Contra Tyrannos by Junius Brutus.* With an historical introduction. London, G. Bell and Sons Ltd., 1924.

Laslett, Peter. *The World we have lost.* London, Methuen, 1965.

Lewy, Gunter. *Constitutionalism and Statecraft during the Golden Age of Spain: A Study of the Political Philosophy of Juan de Mariana, S.J. (Travaux de Humanisme et de Renaissance,* Vol. XXXVI.) Genève, Librairie E. Droz, 1960.

Locke, John. *Two Treatises of Government.* A critical edition with an introduction and *apparatus criticus* by Peter Laslett. Cambridge, Cambridge University Press, 1960.

Lubienski, Z. *Die Grundlagen des Ethisch-politischen Systems von Hobbes.* München, Verlag von Ernst Reinhardt, 1932.

Macdonald, Hugh and Mary Hargreaves. *Thomas Hobbes: A Bibliography.* London, The Bibliographical Society, 1952.

Machiavelli, Niccolò. *The Discourses.* Translated from the Italian with an introduction, chronological tables, and notes by Leslie J. Walker, S.J. 2 vols. London, Routledge & Kegan Paul, 1950.

Macpherson, C. B. *The Political Theory of Possessive Individualism: Hobbes to Locke.* Oxford, Clarendon Press, 1963.

Mathew, David. *The Social Structure in Caroline England.* (The Ford Lectures delivered in the University of Oxford in Michaelmas Term 1945.) Oxford, Clarendon Press, 1950.

Mintz, Samuel I. *The Hunting of Leviathan: Seventeenth-Century Reactions to the Materialism and Moral Philosophy of Thomas Hobbes.* Cambridge, Cambridge University Press, 1962.

Newton, Isaac. *The Correspondence of Isaac Newton.* Edited by H. W. Turnbull. Vol. III. (Printed for the Royal Society) Cambridge, Cambridge University Press, 1961.

Notestein, Wallace. "The Winning of the Initiative by the House of Commons," (Raleigh Lecture on History, 1924). London, published for the British Academy by Geoffrey Cumberlege, Oxford University Press, 1951.

Oakeshott, Michael. *Leviathan, or The Matter, Forme, & Power of a Common-wealth Ecclesiasticall and Civill* by Thomas Hobbes. Edited with an introduction by Michael Oakeshott. Oxford, Basil Blackwell, 1946.

—— *Rationalism in Politics, and other Essays.* New York, Basic Books, 1962.

Ogilvie, Sir Charles. *The King's Government and the Common Law, 1471–1641*. Oxford, Basil Blackwell, 1958.

Osgood, Herbert L. "Political Ideas of the Puritans," *Political Science Quarterly*, VI (1891), 1–28.

Pearl, Valerie. *London and the Outbreak of the Puritan Revolution; City Government and National Politics, 1625–43*. London, Oxford University Press, 1961.

Pease, Theodore. *The Leveller Movement: A Study in the History and Political Theory of the English Great Civil War*. Washington, American Historical Association, 1916.

Peters, Richard. *Hobbes*. Harmondsworth, Middlesex, Penguin Books, 1956.

Pitkin, Hanna. "Hobbes's Concept of Representation," *American Political Science Review*, LVIII (1964), 328–40, 902–18.

Plamenatz, John. *Man and Society*. 2 vols. New York, McGraw-Hill, 1963.

—— "Mr. Warrender's Hobbes," *Political Studies*, V (1957), 298–308.

Pocock, J. G. A. *The Ancient Constitution and the Feudal Law: A Study of English Historical Thought in the Seventeenth Century*. Cambridge, Cambridge University Press, 1957.

Polin, Raymond. *Politique et Philosophie chez Thomas Hobbes*. Paris, Presses Universitaires de France, 1953.

Poore, B. P., ed. *The Federal and State Constitutions, Colonial Charters, and Other Organic Laws of the United States*. Washington, D.C., U.S. Government Printing Office, 1877.

Prothero, G. W. ed. *Select Statutes and Other Constitutional Documents Illustrative of the Reigns of Elizabeth and James I*. 2d ed. Oxford, Clarendon Press, 1898.

Randall, J. H. "The Development of Scientific Method in the School of Padua," *Journal of the History of Ideas*, I (1940), 177–206.

Raphael, D. D. "Obligation and Rights in Hobbes," *Philosophy*, XXXVII (1962), 345–52.

Robertson, George Croom. *Hobbes*. (Philosophical Classics for English Readers.) Edinburgh, William Blackwood, 1901.

Rushworth, John. *The Tryal of Thomas Earl of Strafford (Historical Collections of Private Passages of State, Weighty Matters in Law, Remarkable Proceedings . . . , Vol. VIII.)* London, printed for John Wright at the Crown in Ludgate-Hill, and Richard Chiswell at the Rose and Crown in St. Paul's Church-Yard, 1680.

Salmon, J. H. M. *The French Religious Wars in English Political Thought.* Oxford, Clarendon Press, 1959.

Schlatter, Richard. "Thomas Hobbes and Thucydides," *Journal of the History of Ideas,* VI (1945), 350–62.

Sidney, Algernon. *Discourses Concerning Government.* 3d ed. London, printed for A. Millar, opposite Catharine's-street in the Strand, 1751.

Simpson, Alan. *Puritanism in Old and New England.* Chicago, University of Chicago Press, 1961.

—— *The Wealth of the Gentry, 1540–1660: East Anglian Studies.* Cambridge, Cambridge University Press, 1961.

Skinner, Quinton. "Hobbes on Sovereignty: an unknown discussion," *Political Studies,* XIII (1965), 213–18.

Stephen, Leslie. *Hobbes. (English Men of Letters)* London, Macmillan, 1904.

Stewart, J. B. "Hobbes among the Critics," *Political Science Quarterly,* LXXIII (1958), 547–65.

Strauss, Leo. *Natural Right and History.* Chicago, University of Chicago Press, 1953.

—— *The Political Philosophy of Hobbes: Its Basis and Its Genesis.* Trans. by Elsa M. Sinclair. Chicago, University of Chicago Press, 1952.

—— *What is Political Philosophy? and Other Studies.* Glencoe, Ill., The Free Press, 1959.

Tanner, J. R. *English Constitutional Conflicts of the Seventeenth Century, 1603–1689.* Cambridge, Cambridge University Press, 1957.

Tawney, R. H. *Business and Politics under James I: Lionel Cranston.* Cambridge, Cambridge University Press, 1958.

—— *Religion and the Rise of Capitalism: A Historical Study.* (Holland Memorial Lectures, 1922.) New York, Penguin Books, 1947.

—— "The Rise of the Gentry, 1558–1640," *Economic History Review,* XI (1941), 1–38.

Taylor, A. E. "The Ethical Doctrine of Hobbes," *Philosophy,* XIII (1938), 406–24.

Thompson, Francis. "Lettres de Stubbes à Hobbes," *Archives de Philosophie,* XII (1936), 99–106.

Tönnies, Ferdinand. "Contributions à l'Histoire de la Pensée de Hobbes," *Archives de Philosophie,* XII (1936), 73–98.

—— "Hobbes-Analekten," Parts I and II, *Archiv für Geschichte der Philosophie,* XVII (1903), 291–317; XIX (1906), 153–75.

Trevor-Roper, H. R. "The Gentry, 1540–1640," *Economic History Review*, Supplement I (1953).

Tyrrell, James. *Biblioteca Politica: or, An Enquiry into the Ancient Constitution of the English Government.* London, printed for D. Browne at Exeter-Change in the Strand, A. Bell in Cornhil, J. Darby in Bartholomew-Close, A. Bettesworth in Pater-noster-Row, J. Pemberton in Fleet-street, C. Rivington in St. Paul's Church-yard, J. Hooke in Fleet-street, R. Cruttenden and T. Cox in Cheapside, J. Battley in Pater-noster-Row, and E. Simon in Cornhil, 1718.

Walker, Williston, ed. *Creeds and Platforms of Congregationalism.* New York, Scribner's, 1893.

Warrender, Howard. "Obligations and Rights in Hobbes," *Philosophy*, XXXVII (1962), 352–61.

—— "The Place of God in Hobbes's Philosophy," *Political Studies*, VIII (1960), 48–57.

—— *The Political Philosophy of Hobbes: His Theory of Obligation.* Oxford, Clarendon Press, 1957.

Watkins, J. W. N. *Hobbes's System of Ideas: a Study in the Political Significance of Philosophical Theories.* London, Hutchinson University Library, 1965.

—— "Philosophy and Politics in Hobbes," *Philosophical Quarterly*, V (1955), 125–46.

Wedgwood, C. V. *The King's Peace, 1637–1641.* New York, Macmillan, 1956.

Winch, Peter. *The Idea of a Social Science—and Its Relation to Philosophy.* London, Routledge & Kegan Paul, 1958.

Woodhouse, A. S. P., ed. *Puritanism and Liberty.* Chicago, University of Chicago Press, 1951.

Zagorin, Perez. *A History of Political Thought in the English Revolution.* London, Routledge & Kegan Paul, 1954.

INDEX

Self-preservation: as primary good, 78-79, 86, 93, 108, 121-22, 189-90, 199-200, 206-7; as a natural right, 87-92, 93-94, 96-97, 122, 124, 130, 184-85, 188; natural laws and, 100, 108-9, 113, 116, 122, 125, 202, 246; sovereignty and, 190-91

Sensation, xiii, 5, 48, 111; mechanism of, 2, 35, 61, 243-44; knowledge and, 2, 4, 11, 12-13, 14, 43, 44, 52-53, 119n86; imagination and, 3, 16, 35, 50, 75-76, 243-44; causality and, 10, 12, 14, 21, 24, 35, 37, 39, 59; motion and, 12-13, 16, 31, 50, 59-60, 243; values and, 51-53, 57, 60, 66, 71; *see also* Pain; Pleasure; *and see specific senses*

Sidney, Algernon, 141n20

Sight, 2, 50, 53

Simple circular motion, 33, 34, 36, 37, 38, 42, 46

Simpson, Alan, 239n38

Smell, 2, 37-38, 40, 50, 53

Smith, John, 152

Social contract: necessity for, 129-40; obligation under, 139-40, 141-44, 147, 155, 158, 179, 189; historical survey of theory of, 140-55; in coronation, 141, 143; Hobbes's view of, 155-61; as between master and servant, 162-64, 172

Society, 49, 229; power and, 67-68, 127, 208, 212-14; civilization, 71, 92, 130, 131, 173, 178; security and, 78-79, 86-92, 127-28, 130, 138, 161-62, 166, 173, 181, 182, 185-92, 193, 204, 206-7; human nature and, 84-128, 138, 153-54; natural law and, 93-107, 115, 127, 138, 153, 184-85, 189, 193, 202; order in, 127-28, 129-74, 192-207; incorporation of, 138-39, 143, 144, 148-55, 156-61, 166, 216, 242; patriarchal, 144-45, 154, 155, 166-72; resulting from institution, 156-61; resulting from sovereignty by acquisition, 161-74; *see also* Government; Social contract; Sovereignty; State of Nature

Sophists, 148-49

Sound, 2, 44, 50, 53; medium theory, **37**

Sovereignty: war and, 92, 162-64, 186, 251-52; contract and, 99, 115, 130, 156-74; of the commonwealth, 139-40, 146, 149, 157; of kings, 141-44,

157; patriarchal, 144-45, 166-72; government and, 146-47, 156, 158, 159, 163-64, 175-227, 229-31; power of, 146-47, 156, 158, 159, 176-85, 186-92, 196-97, 223, 229, 233, 235-36, 237; by institution, 155-61, 163, 164-66, 171, 179, 185n30, 186, 248-49; by acquisition, 161-74, 180, 182, 185n30, 240-41; of God, 221-23; Parliamentary, 231n8, 236; English Civil War and, 235-41; twentieth century, 242

Space: concept of place and, 12, 20-21, 22, 47; as imaginary, 16-20, 21; identity and, 23; moving bodies and, 29-30; endeavor and, 33; ether and, 35-36, 46, 173

Speech, *see* Language

State of nature: imaginary dissolution of society, 85; cooperation in, 89n11, 115, 130, 137-38, 139, 154, 173; equality in, 90, 102, 104, 129, 212; war and, 90-91, 92, 93, 100, 126, 130-31, 135, 177, 178, 240, 244; contract in, 99-100, 130, 135-38, 173, 199-200; the individual in, 129-30, 135, 138, 139, 165, 190; life in, 130-31, 187; space analogy, 172, 173-74; *see also* Laws of Nature; Right of Nature

Stewart, J. B., xvn11

Stoics, 27

Strafford, Thomas Wentworth, earl of, 175, 230, 231

Strauss, Leo: cited, 30n43, 72n53, 73nn54-57, 75n61, 125n101, 244, 250, 252; quoted, 67n40, 243

Stubbe, Henry, 249

Substance, *see* Body; Matter

Suicide, 122-23, 132

Sun, 42, 43; dilation and contraction of, 18n6; replenishment, 19n10; motion, 36

Synthesis, 1, 6-7; definitions in, 9-10; scientific knowledge and, 11, 12, 13-14, 16

System: principles, 31-32, 38; theoretical tools, 34, 38; scientific application, 38-47; historical application, 232-42, 251-52

Taste, 2, 38, 50, 53

Taxation, 146, 192, 198, 204; economic policy and, 208, 210-11; English Civil War and, 235, 237

Temperance, 107, 109, 116, 245, 246